# Restructuring Welfare Organizations in Europe

# Restructuring Welfare Organizations in Europe

## From Democracy to Good Management?

Paola Mattei

*Research Fellow*
*Mannheim Centre for European Social Research (MZES)*
*University of Mannheim*

First published 2009 by
PALGRAVE MACMILLAN

Palgrave Macmillan in the UK is an imprint of Macmillan Publishers Limited, registered in England, company number 785998, of Houndmills, Basingstoke, Hampshire RG21 6XS.

Palgrave Macmillan in the US is a division of St Martin's Press LLC, 175 Fifth Avenue, New York, NY 10010.

Palgrave Macmillan is the global academic imprint of the above companies and has companies and representatives throughout the world.

Palgrave® and Macmillan® are registered trademarks in the United States, the United Kingdom, Europe and other countries.

ISBN-13: 978-0-230-21732-4     hardback
ISBN-10: 0-230-21732-X     hardback

This book is printed on paper suitable for recycling and made from fully managed and sustained forest sources. Logging, pulping and manufacturing processes are expected to conform to the environmental regulations of the country of origin.

A catalogue record for this book is available from the British Library.

Library of Congress Cataloging-in-Publication Data

Mattei, Paola, 1974–
   Restructuring welfare organizations in Europe : from democracy to good management? / Paola Mattei.
      p. cm.
   Includes bibliographical references and index.
   ISBN 978-0-230-21732-4
   1. Public welfare administration—Europe. 2. Welfare state—Europe.
   3. Europe—Social policy. 4. Democracy—Economic aspects—Europe.
   I. Title.
HV238.M38 2009
361.94—dc22                                          2008038430

10  9  8  7  6  5  4  3  2  1
18  17  16  15  14  13  12  11  10  09

Printed and bound in Great Britain by
CPI Antony Rowe, Chippenham and Eastbourne

To the memory of Anita and Dino.

# Contents

# Tables

# Preface and Acknowledgements

This book is the result of the dedicated efforts of many people. It was made possible by a community of colleagues who offered me intellectual stimulus. The inspiration of this book emerged in Bremen, Germany, while I was T. H. Marshall Fellow in European Social Policy at the 'Transformations of the State' Collaborative Research Centre 597. The T. H. Marshall Fellowship offered me the opportunity to produce research with cross-national implications for welfare state policy and to build my knowledge of social policy practice in other European countries. The 'Transformations of the State' Research Centre in Bremen and the London School of Economics, through its Department of Social Policy, have supported my research project. I was primarily based there from September 2005 to July 2008, and I have devoted concentrated effort to the T. H. Marshall research project and to the making of this book. Along this journey I had the pleasure to learn from the insights of a great many scholars as well as practitioners.

The policymakers, administrators, managers and practitioners who agreed to be interviewed have been a major source of inspiration for this book. I am immensely grateful to all of them for their time, patience and insights into the empirical puzzle of understanding the specificities of education and health care policy. Among them, special gratitude goes to the civil servants at the German Ministry of Health in Berlin and Bonn, the management and the medical staff at Charité hospital in Berlin, where my journey started. Professor Ganten offered invaluable insights and kindly agreed to open up access to the data. I also wish to thank the patients, pupils, parents, who have shared their views with me, and made my waiting times in hospitals' daunting corridors the most enjoyable. I have learnt from the stories they volunteered to share with me about the limitations of organizational models, and the need for citizenship-based benefits. I wish to thank Gerard Banner, the German 'guru' of New Public Management, for his time and patience with my challenging questions.

My understanding of welfare administration and social policy has been deepened by the comments and intellectual stimulus received from Bleddyn Davies, Carol Harlow, Werner Jann, Julian Le Grand, Lutz Leisering, Jane Lewis, Elias Mossialos, Peter Mair, Herbert Obinger, Kerstin Martens, Ariane Antal, Markus Woerz, Maria Oppen, Heinz

Rothgang, Peter Starke, Anne West, Howard Glennerster, Gwyn Bevan, and Rudolf Klein. I am also much indebted to some intellectual companions and friends, including Sarah Gurr, Pauline Adam. I wish to thank the anonymous reviewers of my book proposal and manuscript for their helpful suggestions.

In navigating the waters of organizational turbulence for the European welfare states, I have benefited enormously from the guidance of Professor Stephan Leibfried, who has combined a strong commitment to his own scholarship as well as a huge inspiration for my book from the early stage to its completion. Professor Leibfried inspired my interest for the welfare state and taught me to understand its institutional peculiarities. I thank him enormously for refreshingly challenging my initial certainties and teaching me that the welfare state is a profoundly different institution from the Pentagon. Without his support and guidance, this book would not have been written. I thank him for his continual and enthusiastic encouragement throughout the three years I was based in Germany for my T. H. Marshall fellowship. I wish to thank him for the many conversations in which he supported me when I was following a rather unexplored territory. Profuse and profound thanks for teaching me intellectual rigour, honesty and passion for European welfare states, which will surely outlive this book.

This project has been supported by the financial and institutional support of the London School of Economics, Department of Social Policy, and the 'Transformations of the State Research Centre' in Bremen, Germany. For the initial research funding, I wish to thank the Committee members who awarded the T. H. Marshall fellowship to my postdoctoral project, and the Volkswagen Foundation. I wish to single out the financial and intellectual support given by the 'Transformations of the State Research Centre', University of Bremen, who hosted most of my research work in Germany, from September 2005. I owe special thanks to all the inspiring research community there associated with the intervention state research group 'C'. I wish to acknowledge the Mannheim Centre for European Social Research, Mannheim, Germany, and all the Selection Committee Members, for awarding me a fellowship aimed at developing my research agenda. The fieldwork in Britain has been facilitated by a visiting fellowship at Somerville College, Oxford University, from February to April 2007. My most profound debt goes to Fiona Caldicott, the principal, for this opportunity and her enthusiastic support at a particular time of the project. Without the financial support of the Wissenschaftszentrum für Sozialforschung Berlin (WZB), the last stage of writing this book would have been more difficult. I wish to thank the President of the WZB for her financial support. She supported an international conference on the core theme and arguments of my book ('Changing Educational Accountability in Europe', WZB, Berlin, 24–5 June 2008).

Philippa Grand, the editor at Palgrave Macmillan, has offered very helpful guidance and detailed suggestions about the book. Her participation has been essential to the production of this monograph. She has seen this book through the different stages, from idea to reality, always with a supportive and enthusiastic eye. I thank all the editorial team at Palgrave Macmillan for their professionalism and efficiency.

This book was also a personal journey of exploration which took me on a most exciting path, travelling to different European countries for fieldwork, interviews and archival work, in Britain and Germany, France and Italy. This also meant extended periods of time away from home. I am hugely indebted to my family for their patience and continual support.

# Abbreviations

| | |
|---|---|
| ARH | Agences Régionales de l'Hospitalisation |
| | (Regional Agency of Hospitalization) |
| BMG | Bundesministerium für Gesundheit |
| | (Ministry of Health) |
| CDU | Christlich Demokratische Union |
| | (Christian Democratic Union) |
| CHU | Centre Hospitalier Universitaire |
| | (University Hospital Centre) |
| CSU | Christlich-Soziale Union |
| | (Christian-Social Union) |
| DEP | Direction de l'Evaluation et de la Prospective |
| | (Department for Evaluation and Future Trends) |
| DfES | Department for Education and Skills |
| DGS | Direction generale de la santé |
| | (General Department of Health) |
| DHA | District Health Authorities |
| DHOS | Direction de l'hospitalisation et de l'organisation des soins |
| | (Department for Hospitalization and the Organization of Care) |
| DOH | Department of Health |
| D.lgs. | Decreto legislativo |
| | (Legislative Decree) |
| D.p.R. | Decreto del Presidente della Repubblica |
| | (Decree of the President of the Republic) |
| EPLE | Etablissement public local d'enseignement |
| | (Local Public Teaching Establishment – Secondary school) |
| GM | Grant Maintained |
| Gmbh | Gesellschaft mit beschraenkter Haftung |

| | |
|---|---|
| HMSO | Her Majesty's Stationery Office |
| JOBS | Job Opportunities and Basic Skills |
| LEA | Local Education Authority |
| LBK | Landesbetrieb Krankenhauser Hamburg (Hamburg State Office for Hospitals) |
| LHA | Local Health Authority |
| MEN | Ministère de l'Education Nationale (National Ministry of Education) |
| MES | Modellvorhaben eigenverantwortliche Schule (Pilot project for self-governing schools) |
| NHS | National Health Service |
| NPM | New Public Management |
| OECD | Organisation for Economic Co-operation and Development |
| PCT | Primary Care Trust |
| PDS | Partei des Demokratisches Sozialismus (Party of Democratic Socialism) |
| PISA | Programme for International Student Assessment |
| KGSt | Kommunale Gemeinschaftsstelle für Verwaltungsmanagement (Local Government Association for Administrative Management) |
| OFSTED | Office for Standards in Education, Children's Services and Skills |
| SPD | Sozialdemokratische Partei Deutschlands (Social Democratic Party of Germany) |
| SNES | Syndicat national de l'Enseignement Secondaire (National Union of Teachers in Secondary Schools) |
| TRUDI | Territorial State, Rule of Law, Democratic State, Intervention State |
| WHO | World Health Organization |

# Introduction

Welfare and democracy are two inseparable questions. Organizing welfare is not reducible to a technical exercise or professional understanding of the services provided. It is fundamentally the result of the institutional struggles of the welfare state through the centuries. To assume that welfare bureaucracies were 'frozen' in the period between 1945 and 1950, when they indeed acquired full-fledged political power of their own in most European countries after World War II, is not an adequate assumption for the study of social policy change. Most of the studies on social administration are limited to the nationalization and institutionalization of the welfare states in Europe in the aftermath of World War II. However, tremendous changes have occurred in the last decades, which require radical adaptations of welfare institutions. Considering those administrative adaptations as technical matters, or management issues, would simply contribute to obfuscate the new hidden threat to the relationship between the welfare state and its democratic structures.

The question of the transformations of European welfare administration as a result of recent changes to the interplay between an efficient and cost-effective state of welfare and democratic accountability is at the core of this book. Since its inception the welfare state has not ceased to pose challenges to democratic institutions. Existing state structures have had to adapt to the transformational forces of new social and political conflicts associated with the development of the welfare state such as suffrage extension and parliamentarianism. The development of the French welfare state is a case in point. From its early days the French welfare state immediately merged social values with the problems of democracy (Hayward, 1959). Despite the centrality of the democratic question in France, in other countries the welfare state was chiefly a bureaucratic product. Local government in England was a bastion of liberal democracy and remained aloof to the political demands generated by welfare needs for a long time. Therefore, in understanding the effects of recent transformations of the welfare state, this book explores the relationship between consolidated democratic structures and new pressing administrative demands on service delivery.

Modern welfare bureaucracies have not formed independently from the pre-existing state structures and organizations. It would be misleading to assume that once new social and economic demands, or new social risks, are created (Beck, 1992; Swank, 2002; Manning and Shaw, 2000; Boeri et al., 2001), the institutional and political context of social policies disappears. The administrative state was originally created as an instrument for delivering welfare services and public assistance. Administrative constraints and opportunities are an essential element to explain how each democracy in Europe has institutionalized its welfare state. During the early stages of the emergence of the welfare state in the nineteenth century, the institutional and administrative arrangements for delivering welfare services were no less intricate than today. Providing welfare services and public assistance was foremost an institutional struggle driven by pragmatic concerns rather than by existential ones. For instance, in the 1870s, the complex administration of public assistance by British localities repelled Edwardian reformers in the civil service (Ashford, 1986). Local government itself was viewed by the central government not as the 'provider' of welfare services, but rather as an institution of local democracy foremost, a cornerstone of liberal democracy in all democratic states. Too often it is neglected that the welfare state was indeed a bureaucratic product, especially in Britain, but also in Germany (Ashford, 1986: 244). The early administrative designs were not shaped to fit political demands (Hennock, 2007). Localities remained distant from the emergence of the British welfare state and did not take much political initiatives.

The concept of 'welfare democracy' transcends different welfare regimes (Rieger and Leibfried, 2003). The purpose of this study is to explain similarities rather than differences in European social policy, as they emerge from the analysis of changing institutional structures of the welfare state. Considering the different historical development of the welfare states in Europe, and the particular institutional and political characteristics in different political systems, it is quite challenging to explain the surprising empirical puzzle of decreasing variance in the administrative structure of welfare service delivery, including education and hospital care. For the purpose of comparative welfare analysis, existing theories are not useful in understanding the transformations of the welfare state in its bureaucratic dimension, for it is shaped by pressures which do not necessarily pertain to welfare per se or to globalization effects. The problem is not whether the welfare state is in retreat or not, in terms of public expenditure, but how it is changing as a result of an internally induced administrative modernization. Therefore, classical welfare state typologies, such as Esping-Andersen's typology (1990), take less relevance in explaining the new question this book addresses.

Unlike the 'mainstream' comparative social policy debate, this book brings the focus of analysis of social policy change mainly on the administrative terrain of welfare state reorganization. This is a dimension of the welfare state which deserves more scholarly attention than it has received to date. Social policy change cannot simply be reduced to the empirical phenomenon of contraction or expansion of public expenditure (Garrett, 1998; Huber and Stephens, 2001; Castles, 2005; Korpi and Palme, 2003) or to the simplistic view of new modes of governance on the basis of supposedly neatly separated public–private providers. Why look only to external variables to discuss the welfare state's challenges? What if the welfare state were challenged *from within* its bureaucratic and institutionally embedded structures, not frozen in the 1950s, but under severe pressure in the post-golden age (Hurrelmann et al., 2007)? System variables do not fully capture the change at the organizational level, which has transformed welfare delivery in the last two decades in many European countries, across different welfare regime types and across specific policy programmes.

This study analyses the problems facing the transformations of welfare democracy from a very different angle than the debate about the challenge posed by globalization to the welfare state (Bonoli et al., 2000). Debate has flourished about the new 'external' challenges to the welfare state posed by globalization (Hirst and Thompson, 1996; Keohane and Milner, 1996; Strange, 1996). Globalization has been a major threat to the continued viability of a generous welfare state, given the pressure created by international trade and the incentives for 'social dumping' caused by the huge increase in international capital flows (Jessop, 1990; 1996; 1998). Economic, social and technological forces are claimed to be uncontrollable factors which risk dismantling the welfare state (Organization for Economic Cooperation and Development (OECD), 1981). However, simply looking at exogenous shocks and their effects on welfare expansion or retrenchment offers a limited understanding of the institutional and political transformations driven by the internal structures of the welfare state. As Jane Lewis has argued with reference to the Blair government's childcare strategy, current debate in social policy revolves less around the welfare state's main goals and more around whether the administrative and financial systems are the appropriate ones to deliver it (Lewis et al., 2005).

The empirical phenomenon under investigation in this book is the introduction of managerialism in core areas of the welfare state, namely education and health care (Marshall, 1950; Titmuss, 1958). These reforms are associated with the organizational axis of the transformation of the welfare state (Zürn and Leibfried, 2005). An organizational change is 'one in which the relationship between state and society changes' (Zürn and Leibfried, 2005: 13). Distinct from privatization and marketization of welfare services, which have been widely discussed by comparative welfare scholars (Le Grand and Robinson, 1984; Hacker, 2002; Pierson, 1994), managerialism does not necessarily imply a cost-cutting strategy. Unfortunately, it is understood only as a narrow financial phenomenon, whereas its scope is far greater and its effects are relevant for the democratic foundations of the welfare state. In this book, I emphasize the importance of studying managerialism as a distinct reform trajectory from privatization and marketization of European welfare states. The distinction is not only empirically driven but also analytically grounded.

The reorganization of welfare bureaucracies at both central and subnational levels of government in Britain, Germany, France and Italy, and also many other advanced industrialized countries, has been associated from the mid-1980s with the shift from bureaucratic to managerial types of public organizations (Pollitt and Bouckaert, 2000). A new administrative paradigm is at the heart of the 'managerial revolution' transforming the welfare state in Europe (Wright, 1994). Its central 'myth' is entrepreneurialism, associated with New Public Management (NPM) (Hood, 1991; Christensen and Laegreid, 2001b). This reflects a programmatic and discursive radical change from hierarchical and top-down government to new modes of 'governance' based on territorial and organizational decentralization of decision making and shifting boundaries between the public and private sector (Jann, 2003; Jann, 2005; Rhodes, 1997; Jessop, 1998). Organizational legitimacy is no longer derived from input and the legality of procedures, but from output and performance. Reform programmes strengthen the discretion of managers in relation to politicians, transfer democratic representation to 'stakeholders' (Peters, 1996) and create structural barriers between political leadership and organizational autonomy (e.g. independent executive agencies, joint executive committees).

Despite the prominence of this empirical phenomenon, the research traditions of social policy and public administration are still viewed separately. This book aims to construct the bridge between these two research communities. It analyses managerialism in European social policy as it applies to state secondary schools and public hospitals in Britain, Germany, France and Italy, from the mid-1980s to 2007, and how the new administrative 'settlement' of the welfare state affects the distribution of power among actors such as managers, politicians, users and professionals. These relationships are shaped by the formal web of accountability arrangements (Sinclair, 1995; Romzek and Dubnick, 1987). It is also influenced by the substantive issues and 'content' of what actors are accountable for (Broadfoot, 1985). I will explore the effects of managerialism on the relationships between actors through the lenses of different types of accountability regimes. In particular, the built-in rivalry between managerial and political accountability (Day and Klein, 1987) is the subject of a detailed conceptual elaboration in Chapter 2. Managerialism is an instrumental logic, made of policy tools aimed at transforming rigidly bureaucratic institutions into flexible, customer-oriented and autonomous organizations of service delivery (Barzelay, 2001). One of the main conclusions of the book is that managerialism in social policy poses a threat to democratic accountability, even if the relationships between the state, providers and users remain within the shadow of hierarchy (Scharpf, 1999). The substantive content of managerial accountability defines the power relationship between actors, increasingly alienating citizens from effective engagement, and politicians from meaningful representation of needs.

The empirical core of the book investigates the reach of managerialism as applied to organizations of welfare service delivery. Contrary to other studies, I will not consider only system variables. This is not a book simply mapping policy trajectories in the management of social policy, unlike others (Clarke et al., 2000). Moreover, the research strategy to study the effects of managerialism on the welfare state needs to move beyond a definition of managerialism as simply a policy fashion (Marmor, 2004), for this characterization would limit the possibility to assess its real implications for the institutional structures of the welfare state. One of the major conclusions of the book is that European welfare states are converging along the administrative dimension towards a new model of the internal governance of delivery units, whereby managerial accountability and organizational autonomy are strengthened. Existing explanations of convergence based on transnational communication

(Holzinger and Knill, 2005) or policy learning, and other 'soft' causal mechanisms, are not entirely useful in studying the outcome of similar ideas when hitting most different administrative structures.

This book proposes to assess whether the shift from a politico-representative organization of the welfare state to an entrepreneurial one (Mattei, 2007b) unfolds mainly at a rhetorical and symbolic level or whether the structural premises of managerialism are such as to lead to a long-term institutional change affecting the relationship between the welfare state and its actors, in particular democratic accountability. How are citizens involved in the new administrative arrangements of welfare provision? How does the new 'settlement' affect their represen-tation? I argue that the organization of the representation of citizens' needs within the institutions of welfare service delivery is changing dramatically. Managers at the head of welfare 'enterprises' are increas-ingly responsible for defining the needs of their clients. Once in the professional welfare state (Klein and Day, 1987), this was the exclu-sive responsibility of doctors and teachers. The client model of public accountability clearly departs both from conventional political account-ability, whereby the ultimate sovereignty rests with the 'citizens' (Mill, 1962), and from the definition of the welfare state and social rights based on citizenship (Marshall, 1950).

Managerialism is far from being a technical matter. It is the ideal alternative reform strategy to welfare state retrenchment, for its costs are totally hidden and it does not necessarily imply benefit cuts. On one hand, it has become more difficult for political parties to endorse neoliberal radical retrenchment programmes (Pierson, 1994). On the other, it is not credible for politicians to be supporting the status quo. Hence, political actors' room for manoeuvring has diminished and par-ties are moving towards centrist positions of 'restructuring', including new means to achieve the same goals (Kitschelt, 2001). Centrist reform efforts revolve around administrative modernization, rather than dis-mantling the welfare state. On the one hand, strong austerity pressures on mature welfare states make cutbacks attractive. On the other, the welfare state generates popular enthusiasm, especially among benefit recipients (Richardson, 1993). The resilience of the welfare state owes much to the electoral incentives associated with programmes which retain intense and broad popular support. Hence, retrenchment is neither a convincing nor a viable policy alternative (Taylor-Gooby, 2004; Boeri et al., 2001), owing to the large size of the welfare state's constituencies (Flora and Heidenheimer, 1982). I suggest that the trade-off between retrench-ment and political unpopularity makes the politics of reorganizing welfare organizations a great opportunity for introducing reforms through the back door and, as such, of great significance for the future debate on European social policy.  but wold undirectt tham tha ?

'Restructuring' welfare public organizations in an era of austerity (Pierson, 2001) is viewed, in the analytical framework of this book, through the lens of a fundamental change to the link between democratic and managerial accountability at the level of the organization. The silent revolution of welfare administrative restructuring has found its way through the breaches of the organizational structure of welfare provision. Welfare delivery institutions are formally designed to make them subordinate to political scrutiny and public accountability (Harlow, 2002). The shift from bureaucratic to managerial organizations has changed the relationship between administrative autonomy and political control and consequently has altered old mechanisms of accountability. In the 1980s and 1990s, the NPM doctrine swept through public administration systems of OECD countries (Pierre, 1995; Pollitt and Bouckaert, 2000; Christensen and Laegreid, 2001b).[1] Its underpinning philosophy emphasized the importance of performance management and called for a redesign of internal control mechanisms. The NPM promised executive politicians to enhance their political control of bureaucratic organizations, by setting priorities and 'steering', leaving civil servants worrying about the details of implementation and 'rowing' (Osborne and Gaebler, 1992).

Although welfare restructuring in Europe has mirrored the wider trajectory of administrative changes (Bouckaert and Pollitt, 2000), including those countries where the scholarly literature expected some institutional inertia and policy immobilism (Crozier, 1970; Hayward, 1975), we know little to date about the national variations of the changing relationship between democratic and managerial accountability, as it applies to the welfare state in Europe. The excessive emphasis on social expenditure and cost containment and the reductionist view of 'efficiency' as a mere financial objective, contrary to the more comprehensive and seminal definition by Herbert Simon,[2] have deflected attention from the wider political implications for the democratic process.

## Outline of the book

The book is divided into three parts. Following this Introduction, Part I sets out the theoretical and methodological foundations of the study of the reorganization of welfare administration. It develops an analytical tool to study the relationship between managerial and democratic accountability. Part II discusses in detail the main changes in the social administration of public secondary schools and hospitals in Britain, Germany, France and Italy. The time horizon will vary because reforms have been introduced at different times. Generally, the time frame runs from the 1983 British Griffiths Report to the French Hospital Plan in September 2007. Finally, Part III discusses the wider implications of new methods of organizing welfare provision and managerialism for welfare democracy in Europe.

By discussing the main theoretical arguments concerning the introduction of managerialism in social policy, Chapter 1 emphasizes the possible hidden costs of recent reform trends in Europe, over-optimism about outcomes, and fundamentally a misleading view of the state, as Wright (1994) pointed out. The book is based on a complex multiple cases design, covering four most different countries and the two social policy sectors. Thus, the methodological approach and methods are set out explicitly in Chapter 1, as well as the research questions and the two main empirical purposes of this book. First, through its empirical original investigation and rich data, the book aims to understand the impact of the managerial revolution on effacing the gap between organizational autonomy and political accountability at the level of the organization; second, it investigates how 'new' types of accountability offer a meaningful solution to the problem of output-legitimated welfare organizations and technocratic dominance.

Some managerial reforms concerning the delivery of welfare services are strictly managerial in nature, but, taken as a whole, the reforms affect the balance of power between managers, politicians, professionals and citizens. Chapter 2 will elaborate a new analytical approach to understand the structural terrain which shapes the effects of the adoption of new organizational arrangements inspired by managerialism. For analytical purposes, autonomy and democratic accountability can be located at the extreme ends of a spectrum. A balance has to be struck between organizational autonomy, which presumably ensures more responsive and efficient local services by putting the experts in charge, and political accountability, which makes these bodies accountable to ministers so that they can answer for their activities in the parliament and to the public more generally (Davies, 2001).

Chapter 3 focuses entirely on public hospitals with an in-depth case analysis of the largest European hospital, namely Charité in Berlin. General management was adopted first in Britain in 1983, with the famous report by Sir Roy Griffiths (Department of Health and Social Security, 1983), which sets out the tenets of a new approach to managing hospitals (Pollitt et al., 1991). Chapter 4 concentrates on secondary public schooling and on the relationship between managers and governors as it has evolved in the last ten years in the aftermath of the performance and standards movement.

Part III of the book consists of two chapters. Chapter 5 analyses the data generated from the two sectors and explains reform patterns in a comparative and cross-sectoral perspective. Are reforms intended to enhance managerial accountability? What is the rationale for their widespread adoption? The chapter discusses the causal mechanisms which are responsible for decreasing variance in social administration in European welfare states. In stressing the role of mimetic isomorphism, my argument represents part of a growing scepticism with efficiency claims. Building upon the empirical findings presented and discussed in Part II, Chapter 6 addresses the wider questions of welfare and democracy, set out in this Introduction and developed in Chapter 1, in light of what we will have learnt from the cases of education and health care in Europe. Given that the reforms analysed in this book are far from being technical matters, to be relegated to the realm of management handbooks, the concluding chapter offers insights into the strong pressure that managerialism poses to existing welfare democratic structures. This risk is magnified by deliberate strategies to couch the debate about welfare administration in terms of politically neutral and technical matters. It is also a credible threat given the empirical evidence provided in this book for convergence of European welfare states on the organizational dimension which defines the relationship between managerial and political accountability.

# Part I  Welfare and Administration: The New Settlement, 1980–2007

# 1
# The New Administrative Settlement of the Welfare State

Administrative arrangements can make a great deal of difference to the outcome of a social policy. Public institutions which deliver services such as compulsory education, health care, and social care are capable of shaping the goals and interests of individual actors, provided certain organizational features are in place. The relationship between professionals, public managers and users is not only a function of contextual conditions or policy orientations. It is also endogenously forged (March and Olsen, 1984). Although doctors, social workers and teachers have extensive contact with the public, they practise within organizations which determine their behaviour and their expectations. Organizational relationships are as crucial as the political and socio-economic context in which they are embedded. Their relationships are not only directed towards users and welfare recipients but also to the various layers of the internal hierarchy of the bureaucratic organization. Frequently, when studying the welfare state as a 'professional state' (Day and Klein, 1987), the administrative variables which endogenously shape the power relationship between actors are omitted. For instance, the coordination mechanism of a hospital or a school is one of the most important factors determining the outcome of reforms geared at granting them greater autonomy from central government controls.

In the current debate about social policy, there is often greater disagreement over the details of administrative arrangements than general policy goals. The public debate about the purpose of public education or universal health care services is kept in the shadow of greater preoccupation with the cost-effectiveness of welfare services and the measurement of performance accountability. The predominant public discourse places the welfare state as an 'object' of the state, an area of governmental activities as any other in a continual process of administrative re-engineering.

13

This study aims at locating it as a subject of the state, inextricably linked to the political institutions of each democracy in Europe. However, the administrative changes of the welfare state are increasingly studied as if they were disconnected from their political determinants. The effects of new organizational arrangements are rarely assessed unless they impinge directly on public expenditure. This was still the legacy of much 'crisis' rhetoric in the 1970s, when the diagnosis of the fiscal crisis of the state emerged in the aftermath of the oil shock.

Although Esping Andersen (1990) challenges the assumption that the level of social expenditure adequately reflects a state's commitment to welfare, most of the 'crises' attributed to the welfare state are still related to the contraction of public expenditure or the financial austerity and cutbacks. Arguably, this reflects the cost-containment strategies of many reforms of welfare services. Crisis and myth seem to reproduce themselves in a cyclical way (Castles, 2004). The 'organizational' dimension of this crisis is most often analysed in strict terms of public–private categories (Backhaus-Maul and Olk, 1994). However, organizational reforms refer to a wider range of mechanisms by which political commitments are turned into welfare outcomes. Moreover, outright privatization has been feasible only in more marginal areas of welfare provision, such as social care for the elderly or housing. As Leibfried argues, 'we see privatisation dominating the sphere of public utilities, while social policies effectively remain mainly with the national state' (Leibfried and Zürn, 2005: 24). There are few remarkable exceptions to a quantitative and predominantly expenditure-based approach. Leibfried has posed the question of the challenge to the golden age welfare state as a process of erosion of the congruence between the political and social space that construed the matrix of the welfare state (Leibfried and Zürn, 2005: 12).

This chapter offers an analysis of managerialism as a separate transformation of the welfare state from the introduction of markets and the privatization of welfare services. 'Privatization' has neither been the most consistent nor the exclusive method of reorganization of public welfare services. The change has not been one-dimensional (Wright, 1994; Le Grand and Robinson, 1984). Reorganizing welfare provision cannot be reduced to the replacement of the state by the market, or reduction in state provision coupled with greater regulation of private providers, or the greater involvement of charities and other non-profit organizations. The introduction of market mechanisms in the provision of welfare has been undeniably one of the most radical departures from the golden age of the 1960s, but another fundamental and more consistent trend since the mid-1980s has been the introduction of managerialism in social policy. Privatization and managerialism are interwoven, but profoundly distinct and analytically very different. The latter has not implied spending cuts, for instance, but has changed the relationship between the state and citizens significantly. This chapter sets out the main characteristics of managerialism and its theoretical antecedents. By doing so, it revisits some of the conventional assumptions concerning social administration, as laid down in the post-war welfare settlement.

## The return of the administrative question in social policy

Governments have set up organizations and large bureaucracies to fulfil their social policy goals. Designing administrative arrangements is a central part of the welfare state evolution. Most of the developments in the late nineteenth century and in the interwar period were social policies imposed 'from above' (Esping-Andersen and Korpi, 1984: 180). The post-war golden age of welfare expansion witnessed the construction of large government bureaucracies employing substantial proportions of the workforce and charged with providing the new social security, health care, social care, education and housing (Glennerster, 1975). This is not to suggest that the institutionalization of the welfare state was merely a bureaucratic development. In the 1960s and early 1970s, there was broad agreement between political parties about the social policies which were needed and this is referred to as the 'post-war settlement' (Lowe, 1999). Thus, besides economic and demographic factors, political ones have shaped welfare state developments (Leibfried and Zürn, 2005). For instance, the Christian Democratic Union–Christian-Social Union (CDU–CSU) hegemony in German politics from 1945 to 1965 has shaped the institutional framework within which post-war conflicts and negotiation were shaped largely by bourgeois forces, with the Social Democratic Party of Germany (SPD) cornered for many years. This contributed to maintaining the occupational division and the institutional fragmentation of the German welfare state (Kauffman, 2002; Seeleib-Kaiser and Bleses, 2004).

In no other European country was the post-war consensus as transformative and as formidable as in Britain under the aegis of the Beveridge Plan (Titmuss, 1968; 1970). The historical conjuncture of the 1940s was a period of convergence between institutional developments and widespread conceptual change, as Marshall argues in his seminal work on social citizenship (Marshall, 1950). He explains the growth of this consensus as the outcome of two important factors. First, the war created a strong sense of national solidarity. Secondly, he suggested that social reforms were carried out at a time of austerity and scarcity in the immediate years after the end of the war, in what he calls the 'Austerity Society'. Paradoxically, Marshall viewed austerity as a condition for the expansion of social rights, a very different conceptual premise to the argument of the 'crisis' of the welfare state from the late 1970s.

The reorientation of law and order types of bureaucracies towards welfare services was a major and formidable institutional change. Although it is outside the scope of this book to dwell on this historical question in detail, for comparative purposes it is worth noticing that whereas in Britain there was not just one bureaucratic voice in relation to post-war welfare state developments, in France the organizational development of the welfare state 'can be traced in a single organisational line' (Ashford, 1986: 115). There were powerful civil servants in Britain, such as Sir Robert Morant, who had tremendous influence on the creation of public education, but there was also the established bureaucracy of the Treasury which resisted social agencies and could inhibit the development of welfare.

On the contrary, in France, the *grand corps* were successful in creating political alliances with the Radical Socialists. In France, the concept of *solidarité sociale* permeated the rationale for social reforms among Radicals, Radical Socialists and Socialists (Hayward, 1959).[1] The civil servants of the *Conseil d'Etat* were socially devoted and some of them formed the nucleus of the Ministry of Labour in the 1920s and 1930s. Despite the fact that French social benefits were smaller than the British ones, from its inception the welfare state merged social values with the problems of the French democracy, like no other European country. In Germany and Italy, after World War II much of the bureaucratic structures had to be reconstructed and revised with the renewed values of democratic governance.

In the 1990s the 'efficient management' of welfare services has gained a prominent position again on the agenda of European governments for two main reasons. First, it is a response to the criticism moved by the public choice school on the rigid, remote and unrepresentative welfare state technocracy (Self, 1993). Secondly, it arises from the need to implement cost-saving strategies and avoid unpopular and politically costly decisions. It is claimed that long years of welfare state expansion from 1945 to 1970 increased the power of public service providers and professionals without improving their weak accountability to customers. A basic goal of this 'attack' on the welfare state was to offer greater choice of service to clients, to undermine the monopolistic position of public providers and stimulate competition in order to reduce the 'gate keeping' function of bureaucrats and their paternalistic allocation of resources.

Therefore, the welfare state was criticized not only for its rising costs but also for its unresponsive administration, which was not in tune with the development of needs beyond bread and butter. These arguments opened a breach for borrowing policy ideas and instruments which were originally adopted in other areas of state activities and mainly by central governmental agencies and the civil service (Page and Wright, 1999).

As I have emphasized earlier, it would be misleading to view the popular support for the welfare state only as a way to meet social and economic needs, or as a rational preference for 'risk avoidance' (Goodin and Dryzek, 1987). Governments consist of a conglomerate of organizations functioning on conformed patterns of behaviours and norms, which eschew rational choice (Allison and Zelikon, 1999). The civil service can have important indirect effects on the content and development of social policies, as Heclo had argued in his study about social politics in Britain and Sweden (1974). Heclo argues that civil service administrators have made greater contributions to social policy than political parties or interest groups.

Although in some countries, like New Zealand (Starke, 2007), office-seeking politicians have pursued unpopular policies of dismantling social contributions, in other countries the normative framework underpinning the welfare state has not even allowed politicians to couch the debate in terms of 'retrenchment'. The political conflict has not been about rolling back the state or the status quo, but about redesigning policy structures and delivery systems (Lewis et al., 2005). Far from the widely held assumption that what is not measured in terms of public expenditure is of little relevance for the development of the welfare state, political conflict has been generated by 'modernising' the existing framework rather than by radical upheavals. This does not only depend on the different types of welfare regimes, namely liberal Britain against conservative welfare systems, but chiefly on the intrinsic character of managerialism.

Therefore, the current politics of social policy centre on the European pressing predicament of restructuring and modernizing the post-war arrangements rather than dismantling them, given that political support for the welfare state is not eroding (Swank, 2002). In social democratic welfare states, we find large constituency groups organized around generous programmes, but also in more corporatist–conservative and liberal welfare states we find support generated by generous schemes of social protections. 'Restructuring', defined in this study as the administrative reorganization of welfare bureaucracies, represents the least politically costly strategy for tackling the financial

strains of the welfare state and improving the quality of public services. For politicians and civil servants alike, the benefits of reform programmes on good management overweigh the financial and political
costs of announcing cutbacks. Political support for the welfare state can
be maintained, if not increased, by enacting, or announcing, policy
reforms aimed at making welfare administration more efficient, and
streamlining heavy bureaucratic organizations. Bureaucracy has, thus,
become the scapegoat of all evils (Suleiman, 2003), and at the same time
the acclaimed solution for many problems.

Reshaping the administration of the welfare state by reducing the size,
scope and resources of the services has led politicians to claim that the
state is in 'crisis'. New public management reforms, namely the deliberate change to the structures and processes of public sector organizations
with the objective of improving public services, has been one of the
most critical issues in contemporary government practice and policy
reform in advanced industrial democracies (Dunsire, Hood and Huby,
1989; Lane, 2000; Stewart and Walsh, 1992). Scholars of administrative
reforms in the 1980s and 1990s have associated the 'crisis' of the state
with new rules of public authority and organization, introduced with
the alleged 'withdrawal of the state' from spheres of intervention which
were previously at the core of its activity and legitimacy (Wright and
Müller, 1994). Most reforms in the 1980s stemmed from economic and
financial tribulations confronting governments unable to pay for public
sector expenditure without increasing taxation. However, the problem of
the crisis of the state does not merely concern its financial capacity, but
involves deep-seated ideological disputes about its nature and purposes.

Whether this reshaping of public sector's functions and processes can
be defined as a 'crisis' should follow a careful evaluation of the specific
challenges that these new arrangements have posed to domestic administrative structures (Page and Wright, 1999). Advocates of the 'entrepreneurial state' (Borgonovi, 1988; Osborne and Gaebler, 1992; Rebora,
1995; Kettl, 2000), however, have devoted less attention towards inves-
tigating the different responses of individual administrative systems.[2]
Hence, insufficient attention has been drawn to the type of challenge
that the alleged 'crisis' poses to firmly entrenched and historically determined bureaucratic welfare traditions. As Wright argued, the general
picture of state retreat 'may mask a partial, nationally differentiated,
limited reality with perverse displacement effects and unintended consequences leading to renewed state activity' (Wright and Müller, 1994).

Managerialism has not only dominated social policy in Britain but
has also been exported to continental European countries (Flynn and

Strehl, 1996; Lane, 2000; Kickert, 1997). NPM is aimed at solving the problems of inefficiencies of the public sector. It is a multifaceted and loose concept, including different doctrinal elements, which policymakers choose according to domestic politics priorities. Thus, it does not represent a coherent movement (Aucoin, 1990). The internal tensions and paradoxes result from the centralizing tendencies of contractualism against the devolutionary tendencies of managerialism (Christensen and Laegreid, 2001a). On the one hand, through contracts political leaders are supposed to specify targets and objectives more clearly, and on the other hand performance should be controlled by the use of indicators for monitoring results and measuring efficiency (Bevan and Cornwell, 2006).

The introduction of pro-competitive ideas, privatization, marketization and managerialism is far from being a phenomenon confined to social policies. It encompasses a wider institutional question for the state in multiple dimensions.[3] The problem of the retreat of the state is not merely an ideological debate,[4] for clearly managerialism has been introduced equally by left and right governments (Pollitt and Bouckaert, 2000). Nor is it a pragmatic problem of cutbacks aimed at containing costs of welfare services under the pressure of the internationalization of financial and industrial circuits and the rise of stateless actors such as multinational corporations. These transformations also have direct consequences for the relationship between the welfare state and its citizens, for representative government and democratic institutions.

The reorganization of welfare bureaucracies in the 1980s and 1990s has witnessed the introduction of new policy instruments, such as quasi-markets (West and Pennell, 2005; Le Grand and Bartlett, 1993; Le Grand et al., 1998). The combination of free access at the point of delivery and decentralized market-like competition between providers of services was the key institutional innovation referred as 'quasi-market'.[5] Despite the ideological commitment of neoliberal governments, market-type mechanisms are introduced for pragmatic reasons, chiefly for cost-containment of public expenditure. Conceptually, it can be argued that the NPM has led to the marketization of public services by incorporating market methods and incentives into the management of social policies (Ranade, 1998). However, this book focuses on a particular and distinctive form of institutional change, which concerns 'privatizing from within', to indicate the extension of private sector management processes into the public organizations of welfare delivery. The next section of this chapter defines the major characteristics and content of managerialism in the context of the welfare state.

## Restructuring the 'old' European welfare administration and new public management

There is an established and comprehensive literature on public management reforms focusing on the comparative analysis of reform trajectories in Europe. One of the most classical works in this area has been C. Pollitt and G. Bouckaert's *Public Management Reform: A Comparative Analysis* (2000). This work presents public management changes concerning the civil service and the core executive. There is little reference to welfare institutions, which remain outside the remit of the book. Countries have differed with respect to the scope and intensity of the adoption of public management (Christensen and Laegreid, 2001), but many governments have adhered broadly to the underlying philosophy, namely running public organizations as private sector enterprise in order to improve their efficiency. The comparative public administration literature does not cover social policy in a comprehensive way, as its main focus is usually the central administrative machinery or specific agencies. This is somewhat of a missed opportunity, given the large bureaucratic organizations which operate in health care, education, housing, etc. This book aims to integrate the debate on administrative reforms with social policy, for the historical development of the welfare state owes much to administrative organizations and arrangements.

In contrast to the public utilities component, the welfare state is clearly being reformed both in the organizational and territorial sense (Rothang, Obinger and Leibfried, 2006). 'Autonomy' has been a recurrent theme of public services reforms since the 1980s. Its normative underpinning and doctrinal legacy have been associated with NPM and entrepreneurial behaviour (Saltman, Busse and Mossialos, 2002). One of its core elements is the preference for more specialized and autonomous organizational forms and 'flexible government' (Hood, 1995; Peters, 1996), which are given a clear set of targets to achieve, and a greater discretion to decide how to go about achieving them. In a restricted sense, autonomy refers to the freedoms of individual public managers, summarized in the slogan 'let the managers free to manage' (Osborne and Gaebler, 1992). A more comprehensive definition of autonomy for the purpose of this book also includes the changes of the organizational management and governance (Ouchi, 1979).

How did it happen that modelling of welfare state organizations has been permeated by rules borrowed by the *transformative* processes of administrative reforms (March and Olsen, 1989; Christensen, Laegreid and Wise, 2002)?[6] In search of solutions, political leaders and social policy advisers in Britain, Germany and other continental European countries have looked at the nearby field of administrative reforms of the civil service for ready-made alternatives to traditional bureaucratic welfare delivery systems. Hence, welfare reforms have become imbued with NPM ideas, including organizational autonomy and decentralized modes of governance (Pollitt et al., 1998).

The idea of 'deregulating' government or 'lightening the burden' or 'hollowing out' the state is central to NPM (Rhodes, 1994). The disenchantment and loss of public confidence in the public sector, the economic and fiscal crises that Reagan's America and Thatcher's Britain were facing and the inefficiency of the administrative machinery (Dunleavy, 1991), due to an overload of rules and bureaucratic formality, have contributed to the pressure for a 'state withdrawal' from its activities (Wright, 1994; Suleiman, 2003). This has implied less state intervention in the economy, privatization of nationalized industries, dismantling of administrative controls and regulations and establishment of new agencies, such as the Next Steps Initiative in the United Kingdom (Rhodes, 1997).

Another feature of the NPM approach is the enthusiasm for entrepreneurial and business-like behaviour in the public management (Osborne and Gaebler, 1992). The public manager should have the same freedom and flexibility of decision making as his private sector counterpart. A change in management orientation from focus on rules and regulations to a greater emphasis on meeting targets is recommended. The position of the civil servant should be one of a line manager with clearly defined operational responsibilities deriving from policy decisions made by politicians. This managerial logic has also been transferred to welfare programmes, such as education (Chubb and Moe, 1990) and health care (Department of Health and Social Security, 1983; Marmor, 2004).

The concept of separating provision from production of public services has also been claimed by NPM, and has been at the centre of the creation of quasi-markets in welfare provision (West and Currie, 2008; West and Pennell, 2006; Le Grand and Bartlett, 1993; Le Grand et al., 1998). In the United States and United Kingdom this has taken the form of privatization, decentralization and creation of independent executive agencies (Thatcher and Stone Sweet, 2002). Separation is claimed to reduce political interference as well as the influence of producers avoiding the risk of 'capture'. In practice, this division means that the strategic functions of politicians and ministers, responsible for setting policy priorities, are clearly separated from the service delivery activities of agencies and departments.

An important aim of the new approach to public management is to give greater weight in service delivery to the interests and needs of consumers (Newman and Kuhlmann, 2007). Vice-President Gore, whose task in 1992 was to put into effect NPM ideas in federal government, said: 'we will measure our success by consumer satisfaction' (Kettl, 2000). It implies more consumer surveys, greater variety of services, higher response to customers' complaints and other mechanisms. Since the customer-oriented approach is clearly borrowed from the private sector, it is not without problems for legitimacy and accountability, as I will discuss at length in Chapter 2.

Local provision for services is also recommended by NPM doctrine because it enables a greater possibility of meeting local needs. A remote agency or a central department is less likely to give customers the public services they want because it is too detached from their needs. The decentralization of service delivery not only results in more flexibility but also in improved efficiency and greater innovation. Such decentralization can be achieved by relying more either on local government or on decentralization within central government itself or by use of third-sector agencies. Foster and Plowden have argued that in backing decentralization targeted at specific client groups, such as providing health services for the elderly, veterans or the poor, rather than for all citizens, NPM seems to support a shift from party to issue politics (Foster and Plowden, 1996). It is certainly less costly to provide services to targeted client groups than the entire population.

During the 1980s and 1990s, the 'marketisation' of the public sector, with its emphasis on customers and competition, seemed the best option for reforming an inefficient public sector (Ranade, 1998). NPM was greeted with enthusiasm from the British Government; in 1991, for example, the British Government published its Citizen's Charter, setting standards for the satisfaction and protection of consumers' needs. Some years earlier, in 1988, the Next Steps Initiative has been launched. It involved the establishment of executive agencies to deliver public services. Nevertheless the introduction of these ideas is controversial and raises serious questions of accountability, re-regulation, policy coordination and the general shift of balance of power in the political system.

Most of the problems stem from the fact that private management methods are applied unmodified to the public sector (Marmor, 2004). The civil servants have a different set of values and orientations from private managers: they are 'community' or 'service' oriented and emphasize security of employment. Besides this cultural explanation, the bureaucracy is not free from political interference and has to take into account external or environmental factors, such as the relationship with other departments, agencies and with the elected representatives. In fact, the economic need for cutting public expenditure, advocated by the Treasury or other departments, does not always coincide with the political interests of parties or Members of Parliament seeking re-election. Nevertheless, in Foster and Plowden's view (1996), there is no doubt that the fiscal crisis and the need to cut public expenditure are at the heart of the radical moves towards the 'hollowing out' of the state, which has given NPM its window of opportunity. According to them, the catalyst for reforms was not it revolutionary thinking inside government, but it was dictated by public dissent in the United States to increased taxes to finance public expenditure's growth. The fiscal crisis was worsened by the low productivity level in public service delivery. Inefficiency seemed to be the major problem to tackle in order to be able to cut public expenditure and continue providing state services to citizens.

Hood identifies the major paradox of NPM in the fact that deregulation in the private sector has been followed by an increase in bureaucratic regulation. He argues that 'the down-grid/down-group movement in service delivery associated with NPM will tend to be paralleled by an up-group and up-grid movement in public sector regulation' (Hood, 1998). The explanation he offers for the 'mirror image' is that the organizational 'unbundling', which is an integral part of NPM, is a precondition for more regulation in order to handle disputes. In fact, regulation has generated conflicts between the regulators themselves, being agencies or core departments, because of their different and conflicting objectives (Baldwin and Cave, 1999).

NPM has also received criticism regarding the implications for administrative coordination (Christensen and Laegreid, 2001b). In fact, by 'disaggregating' central functions with the creation of independent executive agencies, the result is likely to be contradictory objectives and conflicts, which would probably need to be solved by more regulation. Besides the problem for policy coordination, the exclusive concept of citizens as customers and consumers has also been problematic (Pollock, 2004). NPM seems to ignore the fact that the notion of citizenship involves political, legal and social rights as well (Marshall, 1950). It seems that the distinction between the concept of taxpayers, citizens and customers has been blurred by the new approach at the expense of political legitimacy. I will return to this question in Part III of this book.

Devolved managerial responsibilities have been one of the central themes not only of the British NPM but also of the German *Neue Steuerungsmodell* (KGst, 1993; Reichard, 1994; Reichard, 1998;

Jann et al., 2004). I will discuss this in greater detail in Chapter 3. The main elements of the New Steering Model included mainly micro-economic governance instruments, the clear-cut division of politics from administration, contract management, output emphasis, result oriented budgeting and decentralized resource responsibility *(Dezentrale Ressourcenverantwortung)* among others (Banner, 2001, 2005; KGst, 2003). Public managers are let 'free to manage', for politicians are disengaged from running administrative bureaucracies. Reform measures were introduced in many European countries to allow greater bureaucratic discretion for public managers and senior civil servants (Ministero per la Funzione Pubblica, 1982). Schools' head teachers were entrusted with managerial responsibilities as well as public hospitals' managers. This was claimed to improve the efficient decision-making process and encourage managers to take responsibility for output. According to the OECD (1995, 1996), NPM represented a global paradigm for the organization of public services.

The appearance of similar public sector reforms across different administrative traditions has provided a sense of convergence, similar to a 'paradigm shift' (Kuhn, 1962). Certainly common to reform movements is the use of the economic market as a model for administrative coordination (Self, 1993). The claimed promise is to maximize productive and allocative efficiencies that are hampered by 'bureau-pathology' (Dunleavy, 1991), namely by public agencies unresponsive to citizens. However, convergence is a 'myth', as Pollitt argues (Pollitt, 2001). He suggests that convergence is concerned with organizational labels rather than actual practices. Reforms in different countries may attend to the appearance of similar programmes, but, he argues, evidence indicates that substantive content is different. Powell and DiMaggio in their seminal study have also suggested that governments are active in copying organizational forms for reasons that escape global pressures or efficiency gains motives (Powell and DiMaggio, 1991). Political rhetoric and strategy play a pivotal role in the adoption of new public management, more so in countries where they are associated with neoliberal ideologies, such as the United States or the United Kingdom or New Zealand (Castles et al., 1996). However, administrative reforms and changes are not simply empty talk (Christensen and Laegreid, 2001b).

The actual new configuration of political accountability in welfare institutions is changing rapidly and this issue is likely to grow in significance in future years owing to the marketization and privatization of services (Wright, 1994; Esping-Andersen, 1999; Huber and Stephens, 2001; Leibfried, 2005). One of the most distinct elements of managerialism is the challenge it has posed to traditional forms of political accountability. By reshaping the relationship between public managers and politicians, the new managerialism has altered the balance between output-oriented legitimacy and the process of democratic decision making. How to ensure accountability becomes problematic if public managers are excluded from the political arena (Peters, 1996). This is also the case if politicians displace public accountability to senior civil servants, when services do not work. The legitimacy of managers' decisions is increasingly produced by the achievement of performance targets, rather than by the quality of democratic processes. This should not come as a great surprise, as 'new modes of governance can no longer be defined merely in terms of parties, interest groups, parliamentary institutions and a quasi-state monopoly in the ensuing conflict resolution and welfare state arrangements' (Jann, 2005: 153).

In contrast to the NPM focus on internal control, the public governance literature revisits the role of the state as 'enabler', not direct provider of services (Rhodes, 1997; Kooiman, 2003; Jann, 2005). Whereas old traditional 'government' is concerned with a distinction between public and private spheres, new modes of governance are characterized by shifting boundaries between public and private sectors. Negotiated patterns of public–private relations, defined by coordination and cooperation of public and private actors, and a mix of functions between politics and administration supplant the old clear-cut distinction between input and output functions of the state. It is argued that modern governance, contrary to the excessive emphasis on internal administrative control, supports the enhancement of the traditional democratic, representative and bureaucratic Weberian paradigm of public administration and the state (Jann, 2005:152). It becomes possible then to generate public value without state interference, through self-regulated networks and organizations (Rhodes, 1997). Consequently, legitimacy of authority is not based merely on legality and *ex ante* procedural control, but also on *ex post* concerns for results.

This book's analysis on restructuring welfare institutions moves beyond a merely internal management discussion of formal organizational design. The view of public administration in this book is that of an actor inextricably embedded in the dynamic political process of producing legitimacy and accountability (Suleiman, 2003). In contrast to much scholarly work on the introduction of general management in delivery institutions, primarily concerned with microeconomic management, it is necessary to place welfare institutions in their political setting and the traditional structures of political authority (Mayntz and Streek, 2003; Obinger, Leibfried and Castles, 2005). In France and Italy for instance, welfare institutions, such as hospitals and schools, are entrenched in local politics by means of extensive patronage (Eisenstadt, 1984; Wright and Meny, 1985; Tarrow et al., 1979). Public managers and local politicians are part of the same tightly organized policy community. The nature of the political setting in which welfare units are embedded – be it functional or politico-representative, driven by output or procedural legalism – is a determinant of the configuration of the new relationship between managerial and political accountability. If local government is justified functionally (Sharpe, 1970), as in Britain, it is more likely that administrative adjustments and changes geared towards greater efficiency gains and cost containment would be perceived as less of a challenge for political accountability.

## Research strategy, cases and methods: Explaining similarities across most different systems

This section discusses the research design which I adopted for this empirical study, explaining the rationale for analytical case selection, methods and procedures employed to collect and analyse data, and the unusual strategy of comparing different social policy areas across countries rather than different countries along sectors. The book explains with a comparative 'small-N' methodology and predominantly qualitative strategy the reorganization of the institutions of the welfare state along the following three main research questions. First, the study analyses empirically the *reach* of the managerial 'crusade' and its receptivity level in individual countries in a cross-sectoral approach. Secondly, by looking at the *intensity* of the managerial challenge posed to democratic accountability, this book intends to identify the effects of the introduction of NPM on the democratic institutions of the welfare state in different countries. Thirdly, the cross-national and cross-sectoral variations of the actual configurations of the relationship between political and managerial accountability, as reflected in new organizational arrangements of delivery, trigger the wider question about the *convergence* or divergence 'towards' predominantly technocratic-managerial welfare organizational forms. Are we witnessing a definite shift away from political-representative types of welfare organizations, with clear lines of accountability running from managers to elected politicians, towards mainly functionally driven and technocratic accountability, legitimated by 'customer satisfaction', rather than democratic accountability?

This book uses a flexible research design, as a result of the exploratory nature of the study (Hammersley, 2000; Rubin and Rubin, 1995). The effects of managerialism on the institutional structure of the welfare state and democratic accountability cannot be measured exclusively through evaluative studies of final reform effectiveness, for reforms are aimed at improving the running of services through innovative *processes*. New processes of decision making are more easily traceable through flexible research designs, which allow for the qualitative assessment of legislative changes and interview with policymakers, than quantitative designs. Qualitative research has much to offer also because we know little about the phenomena to be explored. We know very little about the introduction of managerialism in social policy in continental Europe, given the strong research bias in the cases towards the United Kingdom, United States and Scandinavian countries. Most of the edited books concerned with comparative administrative reforms focus exclusively on the civil service and central agencies (Page and Wright, 1999), and characterize Germany, France and Italy as the epitomes of inertial systems.

In the 1980s and 1990s many European governments, not only in the Anglo-Saxon world, have devoted a considerable deal of reform effort to the reorganization of the institutional structures of social policy and getting welfare bureaucracies to deliver more efficient services. This book seeks to redress the existing research bias in country selection by studying the reorganization of the welfare state in France, Germany and Italy with a systematic comparison with the British reference, which is the main 'exporting' country of new public management in Europe. Therefore, the exploratory nature of this study is best served by mainly a qualitative and flexible research design (Robson, 2002).

The research strategy in the book is not driven by the verification of rival theories, or fixed pre-specifications, for the design 'unfolds' as the research proceeds through the analytical narratives of the managerial reforms in health care and education in Part II. A flexible research strategy aims to end up with a theoretical explanation and does not start with a fixed one (Hammersley, 2000). Although theoretical propositions are put forward in the next chapter to guide the analysis, by no means are these to be taken as fixed hypotheses. Hence, such methodological approach offers a better grasp because we know little about the phenomena to be investigated, and focus more on the processes and less on the evaluation of outcomes. Comparative quantitative data on policy evaluation of health care and education reforms are provided abundantly by the OECD, particularly as financial indicators of public expenditure. The case analysis will draw on these quantitative datasets, such as *Education at a Glance: OECD Indicators*, but will complement these sources with interviews, documentary analysis, direct observation whenever feasible and other qualitative methods, discussed later.

The methodological approach of the empirical investigation is the case study, grounded in theory and less in ethnographies (Hammersely, 2000). Although I employ the method of direct observation in relation to the embedded case of the largest European hospital chain, *Charité* in Berlin, this is marginal in comparison with interviews, documentary and archival analysis, used extensively in this project. Thus, this book is not an ethnographic study, in the classical anthropological and sociological meaning (Robson, 2000). In accordance with the case study strategy, the research design is evolving, and the analytical categories emerge from the empirical journey (Yin, 1994). This book is not a single case study, but it develops a complex multiple case research design across four different countries (Britain, Germany, France and Italy) and two social policy areas, namely, secondary state education and health care. This will generate extremely rich data and maximize variance on the independent and dependent variables (Ragin, 1987).

The case studies selected do not represent sampling units, but I use them to develop a theoretical framework which will link managerialism to its effects on the institutional structures of the welfare state. The purpose of this methodological strategy is not to enumerate frequencies, but to generalize theories of welfare states and their institutional and administrative structures. I develop analytical propositions in the next chapter to guide the data collection and analysis, but I do not use them as fixed *a priori* laws. Let me quickly explain the case selection strategy, summarized in Table 1.1. Both countries and sectors have been selected *ex ante* on the basis of theoretical expectations. The selection strategy responds to a different method of comparison, as defined by Lijphart (1975), for the task is to find relationships among variables that can survive being transported across a range of very different countries and different sectors of the welfare state.

One of the main purposes of my methodological approach is to explain similarities across most different systems, rather than accounting only for variance. Britain, on the one hand, and the group of continental European countries, including Germany, France and Italy, on the other, constitute two representative cases of different reform patterns concerning state reforms. On the one hand, Britain represents the case of hyperactivity and reforms impetus, in relation to managerialism, but more generally as far as policymaking is concerned, given

*Table 1.1* Case selection strategy: At the extreme of two spectrums

|  |  | Social Policy reform impetus | |
|---|---|---|---|
|  |  | High | Low |
| **Administrative veto points and State tradition** | High |  | Germany, France, Italy Incremental or inertial social policy change; limited possibility of radical change; public authority tradition |
|  | Low | Britain Possibility of radical social policy change; high legislative activism; public service state tradition |  |

its Westminster majoritarian political system, for example, whereas the group of countries composed by Germany, France and Italy represent the cases of immobilisme, and inertia. The widely known characterization of these continental European countries is one of 'laggard cases', as far as public management reforms are concerned (Wöllmann, 2001). Institutional inertia and veto points are claimed to impede reforms in Germany, France and Italy (Crozier, 1970; Tsebelis, 2000; Manow, 2004). Theories predict incremental or inertial change as the predominant policymaking process in this group of countries (Mattei, 2005b). This study aims to explain whether these differences between Britain on the one hand, and three continental European countries on the other play a role in determining the introduction and development of managerial accountability strategies in the welfare state. Furthermore, we know very little about the application of public management to social policy in Germany, France and Italy. The cases of the United States and Sweden are not included here on a systematic basis because, together with the United Kingdom, they are probably the most examined countries both in the public management and welfare state scholarly debate.

Therefore, the selection of countries is not based on welfare state regime types (Esping-Andersen, 1990). Had I adopted this strategy, this book would have included a social democratic system, such as Sweden, for instance. Although the countries selected do vary on the basis of their welfare state type,[7] the nature of this variance is not significant enough for the purpose of this project, which is to explain similarities across welfare state regimes, rather than differences. In fact, one of the problems with the classic typology of Esping-Andersen is that it does not help to explain mechanisms of convergence. Hence, it does not fully capture the most recent challenges to the traditional conceptualization of European social policy.

Another rationale for this country case selection was to discuss case studies which would not only contrast with each other but also relate to each other, and be fully comparable on the basis of the institutional structures of the state. Germany, France and Italy share similar state traditions, which are based on the *Rechtsstaat*, which is claimed to be a possible obstacle to the introduction of managerialism in social policy. The selection of the three main European countries on the basis of their administrative traditions offers the opportunity to compare them directly, and control for extraneous variance.

As far as the policy areas are concerned, education and health care are included. All the income transfer programmes, such as pensions, unemployment, housing assistance and other social assistance schemes, are not. I will now explain the rationale for this sector selection, which is again based on *ex ante* theoretical reasons. Education and health care may not represent the bulk of welfare state public expenditure in the OECD world, but their centrality is undeniable. These are the two public services at the core of Marshall's definition of welfare state in the post-war years (1950). Education and health care are services received as a result of being a citizen, in contrast with the means-tested benefits. The British National Health Service embodied the principles of citizenship that Marshall had claimed for the welfare state as a whole, namely equal rights of access to care, and free at the point of delivery. Most recently, education is coming back in the social policy debate with the prominence which it used to enjoy in the post-war settlement years.

In addition to the significance of citizenship rights to education and health care, the organizational dimension of the delivery system is the second most important rationale for the selection of these two policy areas. As was the case for the countries selection, the most different systems of comparison are adopted also for sectors. Public hospitals and public schools are very different organizations, for the content of the service they provide to citizens, the activities they carry out, their relationship with the external environment and most visibly for the actors involved in the political processes, the different types of professionalism and so on. Most importantly for this study, schools and hospitals are most different in relation to the web of accountability relationships. This will be discussed in the next chapter. Therefore, comparing hospitals and schools offers the opportunity to compare how very different bureaucratic welfare organizations deal with changing accountability mixes. We are able to control, as much as possible, for the exogenous and other contextual factors which may affect individual sectors differently in different countries. Therefore the cross-sectoral comparison is mainly justified by the analytical model proposed here.

Hospitals are organizations with significant structural capacity, whereas secondary schools do not have the same financial and administrative resources. Hospitals benefit from large public budgets and represent the highest share of health care expenditure. The arena of decision making is very crowded in hospital care, with well-organized interests, whereas secondary schooling presents less wide networks with a more limited number of players. As is often the case for large organizations with significant structural capacity, specialization is extremely high in public hospitals. This is a response of the variety of services provided, but also of the network of care organized within a territory. A hospital is an extremely complex organization with conflicting goals (Hasenfeld and English, 1974; McKee and Healy, 2002). It consists of different individual departments, such as emergency medicine and units which have different goals. A hospital is made of a very large number of different occupational groups with an incredibly varied specialized body of knowledge. On the contrary, public schools have fewer organizational layers and are not internally as divided along functions or specialized divisions. Their differentiation mainly consists of different subjects taught.

However, despite their marked organizational differences, schools and hospitals are fully comparable units of analysis. Schools and hospitals are similarly subject to growing and rapidly changing pressures. The old bureaucratic organizational model has become inadequate to meet the new concerns for work productivity, individualized care, increasingly demanding users and evaluation of effectiveness of services. New and similar organizational solutions, inspired by neotaylorian management schools, have been considered in both sectors. Teachers and doctors have similarly changed their professionalism with greater emphasis on managerial practices, based on autonomy, transparency and marketing. Given the centrality of both these institutions in the wider educational and health care systems respectively, they can autonomously affect the broader policies which are adopted. The reforms to which schools and hospitals are subject contribute to determine the wider policy trajectory for the sector as a whole. Wider societal and political pressures on hospitals and schools include financial strains, internationalization of health and educational systems and globalization (Held and McGrew,

2000; OECD, 1996). Schools and hospitals are not only similar in terms of the pressure they are exposed to, but also in so far as they are welfare services in kind. In most industrial countries the post-war years witnessed the construction of large bureaucracies charged with the provision of social security, health, social care, education and housing. Social policies generally use three main administrative forms to achieve their goals: services in kind, cash benefits and regulation. This book focuses on 'services'.

As far as the methods are concerned, the study is based mainly on interviews, participant observations, documentary and archival analysis. Thus, the method is based on multiple sources to increase the construct validity and to allow for data triangulation. From September 2005 to January 2008, I have conducted extensive expert interviews in Britain, Germany and Italy, of which the majority were in Germany, Britain and Italy.[8] The case of France is primarily based on review of the secondary literature and in-depth documentary analysis. Interviews offer an insightful source of evidence, providing the author perceived causal inferences from actors involved in managing the organizational changes of managerialism. The bulk of respondents were selected from 'managers', namely, employees of hospitals and schools with managing responsibilities over the service delivery. In the case of education, I have selected mostly head teachers, who are the object and subject of the type of change analysed in this study.[9] Data will be quoted from interviews to illustrate the categories developed during the analysis.

The second most important source of data is documentary legislation, including acts enacted by parliaments and policy papers, which are more frequent in Britain. These are all official documents, publicly available, documenting the content of reforms and salient issues for political debate. Most of the changes concerning the organizational arrangements of schools and hospitals are decided by law in Germany, France and Italy. Thus, the analysis of legislation is an essential part of the methods employed here, for it does offer a rich and stable source of data, with exact information and broad coverage. The legislation here analysed in both sectors and across four countries covers a period of investigation from the 1988 Educational Reform Act to the 2007 French Hospital Plan. This allows a long-term perspective, not biased on any individual policy event or government's ideological composition.

Another important source of evidence is archival records from individual hospitals and schools. The author's site visits, mainly for the purpose of interviews, were also integrated with the collection of organizational charts, budgetary information and internal documentation of schools and hospitals. The most relevant group of such archival records concern 'strategic plans' for schools and hospitals, which were provided to the author quite openly, differently from financial statements. However, in most cases the latter were available publicly. The analysis of the internal governance structure of schools and hospitals relied in this study also on qualitative assessment of organizational charts and distribution of responsibilities among managers, professionals and all the actors involved in the delivery of services.

# 2
# The Internalization of Accountability

The problem with the legitimating ideology of marketization and managerialism is that it portrays efficiency as a technical problem. The advocates of the managerial restructuring of the welfare state couch their propositions as politically neutral, when effectively they establish priorities between conflicting demands for education and health care. As Broadfoot (1985: 274) argues convincingly, 'the criteria on which accountability is to be based can be couched in terms that conceal the value assumptions on which they are based'. This chapter focuses on the internalization of accountability within organizations aimed at providing services in kind, such as public schools and hospitals. The existing literature on public accountability is noticeably silent about the effects of new managerialism on politicians and political accountability in welfare bureaucracies. Most of the research, on the contrary, is concerned with central departments or executive agencies and with managerial types of accountability.

The purpose of this chapter is to offer a revised model of accountability which takes account of the effects of the structural characteristics of the administrative framework on the mix of accountability regimes formed within organizations. I suggest that the predominance of managerial over political accountability is a function not of policy instruments or policy change, but chiefly of structural and institutional rules. This revised model of accountability investigates the interplay between bureaucratic structural characteristics and the institutional changes resulting from a fundamental transformation of public accountability. Whereas the 'old' public administration emphasizes compliance with procedures and legal rules, the changes of accountability resulting from new public management are characterized by the growing importance of *ex post* 'results' at the expense of processes and input-oriented mechanisms.

The central research question is why the balance between organizational autonomy and political accountability may be altered in different ways across European countries and different social policy sectors, despite converging pressures along the managerial line discussed in Chapter 1. This entails an analysis of the reorganization of the internal governance of welfare institutions, as a result of widespread government' programmes to grant autonomy to hospitals and schools, and discretion to their managers in relation to politicians. Secondary public schools and public hospitals provide fundamental social services which form an integral part of the service welfare state. They are complex organizations with multiple and conflicting objectives, such as providing efficient services under public scrutiny. Until the early 1980s in Britain, and most recently in continental Europe, political considerations were a pivotal element of schools and hospitals' governance systems. Supervisory boards were composed of local councillors and elected local politicians. Political leaders were directly involved in planning activities and making allocative decisions.

Reforms associated with autonomization have changed the mechanisms of political accountability (Verhoest et al., 2004). The adoption of NPM has tilted the balance towards autonomy, at the expense of traditional forms of political accountability. Management boards of public hospitals and schools have acquired new responsibilities and benefited from diminishing political control (Kampe and Kracht, 1989; Saltman, Busse and Mossialos, 2002). However, the balance between autonomy and political accountability at the level of individual institutions is highly differentiated across countries in Europe. The picture is complicated further by cross-sectoral fertilization of NPM ideas. This may increase homogeneity of organizational forms and practices in the same sector across countries, obfuscating national patterns of welfare delivery. A recurrent theme of the reforms of schools and hospitals is the organizational autonomy they gain from central controls. This has been a core element of NPM (Pollitt and Bouckaert, 2000; OECD, 2001; 2005). The theoretical justifications of the process of autonomization are provided by economic neo-institutionalism, such as agency theory (Moe, 1984). Autonomy is also claimed to be associated with decentralized management and empowering local communities and local democracy (Stoker, 2006).

The microlevel operationalization of the changing balance between autonomy and political accountability leaves us, though, with the unanswered puzzle of the effects on politicians and how they respond to these changes. Some scholars have suggested that we witness a reassertion of politics through new methods of political control (Pierre, 1995; Halligan, 1997). New agencies have been created to tighten up policy coordination of autonomous units. The target regime in Britain is also exemplary of the emergence of new forms of centralized political control (Hood, James and Scott, 2000; Bevan and Hood, 2005). Ezra Suleiman (2003) even argues that NPM has been a stimulus to a politicization process. He suggests that 'political affiliation has once again become a determining criterion in appointments to top-level positions' (Suleiman, 2003: 17). Additional evidence is needed though to confirm this hypothesis.

Are politicians capable, beyond will, to reassert 'the primacy of politics' over expert decision making, assuming they try to do so? The atomization and fragmentation of the delivery of social services in specialized single-purpose units (Pollitt and Bouckaert, 2000: 78) has triggered post-NPM attempts at enhancing coordination and centralized monitoring by creating new agencies and new administrative layers of centralized control. Welfare federalism makes this option in Germany less plausible, if not impossible, unlike Britain, Italy and France (Obinger et al., 2006). Yet, alternatives in Germany include the opportunity to bring public hospitals, for instance, within the tight system of corporatism, by a process of 'corporatisation' of autonomous organizations (Döhler, 1995). Employing various instruments, politicians have indeed attempted to curtail the autonomy granted to welfare organizations and their managers.

What is also offered in this chapter is an analytical tool to operationalize the effects of administrative restructuring on political accountability, in order to discern clearly between political rhetoric and practice. As an oratorial slogan, political responsibility is 'decentralised' in favour of local needs and managers are put in charge. Therefore, it becomes increasingly essential to explain the process of establishing new types of accountability in welfare bureaucracies through the lenses of organizational and administrative strategies. In contrast with the claim that depoliticization at the micro level is more transient than other forms (Buller and Flinders, 2005), I maintain that its form within the state has the potential to be a long-lasting change, owing to processes of organizational learning (March and Olsen, 1989). Bureaucratic organizations have a power of their own, and organizational legacies influence the degree of effectiveness of political parties' attempts to reassert control. This book, thus, questions the reassuring prediction that it will be possible to re-establish political primacy in the welfare state, as we knew it before managerialism was introduced.

## 'New' types of democratic accountabilities

This study adopts Mulgan's (2000) approach to accountability and endorses fully the caution in stretching a concept beyond its core meaning (Sartori, 1970). In the context of a democratic system, core accountability refers to the relationship between the citizens and the holders of public office, and within state bureaucracies between politicians and bureaucrats. Thus, it means how voters can make elected representatives answer for their actions, how legislators can scrutinize the executive and how the public can seek redress from government agencies and officials. One of the most fundamental elements of 'core' accountability is its external dimension. This is fully in line with one of the conditions of democratic governance and popular sovereignty, namely the 'visibility' criteria, as emphasized by Schattschneider (1975). I will come back to this point later in the book, as it is crucial for the reorganization of welfare service bureaucracies. For now it is worth noticing that a democratic system is aimed at socializing conflict and the mobilization of interests. Despite its core meaning, political accountability has been loosely and interchangeably used with 'individual responsibility', 'responsiveness' and 'control'. As Mulgan points out, the new reconceptualization of accountability does not appreciate the original central importance of external scrutiny (Finer, 1941). In fact, responsibility is increasingly reliant on the ethical and personal territory of freedom of action and discretion. I refer to political accountability in this chapter in its core meaning, namely the relationship between elected officials and the public and between politicians and bureaucrats.

There is a growing and developing body of literature on 'new' types of political accountability, which expands the classical concept of the Westminster model of 'ministerial accountability'. These definitions emphasize responsiveness to 'users' of services and are particularly suited for application to welfare service administration. 'New' types of political accountability emphasize the need for civil servants to meet people's preferences and enhance their choice, in an analogous way to how private firms respond to their clients. Responsiveness is very different, however, from political accountability because it bypasses elected representatives. This new type of accountability has been also called 'downward accountability' in contrast with the upward hierarchical system by which public servants are accountable to their political masters and superiors. It remains unclear whether in a public system 'users' have sufficient authority to hold state bureaucracies accountable for their services.

## Delegation theory versus internalization

Principal–agent theories point to the importance of certain formal controls, like partisan appointment at the head of executive agencies or budget setting, for elected politicians to limit 'agency losses'. Studies on the politics of delegation have addressed the question of post-delegation political control and agencies' independence from partisan politics (Thatcher, 2005). Thatcher argues that politicians in Europe do not use formal controls such as partisan appointment, dismissal and so on. Rather, alternative methods of control include appointment by personal ties or policy preferences, but not partisanship. Transferring decision making from politicized to non-majoritarian decision making is claimed to enhance the credibility of government policies (Thatcher and Sweet, 2002). The main concern of principal-agent theories is assessing the degree of agency loss, with relatively less emphasis on the wider implications of non-majoritarian institutions for democratic accountability.

However, the problem with the assumption of delegation theories is that depoliticization is not analysed as it happens within the state, for change is viewed simply as a 'shift' in decision making from political to non-political arenas. Decisions are being moved to a different political arena, staffed not by people who are elected, but by experts. Flinders (2004) suggests that institutional depoliticization is based on the principal–agent model, whereby the principal (minister) sets broad policy goals, and the agent (chief executive of an agency) is responsible for executing. The model is based on the division between politics and administration which underpins the liberal British state (Hayward, 1998). On the contrary, the problem is one of emphasis and dominance of expert-rule or traditional modes of political representation. It is more productive to study non-majoritarian modes of governance not as a transition from old party democracy to new forms of governance, but in terms of the relationships between managerial and political account-ability, coexisting in any given accountability regimes.

Delegated autonomy from the state to semi-autonomous agencies at the national and European level is a widely acclaimed reform path. In a report written for the European Commission, Majone (1996, 1998) recommends the creation of powerful regulatory agencies. He argues that there is a need to insulate certain tasks from the political sphere in order to enhance policy credibility. The resulting problems of account-ability can be resolved by employing the right organizational design. The implementation of delegated agencies seems to be a construct of apolitical administrative engineering, which eschews citizens and mechanisms of representation. As Shapiro (1999) argued, 'the creation of apolitical independent agency is rather like the announcement by the demos that it does not trust itself'. This is to indicate that the normative values are inevitably built upon the assumption that apolitical institutions are better suited to 'solve problems'. Delegation not only creates problems for internal control and bureaucratic drift, but also for the normative framework of democratic processes.

Conversely, the focus of my approach is to explain change in the political processes firmly remaining *within* the organizations of the state, without adopting the misleading concept of a 'shift'. The praise of non-partisanship indeed represents a remarkable development of great relevance under Blair's New Labour, though it is not distinctive to British politics. Burnham suggests that depoliticization is mainly determined by exogenous economic circumstances linked to globalization and politicians' inability to control economic conditions. It is understood as 'the process of placing at one remove the political character of decision-making' (Burnham, 2001: 128). The prevailing form that it takes is rule-based economic management, departing from the old Keynesian, politicized and interventionist policies. Flinders and Buller's work adopts a similar definition of depoliticization, as an active 'process' of displacing political responsibility to different decision-making arenas (e.g. 'arena shifting'). Hence, it primarily responds to a strategy of blame avoidance (Hood, 2007; Weaver, 1986), for politicians seek to avoid responsibility for unpopular decisions. As far as the implications of depoliticization for democracy are concerned, arena shifting, they argue, does not necessarily imply a challenge to political legitimacy. The newly created bodies to which politicians shift responsibility for decision making remain intrinsically political institutions. Hence, depoliticization is a misnomer for arena shifting (Buller and Flinders, 2005).

The main problem with this excessively optimistic scholarship on depoliticization of policymaking in Britain is that it minimizes its wider implications for representative democracy. In this respect, it differs fundamentally from the recent work by Mair. He sustains that depoliticization is a symptom of a profound democratic malaise, with far-reaching implications for parliamentary democracies and electoral accountability. He attributes the origins of depoliticization to the failings of political parties by a process of mutual withdrawal (Mair, 2005: 8). Parties are failing in two ways: first, in their capacity to engage citizens, and secondly, in their representative function, as their political leaders retreat in institutions and public office holding. As far as the latter is concerned,

Mair (2005) maintains that over time the dual roles of parties, namely representative and procedural, became separated from one another. He seems to suggest that the ensuing depoliticization is a vicious circle leading to the erosion of popular democratic control and electoral accountability. It leads to putting under stress the traditional and conventional models of representation and party democracy. Thus, depoliticization is not only conceptualized as an instrument and a goal of policymaking, but it becomes a widespread and fundamentally non-democratic mode of governance, so as to 'hollow out partisan politics' (Mair, 2005: 25).

However, public organizations are not instrumental, but institutional actors in my approach. Welfare organizations do often adapt to their institutional context, but they often play an active role in shaping those contexts (Parsons and Smelser, 1956). The proposed study, by analysing the transformation of the internal governance of welfare organizations at the meso and micro level, concentrates on the unintended consequences for political accountability resulting from the organizational conformity with external managerial myths providing organizational legitimacy. Welfare organizations show considerable ability to survive, precisely because they incorporate powerful myths and 'institutionalised rules' (Meyer and Rowan, 1977), like entrepreneurialism and good management. Thus, organizational success depends not only on matching the demands of internal efficiency, but also on conformity to the prevailing normative obligations (DiMaggio and Powell, 1983). These myths are binding on organizations, for they create the necessity to redefine their internal organizational structures accordingly. External institutionalized rules are a legitimate source of organizational structure, which is not only the result of apolitical engineering.

### The welfare state: 'Free' from the 'burden' of democratic accountability?

Educational and health care administration, as well as welfare bureaucracies more generally, have been associated with a corporate management approach, discussed in the previous chapter. As a result, the core meaning of political accountability has been increasingly put under stress and criticised for being inadequate and unfit for the complexity of the tasks at hand. As an alternative, managerial accountability has entered the social policy debate. For instance, as I will discuss in full detail in Chapter 4, state schools have been increasingly preoccupied with the pursuit of bureaucratic efficiency and management techniques (Broadfoot, 1985). Efficiency and 'standards' have been elevated to be the meaning and values of education and health care administration. League tables for schools award and the culture of prize winning to reward 'excellence' is spreading outside the Anglo-Saxon world. For instance, the best German school award in 2008 was given to the Robert-Bosch-Gesamtschule Hildesheim in Niedersachsen, according to a competition sponsored by the Robert Bosch Foundation, which is promoting self-governing schools and great performance accountability.

The rise of managerialism, which I have discussed at length in Chapter 1, has not been accompanied by a conceptual revision of the traditional relationship between bureaucratic and political accountability. On the contrary, the dichotomous view persists, whereby political accountability is linked to the wider institutional level and bureaucratic accountability has mainly an internal dimension. It is widely accepted that there is a built-in rivalry between the two types of accountability, which differ for their accountable actors, holders, content and mechanisms. Table 2.1 summarizes the different types of accountability. Diverse expectations are generated within and outside the organization, creating an internal and external dimension of accountability (Romzek and Dubnick, 1987: 228). In most cases, what pertained to the definition of 'bureaucratic' accountability has been formally changed into 'managerial' to parallel the shifting role of civil servants from administrators to managers. The new relationships generated by managerial accountability, chiefly in relation to political ones, have been neglected, with few remarkable exceptions, such as Day and Klein (1987).

*Table 2.1*  Types of accountabilities in the welfare state

|  | Managerial accountability | Political accountability | Professional accountability |
|---|---|---|---|
| **Accountability holders** |  |  |  |
| *External* | Elected Representatives Users | Voters | None |
| *Internal* | Governing bodies of stakeholders |  | Peers |
| **Accountable actors** | Managers | Elected representatives | Doctors, teachers (professionals) |
| **Content** | Performance and efficiency | Representation | Expertise |
| **Mechanism** | Output measurement | Election | Advice |

The debate about managerial and political accountability has so far reflected the wider concerns about the classical tension between bureaucracy and democracy (Lipset, 1967; Weber, 1991). For this reason, analytically the two types of accountability have been often discussed in an antithetical way, as rivals. Under bureaucratic accountability systems, supervisory controls are applied hierarchically within the organization. The most important element is the relationship between a superior and a subordinate in which compliance with the rules dictated by the superior is its mechanism. Bureaucratic accountability is based on high level of control over behaviours and actions. On the contrary, political accountability is characterized by low degree of control over administrative actions (Romzek and Dubnick, 1987), which leaves ample discretion to civil servants. This feature embraces a wider definition of political accountability, which I refer as 'public', which includes interest groups, constituencies and a broad range of accountability holders beyond elected officials. The basis for public accountability between constituents and representatives is 'responsiveness', as the main mechanism of managing multiple expectations.

### Managerial and political accountability in welfare bureaucracies: Partners or rivals?

Few scholarly works have argued in favour of the empirical and analytical distinctiveness between managerial and political accountability more forcefully than Patricia Day and Rudolf Klein's (1987) *Accountabilities*. One of the merits of that work is to have addressed the specificities of the welfare state and to have focused on the internalization of accountability systems. The analytical approach of this book builds upon their definition of accountabilities in the service delivery state, but it develops further the administrative variables that constitute the structural terrain for the different types of possible combinations of managerial and political accountability. It is their dynamic interplay which shapes welfare bureaucracies, rather than their relative weight in terms of control within organizations. What are the structural characteristics of schools and hospitals which facilitate their vulnerabilities in relation to the transformation from bureaucratic to managerial accountability systems? This is the main question that the revised model addresses. It is likely that each organization will use the form of accountability regime that best suits its institutional mission and values.

Managerial accountability finds its intellectual tradition in the good estate management. As such it is a neutral and technical exercise.

For instance, checking whether the appropriate funds have come in and whether the outgoing money has been spent appropriately is an activity which falls in the remit of neutral experts. As Day and Klein discuss, one of the key historical developments in the system of financial accountability in England was the creation of the statutory Commission for Examining the Public Accounts in 1780, which integrated the notion of balancing the books with the management of resources, namely economy with efficiency (Day and Klein, 1987: 14). In its literal sense of bookkeeping, accountability is an Anglo-Norman practice. It can be traced to the Norman conquest of England after 1066, when William I required all the property holders in his realm to render a count of what they possessed (Bovens, 2006).

What distinguishes managerial accountability from other forms is, thus, neutral and technical expertise. As Day and Klein (1987: 27) suggest, 'managerial accountability is about making those with delegated authority answerable for carrying out agreed tasks according to agreed criteria of performance'. According to this conceptualization, managerial accountability is foremost a technical process by which governments ensure that fiscal regularities, efficiency and value for money have been achieved. Accountable management means holding individuals responsible for performance measured on the basis of objective and agreed criteria. Individual managers and their units are answerable for their performance to the actors who have delegated authority to them, such as politicians and citizens. Managerial models of administrative reforms require those with delegated authority, such as heads of hospitals or schools, to be answerable for producing outputs and meeting targets. The values embodied in managerial accountability are cost-effectiveness, efficiency and managerial autonomy (Sinclair, 1995: 222).

Managerial accountability has different dimensions, discussed by Day and Klein (1987). Mainly they refer to financial accountability, as public managers have become responsible for devolved budgets to schools and hospitals. The delivery of public social services in the last years has been marked by greater devolution of budgets to lower level units within the public sector (Glennerster, 2000). For instance, some schools in England were allowed to 'opt out' of local education authority's control and become more autonomous. Financial accountability consists of spending the allocated money according to appropriate rules within agreed legislative framework. Another important component of managerial accountability is efficiency accountability, which refers to the process of generating value for money. Input- and output-oriented managerial types of accountability depend ultimately on measuring performance and assessing organizational efficiency. In the case of most social services, outputs are not easily measurable, nor are production processes clearly understood. The nature of managerial accountability, thus, depends not only on the unilateral shift from political to technical decision making, but also, and most importantly, on the type of organizational governance which prevails within any organization (March, 1988).

In contrast with managerial accountability, political accountability rests upon debatable criteria based on 'reasons, justification, and explanation' (Day and Klein: 1987, 27). They emphasize the different tradition of the concept which was forged in the Athenian state. Officials there had to explain and justify their actions and conduct to the public. Political accountability is essentially defined in accordance with the classical notion offered by John Stuart Mill, which hinges on the concept of ministerial accountability and representative government. The element of deliberation is much stronger than performance in the political definition of accountability. Accountability is a fundamental and constitutive element of parliamentary government, which refers to the institutional arrangements by which the executive is accountable to Parliament (Bergman et al., 2006). The policy process in a democratic system is viewed as a process of delegation by which citizens delegate to politicians first and foremost through elections. In a parliamentary government, the fear of electoral punishment is a strong incentive for incumbents to remain in tune with their voters' demands.

Sinclair (1995) advances an interesting distinction between public and political accountability. Whereas the former entails direct accountability to the public and may take various forms, such as hearings or other consultative mechanisms, political accountability is understood as a chain (Sinclair, 1995: 225) which runs from civil servants to minister, accountable to Parliament and to voters. This distinction is useful as it reinforces the demarcating factor of 'representative government' in the definition of political accountability. However, the ultimate source of authority remains the same in both cases, namely the people. Therefore, the external dimension is valid in both cases. Yet, the mechanism changes and in the case of 'public' accountability it eschews elected representatives. Table 2.2 summarizes the different values of managerial, political and professional accountability.

As Day and Klein argue, the development of the welfare state has made the original conceptualization of political accountability subject

*Table 2.2* Values of accountability

|  | Managerial accountability | Political accountability | Professional accountability |
|---|---|---|---|
| **Values** | Efficiency Cost-effectiveness | Representation Election | Autonomy Expertise |

to severe pressure. Ministers are accountable for the actions of their bureaucrats to Parliaments, and political accountability in a representative democracy constitutes the main chain between the executive and the legislature. However, accountability in the service delivery state gave rise to new concerns, as the 'estate' had enlarged its size and demanded to revise the traditional accountability arrangements to take into account that 'the Welfare State was the Professional State' (Day and Klein, 1987: 16). Professional accountability, based on expertise, does not fit the hierarchical and 'chain' notion of accountability, be it political or managerial. It is a horizontal type of regime whereby actors are answerable to peers rather than superiors. Teachers and doctors, for instance, define their own actions and policies with a large degree of 'discretion' from local or central bureaucracies. In the nineteenth century the growth of professionalism has broken the old chain between executive and legislative accountability introducing professionalism and the assertion of the value of autonomy. Being professionally accountable means to represent the interest and values of particular occupational groups, like teachers or doctors, rather than the public interest (Sinclair, 1995).

Professional and public accountabilities are not necessarily conflicting. However, responding to professional codes of conduct and internal rules does not necessarily reflect the needs or preferences of citizens or group of citizens. Studies about the implementation of professional discretion in the welfare state show that clients have no capacity to enforce accountability (Brodkin, 1997; Diller, 2000). As Brodkin (1997) has argued, when the 'clients' are the poor unemployed in the case of the Job Opportunities and Basic Skills (JOBS) programme in Chicago, they are limited in their ability to 'exit' and they are not fully able to hold states accountable for delivering on their policy promises. She has convincingly shown that accountability depends on the clients' expectations that, if they are perceived as troublemakers, they are subject to retaliation by professionals (Brodkin, 1997: 21). In light of professional misconducts, professional accountability comes under severe criticism.

The relationship between managerial and political accountability is of particular significance because it impinges directly on the question of democracy. Day and Klein (1987: 18) suggest that 'managerial accountability should be put into the service of political accountability', for independent experts would provide information and support to decision makers in the legislature. Accordingly, effective political accountability is enhanced by managerial accountability, the two being mutually reinforcing. However, this supposedly harmonious and non-conflictual relationship does break down when public managers acquire discretion and autonomy (Diller, 2000), as has been the case in the recent managerialist wave of reforms in Europe and the United States.

Day and Klein mainly resolve the tension between bureaucracy and democracy and between managerial and political accountability by harnessing the former to the latter. They argue that accountability should not be seen exclusively as a function of electoral politics and that managerial accountability should be a necessary condition for effective political accountability. This proposition is based on their definition of what 'politics' is and what the content of accountability should be. If one assumes that welfare services, like education and health care, are consumable goods supplied to customers, then this view of the welfare state would be fully compatible with a very loose definition of 'political' accountability, taken as 'responsiveness to users'. Then, managerial accountability could indeed be used for enhancing this extended use of the concept of democratic accountability.

However, there are two main problems with this approach. First, citizens should be part of the decision-making process regardless of their status as 'users' or not of welfare services, especially in those welfare systems in which social rights are an established constitutive element of the political system. Citizens should participate in the input side of the process and not only in virtue of what output is produced. Secondly, the problem with stretching political accountability so as to make managerial accountability its support is that it does not establish the contrary, namely that the effectiveness of managerial accountability depends on political accountability, among other conditions. The argument in favour of a mutually supportive relationship between the two types of accountability seems to run only in one direction, which leads to suggestions for strengthening managerial accountability. However, it is unclear how political accountability can foster managerial accountability or at least not be its impediment. This silence is particularly noticeable in light of the claim that efficiency and accountability are two sides of the same conceptual coin (Day and Klein, 1987: 42).

## Limitations of actor-centred theories of accountability

The web of managerial accountability is more extended than a simple hierarchical model, and more so in the case of welfare programmes (Page, 2006; Pollitt, 2003). Each welfare bureaucrat has accountability relationships with numerous parties, including administrative superiors, the legislature, interest groups and clients. Thus, managerial accountability is multidimensional (Romzek, 1996). Civil servants have to answer for their performance and outcome through different channels. The high number of accountability holders does not say much about the nature of those relationships though and how they have changed from the past. The argument is simply that the web is getting larger and more complex, but it does not advance our understanding of how different lines of accountability interplay with each other. Adding one layer of accountability over the others increases the complexity, but whether it makes accountability more effective remains ambiguous. More research on the evaluative frameworks of accountabilities is needed. It may be that in fact each line of accountability is diluted in a multi-layered system, whereby public managers can resourcefully play one accountability holder against the other. The 'web' of accountability is a limiting factor as it puts more constraints on civil servants. It is also a resource as it dilutes the authority and power relations deriving from the political 'chain'.

Bovens contributes significantly to the debate on accountability by analysing the social relationships between actor and forum which accountability relationships entail. He defines accountability as 'a relationship between an actor and a forum, in which the actor has an obligation to explain and to justify his or her conduct, the forum can pose questions and pass judgement, and the actor may face consequences' (Bovens, 2006: 9). There are two fundamentally different ways to classify the relationship between managerial and political accountability. The first one focuses on 'to whom' the account is to be rendered (Bovens, 2006: 15), namely the accountability holder. Under this type, the stress is on the locus of authority which holds actors accountable. In the case of political accountability, it clearly refers to being answerable to elected representatives, political parties and voters. In a democratic system this is the most important source of public accountability. The second classification type, according to Bovens, focuses on 'who' is the actor and who should take the credit or blame for programmes. For instance, public managers are responsible for efficient and effective processes and outcomes. What emerges from this classification developed by Bovens (2006) is that 'to whom' the account is to be rendered is not easily identifiable in the case of managerial accountability, for it is the actor end of the accountability relationship and not the forum end which is emphasized by the model.

However, this is an extremely problematic classification because it puts excessive emphasis on the social relationship between actors, and less on the substantive 'content' of accountability and on institutional structures. I will come back to this crucial point in the course of the empirical analysis and in Chapter 6. For the time being, it is worth noting that the formal arrangements of accountability relationships can remain in place even when the content of accountability is radically altered. What are managers accountable for? The relationship between them and politicians may remain stable within organizations, in formal terms, but may be transformed by its new substantive content. Hence, the 'what' question matters.

Should public managers render account to elected politicians or to clients or to independent regulators? The apparent crumbling of hierarchical accountability partly justifies the confusion of the 'to whom' classification, especially when applied to managerial accountability, not investigated by Bovens. The 'to whom' question for managerial accountability becomes the more problematic one in light of recent reforms associated with NPM. As a result of greater discretion given to managers, elected officials find it increasingly difficult to have insights into the process of welfare administration. Moreover, the 'reinvention of government' (Osborne and Gaebler, 1992) renders welfare recipients paradoxically more accountable to administrators. Thus, actor and forum are almost reversed, and the accountability holders become the managers. New opportunities for weakening the classical concept of accountability have been created by granting autonomy to agencies, organizations or individual managers. 'To whom' remains the key accountability question for a democratic state and for the external dimension of accountability. This is the original sense in which Finer couched the debate about accountability (Finer, 1941). The elemental notion of accountability is a process by which a government has to present itself at regular intervals for election, and can be ousted by the electorate.

On the one hand, due to the increasingly complex web of accountability, confusion arises over 'to whom' managers are accountable and what for. On the other, political accountability is stretching its scope and application to a wider range of stakeholders, beyond its historical core meaning of the relationship between public office holders and citizens, and more specifically between elected politicians and bureaucrats. In this book I use political accountability in this core meaning, which leads to issues about the balance between accountability and efficiency and about the distinctions between political and managerial accountability.

Hence, one of the key dimensions demarcating managerial from political accountability is the internal–external one. Despite the transformation from bureaucratic to managerial accountability, I maintain that the external/internal is still a crucial dichotomy, although some recent conceptualizations have suggested that the arrangements are becoming too complex to be defined in dichotomous terms. Public accountability is a public procedure in all its forms. Moreover, the pyramidal and hierarchical assumptions that underpin traditional accountability theory may no longer be empirically adequate (Harlow and Rawlings, 2006). However, in practice internal governance arrangements of public organizations are sometimes designed to minimize the participation of politicians or patients' groups in light of purely internal managerial accountability.

The existing literature on internal accountability remains scarce, as 'new' types of 'political' accountability have attracted much more attention. Hence, what happens at the institutional level within organizations remains unclear and whether 'new' forms have replaced the 'old' ones or not is an open question, which this book aims to answer. Another important rationale for maintaining the distinction between internal and external is that a fundamental component of accountability is the authority structure (Mulgan, 2000). Most of the recent reformulations of accountability do not sufficiently analyse power relationships and public authority structures as organizing variables. The next section aims to identify the structural dimensions of accountability and, as such, contributes to developing an analytical framework which is less based on actor-centred interpretations and relational views of accountability, and more on administrative and structural conditions.

## Accountability regimes and internal structures

If one adopts the widely accepted and broad definition of political accountability to include any relationship which provides responsiveness to 'clients', then it becomes more plausible to sustain that NPM, with its emphasis on performance-oriented administration, may strengthen the political accountability. I do not adopt the commonly used definition of political accountability, which has been subject to significant conceptual stretching (Sartori, 1970), and I retain instead the original conceptualization for which the electoral dimension is the basic link between the citizens and the state. This has a long tradition in Europe going back to the abolition of monarchical power and absolutism. Thus, 'political' means foremost representation of voters and not simply responsiveness to clients. By assessing the impact of NPM on the accountability regimes, it seems more rigorous not to bend the criteria of accountable power to fit the performance-oriented basis of the relationship.

Sociological definitions of accountability are based on a social relationship between actor and forum, as discussed in the previous section. Thus, it is bidimensional at the core. It entails expectations that a forum has from an actor. This sociological definition is also accepted by scholars like Harlow, in her work on network accountability (Harlow and Rawlings, 2006). According to the relational type of accountability, an actor fulfils a specific role and function within the frame of a formal relationship with the forum. For instance, a politician is the actor accountable to the electorate and managers are accountable to their superiors. Accordingly, political accountability is the relationship which links public office holders, a minister or a member of Parliament, to the people. The key mechanism of political accountability is representation, as indicated earlier in Table 2.1. Conversely, bureaucratic accountability relates public servants to their superiors and is based on supervision and hierarchy. Obedience and compliance with rules and procedures are its main mechanisms.

The problem with the predominantly relational approach to accountability is that it is excessively actor-centred and based on 'who' the actor is, what the actor's role is and how this changes. This contributes to some analytical clarity, but is not useful to understand the dynamics of the relationship, when the actor becomes the forum and the two roles can be exchanged easily on the basis of power relationships. In short, Boven's definition is static and unidirectional. On the contrary, a politically appointed head of a hospital is not only an actor politically accountable to the local administration or to the Ministry of Health, but also fulfils the role of the managerial forum to which all staff of the organization are accountable. The level at which the interaction between actor and forum takes place is thus very important.

Against an excessively actor-centred definition of accountability, the model here developed conceptualizes the relationship between managerial and political accountability as structurally determined by internal organizational arrangements. The internal dimension of accountability creates the conditions for the external one, and any attempt to focus exclusively on the latter is limiting. Relationships between actors in a social and political system cannot be conceived without the institutional and organizational context which produces preferences and interests (March and Olsen, 1989). Therefore, I define the problem in terms of accountability regimes rather than relationships, referring to the structural terrain of the interplay between different types of accountabilities within an institutional context. In the revised model of internalized accountability, administrative capacity, specialization and methods of coordination are the three main contributory factors and conditions in the making of any accountability regime.

Therefore, in this model I focus on the internalization process of accountability, namely how the different types are combined as a result of the internal administrative structure of a public organization which delivers welfare services. In practice, there is often a combination between the different types of accountability in any organization. However, to date there are no analytical attempts to study the determinants of any mix of these combinations. The predominant focus in the existing literature remains on individual welfare programmes and sectors, rather than on the administrative determinants of accountability arrangements across sectors of the welfare state.

## Bureaucratic capacity, specialization and coordination

Three main administrative dimensions are hereby identified as contributing to the accountability regime within any organization of welfare delivery. They are bureaucratic capacity, specialization and administrative coordination. The impact of structural capacity refers to the degree to which welfare administrations are able to mobilize interest and resources in order to direct policy outputs towards the fulfilment of their institutional mission, whether it is educational attainments or health care. This may lead to policy outputs which are not intended by the government though. Organizations do vary in their planning and managerial capacity, and this study will assess the degree to which varying structural capacity influences the predominant accountability mix in its form and content. The indicator of capacity is 'size', intended in budgetary terms and system complexity.

The second organizational variable, namely specialization, refers to the way in which tasks and policies are divided across units of an organization. It is a significant determinant insofar as the organizational boundaries determine the level at which conflicts are resolved. For instance, a very high degree of specialization, as found in hospitals, is likely to move the processes of leadership upward in the organization, making the head more involved in technical decisions and more powerful for his coordination role. In organizations where horizontal specialization is very high, serious information deficits may occur and conflicts over substance may be more frequent, as Egeberg notices (Egeberg 2003: 121). In this context, there is an increasing upward pressure which augments the influence and intervention of the head of the administration in the internal divisions. For instance, a hospital is a very complex structure and highly specialized internally in different divisions, headed by professionals. In theory, professional accountability predicts that they would resort to horizontal types of peer-based accountability. However, in practice, the endemic conflict between the heads of divisions in a hospital is pushed upward to the management team, sometimes even to the politicians in the supervisory board. In fact, a way to overcome endemic conflict within very complex welfare bureaucracies with a high degree of service specialization is for the manager to influence the composition and appointment of the heads of divisions, as I will discuss in Chapter 3 for public hospitals.

Given the nature of 'expertness', welfare bureaucracies are particularly affected by higher than average degrees of specialization and fragmentation. One of the distinctive features of welfare administration, in comparison with other government ones, is its 'expertness', to use Gouldner (1954). Welfare delivery is a type of bureaucracy which provides public 'services', and as such it differs significantly from other administrative organizations which are 'punitive' and of the Weberian type (law and order bureaucracies). The service is provided by professionals, whose values are based not on hierarchical control, but on cooperation and ethical responsibility. Professional accountability is of particular significance in welfare bureaucracies. For instance, teachers in schools may be more loyal to their individual subject than to the institutions, as is the case in France, as I will discuss in Chapter 4.

The third most fundamental variable for the analysis of administrative life is the type of administrative coordination. It is the structural expression of how conflict is resolved and how interdependencies are dealt with in bureaucracies. It defines a chain of command and makes possible the administrative integration of specialized functions (Selznick, 1948: 25). Delegation is the elemental organizational act by which roles, functions and powers are formally assigned to individuals. Conversely, control is the system of procedures and rules in place to provide a level of integration which permits the organization to function. Delegation and control, thus, constitute the systemic elements of the organization. Coordination is the system of formal arrangements within an organization, which allows for its maintenance, stability and organizational survival. As Selznick (1948: 28) proposes, organizations are cooperative systems, which 'are constituted of individual interactions as whole in relation to a formal system of coordination'.

Vertical integration is an important indicator of coordination (Hayward, 1998). Complex organizations are internally specialized in different units in relation to function (process) or clientele served or purpose (sector). In general, vertical specialization diminishes the potential for centralized political steering and control. NPM has advocated greater specialization and fragmentation within organizations and decentralization of management, as discussed in Chapter 1. This loss can be compensated by mechanisms of coordination. Centralization is an important means of eliminating discretionary personal power within an organization (Crozier, 1964: 190). The structures of coordination can be collegial or hierarchical, as Table 2.3 shows. Advisory boards in public organizations represent arenas for political steering from above, but also for the articulation of group interests and expert appraisals. In the case of chain and command modes of coordination, the executive leadership derives authority often directly from the ministers or elected politicians.

From Table 2.3 we can derive the following three analytical propositions, which relate the structure of welfare bureaucracies to their internalized accountability regime mix. These propositions are not intended and used as hypotheses, but rather theoretical expectations which guide the author through data collection and empirical analysis. First, a welfare organization with strong structural capacity is more capable of autonomous planning, constructive input into the policy process and mobilization of key interests for the success of reforms, than organizations with more limited resources for autonomous planning. Managerial autonomy is more likely to be effective in delivery units supported by a strong bureaucratic capacity, in terms of financial and human resources and institutionalized bureaucratic systems. Managers have an ample range of internal resources and their relationship with external accountability holders is less relevant. They have the power to implement the reforms with large deviations from the intended policy goals. Conversely, elected politicians and users find it more difficult to serve as effective accountability holders if the unit has strong bureaucratic capacity. Therefore, the stronger the bureaucratic capacity

*Table 2.3*   The administrative framework of accountability regimes

| | Significance for managerial autonomy | Effects on political steering capacity by politicians | Propositions on accountability regime |
|---|---|---|---|
| **Bureaucratic capacity** | | | |
| *Large structural capacity* (e.g. hospitals) | Strong capacity for autonomous planning and policy initiatives, supporting managerial autonomy. | Great number of positions and interests to mobilize. Crowded policy arena with multiple veto players. | P1: The greater the structural capacity of a welfare delivery organization, the greater opportunities for its transformation into an institutionalized managerial system, which may eschew political control by the internalization of accountability. |
| *Small structural capacity* (e.g. secondary schools) | Fewer opportunities to initiate policies, and to develop alternatives from centralist strands. Managers are agents of central control systems. | Greater opportunities for local councillors or politically elected governors to interfere in the day-to-day running of schools. | |
| **Specialization** | | | |
| *High fragmentation of tasks* | Serious information deficits and conflicts over policy substance. Demand for coordination pushes conflict resolution higher up in the hierarchy. Greater opportunities for managerial power. | Diminishes potential for centralised political steering due to need for delegation. Reduced capacity of conflict resolution by traditional political instruments (such as appointments). | P2: The more internally specialized a welfare organization, the more isolated management structures become from external political influence, for fragmentation invests managers of greater coordination powers |

| | | | |
|---|---|---|---|
| *Low decoupling and despecialization* | Weaker demand for internally centralized controls and managerial coordination. | Political signals remain high and political leaders are highly involved in governing bodies. | and conflict resolution is pushed 'up' (not 'outside') the ladder of the organization. |
| **Administrative coordination** | | | |
| *Collegial* | Managerial decision making is through arguing, voting, bargaining. Consultation with advisory boards, committees, project groups, etc. | Articulation and representation of consumers by lay members in advisory boards. | **P3:** The greater reliance on governing bodies as means of democratic control, combined with lay members 'in' and politicians 'out', the more diluted is the opposition to potentially autocratic managers. |
| *Hierarchical* | Decision making is through control and command. Truncation of consultative layers. | Greater use of traditional forms of political control, such as appointment of heads and reconstructed hierarchies. | |

of welfare service unit the greater the opportunities for managerial accountability to prevail and escape external forms of accountability. The accountability regime is predominantly internalized and the accountability mix may eschew traditional forms of political accountability.

Secondly, when organizations are highly specialized, conflict arises between different units. As this is frequently the case in complex delivery institutions, the resolution of conflicts over resources of substantive policies is fundamental. The higher the fragmentation the more likely it becomes that the conflict resolution is pushed up the ladder of hierarchy and that the management team has to intervene to mediate and resolve it. Therefore, political signals are given heavier weight in organizations which have a low level of vertical or horizontal specialization. The outcome for the accountability mix is that greater specialization diminishes political steering capacity and, thus, invests management structures of greater powers by isolating them from political intervention.

Thirdly, when organizations have hierarchical leadership structures, namely a strong executive at the top, it is likely that the chain of accountability flows directly from the minister or the elected representatives who have appointed the management structures. 'Old' types of political accountability are more likely to survive when the organization retains the fundamental properties of internal hierarchical coordination. On the contrary, collegial instruments of coordination facilitate the articulation of different interests and voices, including that of users and professionals. This results in clear lines of demarcation between managerial and political accountabilities and in the participation of professionals and users in the decision-making system of the organization.

When we combine the effects of the three main dimensions of structural capacity, specialization and coordination on the final relationship between managerial and political accountabilities, I propose the following theoretical expectation. Those welfare service bureaucracies which have a strong bureaucratic capacity, are highly specialized and have mainly collegial methods of coordination are more likely to replace external political accountability with internal managerial accountability, as a result of diminished political steering capacity by politicians within the supervisory boards of the organization and greater opportunities for managerial discretion. However, when coordination structures are more hierarchical, despite the presence of high structural capacity and high specialization, traditional forms of political accountability are more likely to survive.

## Appointment and composition of governance structures

Organizations are more than mirrors of societal forces and interests and have a life of their own. Accountability relationships which are formed in administrative institutions are not merely the result of distribution of resources or exogenously determined preferences. The pattern of systematic relationships between managerial and political accountability is endogenously shaped by the organizational structures created to coordinate the governance of institutions. The model proposed in this book adds this important dimension to the study of accountability in welfare bureaucracies. Many of the contemporary studies on governance emphasize the exogenous factors of the external environment as determinants of political processes and institutions. Conversely, the relationship between managers and politicians develops also within the context of institutional action and organizational structure of administrative systems.

In practice, political steering of complex welfare organizations is operationalized in this study through the leadership structures, namely the supervisory boards, made up of stakeholders, and the chief executive and management team. Professionals have also been part of the management process, and, if so, this will be fully taken into account in the empirical study in the next three chapters. These leadership structures represent the organizational arena where conflicts arise and are mediated, where power is distributed within the organization, and relationships between actors formally forged and institutionalized. Thus, the internal governance of schools and hospitals will be our primary unit of analysis. The arrangements of supervisory boards, advisory boards, chief executives and management teams of schools and hospitals are not merely legal technicalities. They have a long-lasting and profound effect on the systems of social relationships between actors and on the need of citizens.

There are two dimensions of internalized accountability which are here analysed for their relevance on political accountability: appointment and composition of supervisory boards of stakeholders. The former is an indicator of the steering capacity of politicians and of hierarchical lines of accountability. The latter reflects the degree of representation of societal interests. Supervisory boards are here studied in their political significance as a conflict-mediating arena among actors, which in turn determines the internal system of relationship between managers, professionals, politicians and users. This is not an evaluation study of the effectiveness of management or leadership system, as this would be the remit of management studies.

Appointment is traditionally held as an important dimension of political control of the administration (McCubbins, Noll and Weingast, 1987). Organizations with their chief executive appointed by the minister or government see a positive influence on their accountability, according to a study of accountability in Flanders (Verhoest et al., 2004: 14). A direct link between the board and the external political source of authority, be it the minister or Parliament, is claimed to strengthen political accountability. Appointment can be based on policy preferences or openly on party political affiliation. Another related feature is the provision for dismissal of heads of the organizations. In some cases, Parliaments are involved, whereas in others it is exclusively a government decision. This is particularly relevant when managers have fixed-term contracts which are renewable on the basis of political approval (Mattei, 2007a). In some cases, the term of office can even coincide with the electoral process. The empirical investigation in the book analyses the mechanisms of appointment of the members of the leadership structures of schools and hospitals and to whom they are ultimately accountable.

The composition of supervisory boards of stakeholders in hospitals and schools reflects the underlying institutional choice which has been taken by the government in relation to the representation and mobilization of interests. It is another element which is indicative of the sort of incentives created by the government and elected politicians for enhancing a specific accountability regime. In some cases, professionals are represented in the supervisory boards. In others, they are excluded. This, for instance, reflects the institutional expectations in relation to the relationship between managerial and professional accountabilities. Hence, the research questions pertaining to the composition dimension are: Who are the members of the supervisory boards? Is a majority of members representing central government, local government or interest groups? Are the members of the schools and hospitals' boards appointed by the government or elected by the users, such as parents or patients?

It is worth noticing that it is not infrequent to find governance structures where the boards have been abolished and a single executive chief replaces all their functions. This is a radical institutional design, but in highly politicized administrations, such as the Italian one, it was introduced as a way to shield the administration from partisan colonization, traditionally blocking decision making in collegial boards (Mattei, 2005b). This is a radical form of organizational change, which I will include in Chapter 4, in relation to the 1992 health care reform in Italy (Mattei, 2004).

# Part II  State Schools and Public Hospitals in Europe

# 3
# Enduring Managerialism in the Internal Governance of Public Hospitals

As Paul Pierson suggests, 'hemmed in by popular sensitivities, powerful interests and economic realities, governments generally find health care to be a cause of political headaches rather than a target for successful retrenchment' (Pierson, 1994). In a few areas of the welfare state has the reform of welfare administration been so vigorously dominated by the logic of the market and competition as in health care (Le Grand and Robinson, 1984; Ranade, 1998). In the 1990s economic efficiency was the *leitmotiv* of health care reforms around the world (Saltman and Figueras, 1997; Saltman et al., 1998; Moran, 1998). Productivity and efficiency imperatives originated from the search for ways to meet rising health care demands while limiting public expenditure. The literature on comparative health care systems has grown exponentially in the last 20 years. A spate of comparative reports by international organizations such as the OECD and the World Health Organization (WHO) has provoked commentary and controversy, supplying a wealth of comparative data.

However, hospitals as units of analysis have received scarce attention beyond a brisk trade in the economic analysis of the real and imagined ills of modern health care systems. This chapter's purpose is to analyse the transformations of the governance structures and processes within hospitals resulting from the adoption of corporate management rules, demarcating them from the supposedly inefficient bureaucratic account- ability of local or national authorities. It is a rather under-researched ques- tion, for most scholarly attention has been directed towards the study of systemic political and institutional factors (Immergut, 1992; Tuohy, 1999; Bandelow and Hassenteufel, 2006; Doehler, 1997; European Observatory for Health Care Systems, 2001) and the public–private blurring in the finance and delivery of health care services – a mixed economy of welfare

(Department of Health (DOH), 2000; Dixon and Mossialos, 2002; Lewis and Glennerster, 1996; Mossialos and Thompson, 2004).

Public hospitals are not only units of production where professional and technical advice is provided, they are also institutions embedded in contextual governance systems within a wider set of political institutional rules (Cipolla and Giarelli, 2002; Ferrera, 1995; Olla and Pavan, 2000). Unfortunately, existing studies rarely analyse hospitals as bodies of welfare administration legitimated by norms and practices of democratic accountability, deeply entrenched and constrained by complex and multiple accountability relationships. The conventional political accountability mechanism for a public hospital is the hierarchical relationship between the Minister of Health and the supervisory board of the hospital. Stakeholders on the board include health authorities, politicians and local interests. Public hospitals also are politically salient local institutions where issues of local ownership matter. Citizens are attached to their local hospital and are likely to oppose closure and mergers motivated by financial pressure or poor performance (Le Point, 2008).

Recent reforms, as this chapter investigates, are directed at introducing new accountability regimes by strengthening management boards at the level of the individual organization and devolving decision-making power (Pollitt et al., 1998). One of the main reform objectives is to design internal governance structures that hold hospitals accountable and enhance efficient decision making. Overall, the model is inspired by a separation between strategic and operational responsibilities. On the one hand, to improve accountability hospital supervisory boards should be responsive to the demands of the local community via new types of 'local ownership' (Department of Health, 2002; 2003). On the other hand, to augment efficiency the relationship between managers and doctors has changed to include performance-related objectives and rewards.

The purpose of this chapter is to discuss the changes of the internal accountability mechanism in British Foundation Hospital Trusts and in German, French and Italian public hospitals within the analytical framework developed in Chapter 2. The micro-institutions through which we can trace change are the management team and supervisory boards. The supervisory boards have two main functions: stakeholder representation and management oversight. As a representative body, the supervisory board ensures that the different, often conflicting, interests of stakeholders are represented. Boards that emphasize this function tend to be larger and exercise self-restraint in the decision-making process. Political accountability is guaranteed by the membership of elected officials. Boards that emphasize their role in evaluation and supervision make long-term strategic decisions and hold the management of the hospital accountable for performance and for delivering the agreed targets. These boards are usually smaller, and elected representatives may or may not be present. Some hospital care reforms have gone as far as to eliminate supervisory boards all together and delegate all their responsibilities to one general manager (Mattei, 2006; Borgonovi, 1988; Rebora, 1999).

The changes to the internal management structures illustrate the effects managerialism has on the relationships and power distribution among politicians, managers, users and professionals. The internal rules and governance framework may be designed by legislation, as it has been in France, Italy and Britain, or it may be left to the discretion of individual hospitals, as is done in Germany. This chapter will look at legislation, rules and directives that have stimulated the entrepreneurial formula in public hospitals. By this I refer to the structural opportunities for managerial discretion, which marks a departure from bureaucratic-style organization (Saltman, Busse and Mossialos, 2002; Bundesministerium des Innern, 2006; Capano, 1992; Health care Financial Management Association, 2007). In the first section, I will focus on managers' changing roles that affect their relationships with the other actors, in particular with the governing boards, but also with professionals. The case studies will analyse the effects of reforms aimed at introducing organizational autonomy (Mattei, 2007c) on the rules and structures which facilitate managerialism as an alternative to traditional administrative arrangements. The cases of Britain, France, Germany and Italy will be analysed in sequence. I will start with managerialism in Britain, which provided the blueprint for the introduction of 'general management' in health care delivery.

## New system of internal governance of hospitals

As Table 3.1 indicates, managerialism refers to the transformation of the internal governance of public hospitals in Europe, inspired by the freedoms enjoyed by managers in private firms. The definition adopted in this study draws mainly from Hood (1991), who has, in a seminal article, conceptualized the different strands of NPM. Managerial autonomy forms an important part of it. The blueprint of managerialism is the Griffiths Report, which was introduced in the British NHS in 1983 (Department of Health and Social Security, 1983). By 'general management', Griffiths meant the responsibility of a single-headed chief executive for planning, implementing and controlling hospital performance. By 1987, two-thirds of management boards in the British NHS involved a senior manager with primary responsibility for promoting

*Table 3.1* Managerialism and typology of reforms in hospitals

| Dimension of reform | Type of reform | Aim of reform |
|---|---|---|
| **Composition of internal bodies** | Reduction in size of boards | To lift veto points and make decision making more efficient. |
| **Role of actors** | Power shift from stakeholders and representatives to managers | To facilitate the decentralization of management responsibilities. |
| **Style of decision making** | Shift from consensual/ collegial to adversarial | To challenge possible opposition to cost-efficiency imperatives and unpopular decisions. |
| **Appointment of internal bodies** | Shift from direct appointment to election | To make public hospitals more responsive to local communities via 'local ownership'. |

service quality and consumer relations (Pollitt et al., 1991; Day and Klein, 1987).

What follows in this chapter is not a description of techniques or managerial systems, but an understanding of how the governance structure of hospitals has changed as a result of recent organizational transformations in welfare administration more generally. The last 15 years have been a period of substantial organizational reconfiguration in the health sector, and increased entrepreneurial activity has been at the core of the process (Saltman and Figueras, 1997). The major goal is to increase the operating efficiency of the organization of the hospital (Harding and Preker, 1998; Das Krankenhaus, 1997; de Pouvourville and Renaud, 1985; Ruef and Scott, 1998). In a World Bank publication, Harding and Preker (1998: 6) defined organizational reforms in hospitals as those which 'move public hospitals out of the core public bureaucracy and transform them into more independent entities responsible for performance, keeping ownership in the public sector'.

Autonomy is an essential element of innovation, claimed to improve performance of the hospital. The degree of autonomy hospitals enjoy provides the first key to the organizational structure of health care delivery. Autonomy can be about inputs (hiring decisions, investment and sale of assets, procurement of pharmaceutical), outputs (volume of services and mix of service provided), outcomes (public health targets) and processes (strategic management, financial management, setting users' charges, clinical management). The organization of health care systems in Europe varies significantly, creating a greater demand for autonomous public hospitals in centralized and Beveridge-type health care system (Ranade, 1997; Glennerster, 2000). This is not to suggest that the change has been uniformly intense or synchronous. For instance, in Britain the Griffiths Report was introduced in 1983,[1] whereas France has adopted managerialism with the 2007 Hospital Plan.[2] In Germany's social insurance system, for instance, public hospitals have traditionally enjoyed an ample degree of autonomy in the delivery of health care services (European Observatory, 2000).

Managerialism is different to other market-type mechanisms, and certainly it does not imply privatization (Le Grand and Bartlett, 1993). Frequently it has indeed been part of a wider package that includes market mechanisms, but in this study managerialism is distinct from marketization, as discussed in Chapter 1. Despite different meanings attributed by different countries to the terms 'markets', 'competition' and 'private sector' (Ranade, 1998), the universal logic of health care reforms in the 1990s was that market competition would contribute to an optimal allocation of resources (Mapelli, 1999). The internal market belongs to the 'marketization' category of public management reforms because it does not mean selling public sector assets to private providers (privatization) but rather 'privatising from within', namely adopting organizational arrangements and management systems tested and developed in market conditions (Le Grand et al., 1998).[3] The strand of NPM which deals with managerialism is concerned with hands-on management, autonomy, clear objectives and performance, and it is different to the strand related to new institutional economics, which is based on competition, public choice and transaction costs analysis and which is not the focus of this book.

Whereas market mechanisms such as the internal market have been adopted in a stop-and-go fashion, managerialism has been a consistent trend which has not withered, but rather has spilled over into other sectors, like education, as I will discuss in Chapters 4 and 5. There are three types of organizational reforms in relation to the introduction of managerialism in public hospitals: first, the transformation of collegial and plethoric decision-making structures, such as supervisory or management bodies, into small and flexible governance instruments (Pierre and Peters, 2001); secondly, the redistribution of power between the management team of public hospitals and the supervisory board in the direction of strengthening the authority of the former; thirdly, the creation of a new managerial caste with new operating autonomy and performance accountability. The new arrangements are supposed to get away from multiple and conflicting goals and, instead, set clear and transparent missions and guidelines, leaving managers 'free to manage' within clear parameters. It is claimed that consensus decision making leads to long delays in the management process (Department of Health and Social Security, 1983). The common denominator of all types of entrepreneurial transformations of public hospitals is that managers acquire substantial decision making. However, there remains little support in the academic literature for the idea that policymaking and implementation can be kept in separate compartments (Baumgartner, 2002; Barzelay, 2001).

The advocates of NPM argue that it brings greater transparency and performance accountability to customers, who are informed by the greater publicity of ranking and league tables. The enhancement of accountability to customers occurs via the creation of performance indicators (Power, 1997; Hood, 1998; Barzelay, 2001; Bevan and Hood, 2005). A way to read NPM could be to argue that it sharpens account-ability by distinguishing between policy setting and operational respon-sibility. However, whereas the rights of customers can be enhanced by performance-accountability, for they are based on service-provision, it is important to remember that in democratic societies the state derives its power from the citizens, and that the rights of citizens are political and social (Marshall, 1950). As Peters (1992) argues, offering hospitals more autonomy may be an attractive option for the critics of bureaucracy, but it does not address the problem of accountability.

The 'old' bureaucratic framework of the hospital administration has been slowly supplanted by the new organizational ideology of managerialism, almost everywhere in Europe. As Pollitt suggested, two models were incorporated: 'scientific management' and the 'excellence' model (Pollitt, 2003). With regards to the former, NPM is viewed as an updated version of neo-Taylorism and of its emphasis on perform-ance management. Underlying Taylorist assumptions that employees respond only to rewards, performance-related pay has been spreading to welfare organizations and hospitals. As Metcalfe and Richards argue (1987), governments drew the wrong lessons from the private sector by implementing a neo-Taylorist model inappropriate for new conditions, increasingly abandoned in the commercial world. In relation to the 'excellence' literature (Peters and Watermann, 1982), the key to success is the focus on customers, quality of services and creating a culture of excellence. The case of German hospitals illustrates this second model of managerialism and the shift from producer to consumer values (Newman and Kuhlmann, 2007).

The customer-driven hospital organization is the basis to formulate an alternative to the bureaucratic paradigm upon which health care administration in many European countries has been based. The post-bureaucratic paradigm emphasizes production against administration, improvement of process against complying with rules and procedures (Barzelay, 1992). The introduction of managerialism in European hospitals increases the tension between efficiency and professional accountability. However, as Klein (1982) suggests, the health care organization does not simply respond to consumer-demands, but to a large degree it creates them through the clinical decision of professional providers. Until the early 1990s, doctors were all powerful, and their's was one of the most delegated professions from the state (Freddi and Bjorkman, 1999; Richardson, 1993).

Some scholars have characterized managerialism as a 'policy fad' (Marmor, 2004). Indeed, as a *Zeitgeist* it has been diffused by international bodies such as the WHO. By 'fads' Marmor (2004) means 'enthusiasms for particular ideas or practices'. In his Rock Carling lecture, Ted Marmor launches his fierce attack on the language of business management, which affects doctors as well as hospitals' administration. The vision of a hospital as primarily a business affected the way Americans regarded medical care from the 1970s. Hospitals are viewed as business firms. As Marmor (2004: 10) argues, financial monitoring is a useful tool. Yet conceiving of a hospital as another business undermines the philosophical and normative values of medical care. The argument of policy fads is more persuasive, if we move beyond simply the consideration of linguistic devices and analyse the organizational changes caused by these fads. This is what I set out to accomplish in the empirical analysis which follows.

## Britain

In 1983 Roy Griffiths led the National Health Service (NHS) Management Inquiry, which resulted in the well-known report aimed at transforming radically the management style of the NHS. The report lamented the deep institutional crisis the NHS was suffering (Klein, 2001: 124). For instance, the report suggested that consensus decision making led to 'long delays in management process' (Department of Health and Social Security, 1983). The diagnosis was not new, but the solution was a radical upheaval of the management arrangements of hospitals and the entire health care system: the introduction of new managerialism. The solution was a clear general-management structure whereby managers at all levels were responsible for results. Everywhere in the system, at national, regional and local levels there had to be managers, recruited from outside the civil service.

The underlying idea of managerialism was to separate politics from operation. This was based on the belief that NHS management could be depoliticized by handing it over to independent managers. The Griffiths Report's recommendations were implemented by the creation of a stratum of newly appointed managers, who were pressured to deliver good service. If they did not, they risked not having their contracts renewed. In the new management arrangement the medical and nursing representatives on the management boards lost their veto power (Klein, 2001). By 1987, 61 per cent of the new managers were former NHS administrators or finance officers, and only 25 per cent were doctors and nurses. A further 12 per cent were recruited from outside the NHS (Pollitt, 1991).

The management task of the NHS, as set out in the report, was to assure quality and delivery of a good product to the 'consumer'. As business managers were concerned mainly with customer satisfaction, likewise NHS managers had to be more responsive to patients' demands. The NHS had to behave as a supermarket, trying to satisfy its customers. The new organizational culture had to be based on customer values and value for money (Milewa et al., 1998; Gray and Jenkins, 2003; Kaboolian, 1998). The Griffiths Report, then, became the symbol of the new organizational culture inspired by the private sector. Its significance rests in having set a new agenda for the health care sector.

Although the implementation of the Griffiths Report was not as radical as its goals, the power of the manifesto survived and formed the underlying philosophy for subsequent reforms of the NHS. The premise of reforms is that the needs and demands of patients are essentially defined by managers and no longer by doctors (Clarke, Cochrane and McLaughlin, 1995: 5). To ask whether the right goods were being produced and whether they were produced according to adequate levels of standards was perceived as an inroad into professional territory and clinical autonomy. The Griffiths Report laid the foundations for the 1989 *Working for Patients* White Paper, and the 1990 *NHS and Community Care Act*, which introduced the quasi-markets in health care provision. Having contracts meant introducing line-management arrangements, including a reduction in the representation of health care professionals on management boards (Ferlie, 1996). The 2001 *Shifting the Balance of Power* makes substantial reference to the notions of 'autonomy', and 'empowerment of managers'.

NPM, introduced by the Conservative governments in the early 1990s (Klein, 2001), continued unabated even with the recent New Labour reforms. NHS Foundation Trusts were established by the 2003 *Health and Social Care (Community Health and Standards) Act* as independent public benefit corporations modelled on cooperative and mutual traditions. This was a new type of organization in the British NHS, a departure from the NHS Trusts created in the early 1990s to give them operational independence from their local District Health Authorities (DHAs).[4] New Labour has maintained the reform commitment of previous governments to the principles of decentralization and the devolution of managerial responsibilities to local public hospitals, which were not found to be sufficiently free from central government interference.[5] In fact, one of the main characteristics of the British NHS is that Trusts had a direct link of accountability with the Secretary of State for Health, who could give legally binding direction to a Trust and could dismiss the Trust's Chair and non-executive directors. The 2003 Act established that hospitals could be given 'Trust' status on the basis of meeting strict application guidelines, whereby hospitals need to show that they have met the standards and requirements set by the newly established independent regulator, called Monitor.

The purpose of establishing NHS Foundation Trusts is to devolve power and greater autonomy to the local level so that hospitals are better able to respond to the needs of their patients and communities. This is achieved in two ways: through a new system of accountability and through greater autonomy from the Secretary of State's direct control. The new system of devolved accountability to local 'stakeholders', including patients and staff, is intended to replace the traditional political accountability to the central level of government. The new governance arrangements offer members of the community the opportunity to participate in and influence the strategic development of the organization. Foundation Trusts are not answerable to the Secretary of State, but to local people and Monitor, the new independent regulator. They are free to pursue their own agenda in accordance with the priorities set by the community.

The 2003 Health and Social Care Act sets out the minimum legislative requirements for the internal governance of NHS Foundation Trusts (Department of Health, 2003). The organizational governance structure reflecting this newly created accountability to local people is represented by the new Board of Governors, to which the Management Board of the Foundation Trusts will be directly accountable. The board is made of representatives elected from among the 'members' of the Trust—that is, registered residents and patients in the areas served by the NHS Foundation Trusts. Membership is open to all who wish to register with the public hospital and participate. The legislation encourages that membership be representative of the community. Membership is open to people who live in the area, staff and patients and carers of patients treated in the NHS Foundation Trust. Members are able to stand and to vote in elections to the Board of Governors of the NHS Foundation Trusts. This body is intended to represent the interests of all stakeholders. Some places will be reserved for nominees of other local health authorities, such as Primary Care Trusts which commission services from the hospitals.[6] The Board of Governors is responsible, thus, for respecting the interests of the community in the management and strategic development of the NHS Foundation Trust. It is expected to receive regular information about the Trust and to be consulted twice a year for future development. The board has important powers in appointing the Chair and the non-executive directors of the Board of Directors, which has exclusive responsibility for operational matters, for example, setting budgets, staff pay and others. It has also the power to approve the appointment of the chief executive for the Chair of the Foundation Trust.

The management of a Foundation Trust is the responsibility of its Management Board, made of executive and non-executive directors. The directors of each Foundation Trust are accountable to the Board of Governors elected by local people and staff. This mechanism is claimed to ensure accountability to the public, in that the Board of Governors represents the Foundation Trust's stakeholders. The majority of seats must go to governors who are representatives of the public and patients, although a few seats are reserved for nominees of Primary Care Trusts. Thus, the members of the Foundation Trusts are drawn from the staff, patients and community where the hospital is located. The group of stakeholders is, thus, very broad and diversified. Governors are eligible to serve for up to three years and to stand for re-election. Members can vote in elections and can stand for elections themselves. This new system of 'membership' of Foundation Trusts is claimed to ensure representation of local interests and political accountability. The models which have inspired this new type of accountability regime, namely representative membership, are cooperatives and voluntary organizations (Davies, 2004: 820).

With regard to the relationship between this type of political accountability and managers, it is not certain that members of the Board of Governors have the power to hold directors accountable, especially if the Management Board has the power to set the agenda and decide which issues to refer for consideration to the governors. Formally the Chair and the non-executive directors of the management board are appointed by the supervisory board, which also approves of the appointment of the chief executive. The latter is appointed by the Chair and non-executive directors. The supervisory board and the management board meet twice a year to set the hospital's strategic direction, but on a daily basis the management board is in charge of running the service. The legislation is very clear in establishing that the Board of Governors will not be involved in day to day management, such as setting budgets, staff pay and other operational aspects.

NHS Foundation Trusts are claimed to enjoy greater freedom and flexibility from Whitehall control and performance management by Strategic Health Authorities. They have freedom to access capital on the basis of affordability instead of the current system of centrally controlled allocations. Moreover, Foundation Trusts can invest surpluses in developing new services for local people. Granting autonomy to NHS Foundation Trusts has meant mainly a 'negative' freedom that lifts managers from the direct interference of the Secretary of State in the daily operations of local hospitals. This autonomy is enhanced, arguably, by the creation of a new independent regulator, Monitor, which acts as a new institutional buffer between Foundation Trusts and the DOH. This new public body, which is at arms' length from the DOH, should serve as a safeguard against direct ministerial encroachment and political pressures. The regulator accounts directly to Parliament through an annual report. The main role of Monitor is to grant a licence to an applicant for Foundation Trust status, to monitor compliance with the terms of the licence and to intervene in the event of breach of the terms. Monitor may issue warnings and, in the most serious cases, dismiss members of the Board of Governors or Board of Directors and appoint interim members.[7]

### Tension between the Board of Governors and Board of Directors

The institutional instrument of representation of interests within the NHS Foundation Trusts is then the Board of Governors, which in some hospitals are called council of members or council of governors. The average size is 33 members. The size of the boards of governors ranges from 18 to 53 members (DOH, 2006). The government does not discourage a large and plethoric board, because it is necessary to ensure inclusiveness of the communities represented by the Trust. For instance, the Basildon and Thurrock NHS Foundation Trust has decided that the optimum number of its Board of Governors is 53, to be built up over three years (2004–7). In general, Foundation Trusts do have a lot of room to manoeuvre in deciding the proportionality of interests represented.

The large majority of members are then elected by their constituencies, with the exception of at least three governors, one appointed by the primary care trust, one by the local authority and one by the university. In terms of numbers, each NHS Trust has margins to decide how many governors will be appointed from those primary care trusts to which NHS Foundation Trust provides goods and services. There is no reserved seat for local politicians in the Board of Governors, although obviously this does not exclude them from being elected in their personal capacity. The DOH has detailed the process of elections of members at length and, more generally, the governance arrangements of NHS Trusts are established by the central government (Department of Health, 2002). It is worth noticing that 'election' is very much emphasized as the most important mechanism for membership to the Board of Governors, despite the adoption of 'new' types of accountability based on local engagement.

As far as the election of members on the board is concerned, the Foundation is free to decide how many governors it wishes to draw from the public, patient and carer constituencies. The only legally binding provision is that they must constitute a majority within the board. This means that the Foundation can decide autonomously how many representatives of patients it has on the Board of Governors. The same applies for staff governors. There is no maximum number of staff governors in an NHS Foundation Trust, so long as the public, patient and carer governors are in the majority. The average of staff governors is five (DOH, 2006: 40). The principles of the workings of the board are 'stakeholder engagement, consultation and participation' (Monitor, 2006).

Governors have three roles: advisory, guardianship and strategic. With regard to the first responsibility, governors maintain a dialogue with the community they represent in order to create a channelling mechanism between the local community and the hospital's decision-making structures. Acting as guardians, governors ensure that the NHS Trust operates in a way that is consistent with its authorization terms and with its statement of purpose. In its strategic role, the board of governors advises on the long-term direction of the NHS Trust so that the board of directors can effectively determine its policies. For this purpose, some NHS Foundation Trusts have delegated the responsibility for strategy to a subcommittee.

The Board of Directors, which is responsible for running the hospital, is made up of non-executive and executive directors. The average size is between 10 and 16 members. This is relatively large compared to the smaller size requested for effective decision making. Among the executive directors we find a chief executive, a finance director, a medical practitioner and a registered nurse. The non-executive directors are appointed by the Board of Governors at a general meeting. There is no limit on the number of non-executive directors an NHS Foundation Trust may have. Monitor may issue guidance on good practice for non-executive appointments, but the NHS Appointments Committee plays no role in the appointment of the Board of Directors. Only a member of the public or patient constituencies is eligible for appointment as a non-executive director. Non-executive directors are expected to bring independent judgment from their experience outside the NHS. They may question and probe the executive directors (DOH, 2006: 59). They are appointed for a minimum of 12 months. The DOH recommends that the non-executive directors, as well as the Chair, be appointed for a period of office not exceeding three years, but they may be renewed.

It is the responsibility of non-executive directors, subject to the approval of the Board of Governors, to appoint the chief executive. Together with the non-executive directors and the Chair of the hospital, the chief executive of the hospital appoints and removes the other executive directors. The Trust has to establish a committee made of non-executive directors to act as an audit committee. This committee should be responsible for audit monitoring. The Trust is also to establish a committee of non-executive directors to decide the remuneration and terms and conditions of employment for the executive directors.

Therefore, it becomes clear that within the Board of Directors the non-executive members counterbalance the power of executive directors and the chief executive. The Audit Commission (2007) has identified a crucial area of tension in relation to non-executive directors. On the one hand, they are part of a corporate body, such as the Board of Directors, and as such they need to be supportive of the chief executives, but on the other hand they must balance that managerial power. Moreover, non-executive directors need to ensure the efficient operation of the board. They also have a particular role in monitoring the performance of executive directors, and this raises the potential for conflict. The problem is that the dividing line between strategy, which the non-executive directors are responsible for, and operation is by no means clear.

The Board of Directors exercises a strong planning role, strategic decision making and resource allocation. It is responsible for the financial, environmental and social management of the hospital. The directors have to monitor the performance of the organization and hold other management structures to account. The board is also responsible for the supervision and appointment of senior executives and for setting out their salaries. It is also the sole responsibility of the directors to establish the organizational structure of the hospital. The board is accountable as a whole to the members of the Board of Governors.

The 2003 Health and Social Care Act clearly establishes that all powers of a NHS Foundation Trust are to be exercised by its directors. The Board of Governors cannot veto the decisions approved by the Board of Directors.[8] The link between the directors and the governors is vital to the effectiveness of accountability mechanisms, which remains a top priority of the governance arrangement of NHS Foundation Trusts. The DOH advises that the boards must be complementary to each other, and not hierarchical or competitive, and the Chair of the Foundation must provide a critical link between them at the highest level of the organisation. The Chair in fact presides over both the Board of Governors and the Board of Directors. The Chair and the non-executive directors appoint the chief executive. The chief executive's role is pivotal in getting the relationship between the governors and directors right. Tension can arise from the different objectives of these two boards. Some foundation hospitals have made the directors' meetings a closed affair to governors. The demarcating line is that the governors focus 'outwards' to represent stakeholders, whereas directors are responsible 'inward' for the effective running of the hospital enterprise.

The DOH has set out detailed guidance on governance arrangements, including the electoral process of governors which ensures a democratic control of the decision-making process. Despite the legislative provisions, some scholars have cast doubt about the representativeness of the membership from which constituencies are drawn (Klein, 2003). This scepticism is based on the difficulties that mutual organizations experienced in England in overcoming the apathy of their members. Klein (2003: 174) states that 'the first safe prediction is that membership will be unrepresentative'. It will be skewed in favour of those interests which are intense and have greater resources to be mobilized. Ray Robinson (2002) shares similar sceptical views on the possible success of the new governance arrangements. On the one hand, they are meant to transform centrally controlled organizations into locally owned hospitals by operating in a business-like way. However, as he argues, these proposals are not new. They were originally introduced with the NHS Trusts by the Thatcher government in 1991. Devolution of decision making to the local level and new freedoms over pay and conditions and capital spending were important elements of those reforms too (Robinson, 1989). The history of granting freedoms to NHS Trusts, however, is not a success, given the legacy of centralized command and control that has proved stubbornly resistant.

Trusts have reported disappointment in the general level of commitment from appointed governors and have found that they have the poorest attendance record at meetings (DOH, 2006: 47). The problem is lack of interest in becoming members and the consequential self-selection of members (Klein, 2004) who are not representative of the community. Klein argues that even hospital staff have been slow to respond enthusiastically to the election of members on the supervisory boards. He suggests that their behaviour may be justified by the decorative role of supervisory boards, while the real power is concentrated in the hands of the executive team and the Board of Directors.

## France

Judging from a parliamentary inquiry carried out from November 2002 to March 2003, the French public hospital is an institution in severe 'moral' and managerial crisis (Assemblée Nationale, 2003, Les projets de loi de financement de la sécurité sociale, Paris: Assemblée Nationale.). This suggests that the reforms in the 1980s and 1990s have not been able to deliver the intended changes. '*L' hopital public va mal … l'hopital est en crise …* '. The inquiry clearly points to the alarming conditions in public hospitals. The crisis is claimed to be particularly serious in relation to the lack of strategy, direction and organizational authority within the hospital structures. The so-called *pilotage* of the public hospitals suffers from a lack of attribution of clear responsibilities and authority. The hospital is described as a '*machine à déresponsabiliser*'. The metaphor of the crisis is apparent in the public debate (Le Point, 2008).

Factors internal to the organization of French hospitals are claimed to be responsible for the crisis. Excessive bureaucratization and lack of authority are viewed as the primary obstacles to the transformation of the hospital into an 'enterprise'. These are cultural inhibiting traits of French hospitals. In the parliamentary inquiry one doctor in a managerial position illustrates the problem in this way:

> Nowadays, we are confronted with the problem of the '*patate chaude*': who has responsibility for solving it? The director of the hospital? The director of the regional hospital agency? The president of the doctors? Who has responsibility for decision making within hospitals? The confusion of roles and responsibilities is the source of an alarming demoralisation among staff.[9]
>
> (Assemblée Nationale, 2003: 19)

The ministerial circular of February 2004 and the related ordinance no. 2005-406, enacted in May 2005,[10] concerning the simplification of administration of public hospitals, attempts to address this problem by clearly adopting new managerialism and strengthening managerial accountability, not at the expenses of political representation though, as I will argue in this section.

The French health care system shares some of the main features of the Bismarckian health insurance model with Germany and the Netherlands. In France the social security system is still identified with the health insurance system. For most of the French people, the *sécurité sociale* signifies health care protection (Hassenteufel and Palier, 2007). The French health care systems share with Germany traits such as social contributions paid by employees and employers, access to services based on work and administration by sickness funds. However, the French system is much more centralized and directed by Paris and the Ministry of Health. The negotiations between sickness funds and doctors and trade unions are more controlled by the state than in other social insurance systems. No *convention médicale* can be adopted without the approval of the state, which always takes an important role in negotiation. In Germany, sickness funds enjoy a relatively greater autonomy (Rothgang, 2005).

Managerialism and the reforms of organizational governance have been at the top of the health care reforms agenda in France since the beginning of the 1990s (Ministère de la Santé, 2003, 2004, 2005; Sobezak and Chastagner, 1998; Soubie, 1993) and have been widely discussed by the public. Hospitals have been the centre of attention of reforms aimed at improving their management structures, quality of services and performance. Among the different themes, managerialism and autonomy have witnessed a consistent centrality in the policymaking process (Pierru, 1999). Most of the changes with regard to the internal governance of French public hospitals have been adopted at the national level through legislation and executive directives, here analysed.

### The 1991 Hospital Reform Act: The new decentralized hospital system

In contrast to the large degree of freedom that prevails in ambulatory care, the French hospital system is centrally directed from the Ministry of Health in Paris, in particular with regard to capacity and standards, but more recently also management issues, the so-called *gestion*. Since the 1980s, public hospitals have been the target of ambitious and at times radical reforms of cost-containment, in order to improve their financial conditions. However, as I will discuss in this section, more recent reforms, such as the 2007 Hospital Plan, are increasingly focused on managerialism and the adoption of NPM as a solution to the malaise that hospitals suffer (Assemblée Nationale, 2003).

The introduction of global budgets in 1984 altered the management of public hospitals. This squeeze of resources raised tension in the internal hospital organizations and created opportunities for greater managerial assertiveness. Cremadez argued that the intensified conflict between management and the medical staff has encouraged hospital management to establish clearer objectives and to decide priorities for funding (Cremadez, 1991). Thus, global budgets resulted in a strengthened role for the hospital directors. Since the mid-1980s the managers of French hospitals have sought to increase their autonomy, especially against the medical chiefs of service, who were appointed for life and were very powerful in the organization of the hospitals. The tension between the management and the medical profession frustrated the managers, who faced insurmountable difficulties in challenging the fiefdoms of the hospital 'departments' (de Pouvourville, 1986; Bach, 1993).

As Bach has argued, the reform experience of the 1980s revealed the limitations of a reform strategy only focused on cost containment. Subsequent reforms, in 1991, 1996, and most recently in 2005 and 2007, have emphasized the significance of internal governance arrangements and restructuring of the public hospitals for the wider institutional system. The 1991 reform aimed at increasing the autonomy of hospitals and developing clear responsibilities of the actors in the hospital system. The 1991 *Hospital Reform Act* introduced the *projèt d'établissement*, an instrument that was intended to strengthen hospital planning. Hospitals are required to draw up a business plan spelling out their objectives, negotiated with the medical and nursing management and the regional administration. The reform also focuses greater attention on the evaluation of medical staff, including the powerful chiefs of service. Their performance is to be evaluated after five years and their lifelong contract of employment has been changed to a five-year fixed-term contract. They are evaluated and their contract renewed upon the decision of the hospital board (*Conseil d'Administration*). This provision has potentially given the hospital director greater influence in the appointment medical staff in managerial positions.

The *Cour des Comptes* and its regional branches conducted an investigation in 2001 and 2002 to assess the state of the implementation of the *projèt d'établissement*. The report suggested that many hospitals had not yet introduced a business plan (Cour des Comptes, 2001). Only 45 per cent of hospitals financed by global budgets had adopted a business plan by January 2002. There were significant regional differences: 21 per cent in Basse-Normandie and 81 per cent in Nord-Pas-de Calais, for instance. It also noted that the Ministry of Health had not paid enough attention to this problem. The court emphasized the significance of this instrument as a five-year planning mechanism whereby clinical and research objectives were defined. Human resources management was also to be included in the business plan. Some hospitals were making an effort, but often this was an unrealistic list of objectives, as it was the case at the University Hospital Centre (CHU) in Bordeaux, where a business plan was adopted as early as 1994 (Cour des Comptes, 2001).[11]

The 1991 reform strengthened the hospital management in an attempt to innovate the internal governance of French public hospitals. In particular, the authority of the hospital director was reinforced by the autonomy provided by the law for financial resources, the responsibility for the elaboration of the *projèt d'établissement*, and the introduction of the notion of evaluation not only of services, but also of individual doctors. One of the merits of the reform was to tackle the internal dynamics of the public hospital and the relationships between actors, rather than closely pursuing cost-containment. This has been the case for most reforms of the health care system in France in the 1990s. There has been consistent attention and understanding of the significance of internal governance arrangements as a prerequisite for any further innovation and policy change. The organizational dimension of delivery is viewed as the core of health care reforms and welfare politics in France, unlike in Germany where narrow strategies of cost-containment dominate the debate.

### New governance structures of French hospitals

The management structures of a French public hospital are: the *Conseil d'Administration*, and the *Conseil Exécutif* headed by the hospital's directors. Traditionally, each hospital has its own governing board made up of representatives from the Ministry, from the local social security boards (*Caisses primaries d'assurance maladie*) and from staff. The mayor normally presides over this governing board in the case of hospitals that are managed by the municipalities. Elected local officials are key players on the supervisory boards of French hospitals. In contrast, the hospital director has traditionally been a civil servant trained in hospital management at the National School of Public Health in Rennes, nominated by the Ministry and approved by the governing board. The position has been fairly ambitious in terms of authority within the organization. Therefore, the administration of French public hospitals has been highly

centralized, with political control exercised through ministerial appointment of hospital directors and hospital supervisory boards presided over
by the local mayor.

The *Conseil d'Administration* is composed of three categories of members. First, the elected officials include the mayor, a regional representative, a departmental representative and a member elected by the
intermunicipal association. The second group of members is appointed
by the regional hospital agency to represent users and experts. Third,
representatives of the staff of the hospitals are members of the *Conseil
d'Administration*. The total number of members ranges from 12 to 18.
The ordinance no. 406, 2 May 2005, establishes that there must be an
equal number of members representing the politicians and the professions (first and third categories).[12] Elected officials are chosen by the
local, regional and departmental councils. In addition, some members
are observers: the hospital director and the director of the regional hospital agency. The *Conseil d'Administration* adopts the business plan, the
internal organization of the hospital, the financial objectives and the
budget. In addition to a strategic management role, it also has power
with regard to the evaluation of performance.

The ordinance establishes that the president of the *Conseil
d'Administration* of municipal hospitals is the mayor, and the president
of departmental hospitals is the president of the departmental council.
Only in the case of big hospitals, namely the intermunicipal and inter-
departmental ones, is the president of the Conseil elected by the members of the *Conseil d'administration* belonging to the elected officials and
users' categories. The legislation is explicit in its endorsement of strong
political accountability mechanisms. Unlike the NHS Trusts, the French
*Conseil* prefers representative mechanisms to direct representation of the
public and participatory mechanisms. Elected officials, for instance, have
opposed the restructuring of the hospital system in Marseille, in particular the hospital Sainte-Marguerite, and delayed the process of hospital
restructuring (Cour des Comptes, 2001). Locally elected representatives
on the boards of hospitals use their political position to contact ministers, for instance, to obtain the installation of costly imaging equipment
in their hospitals (Minvielle, 1997: 756). Although hospitals are embedded in a centralized hierarchical system, they are of great relevance for
local politicians, due to their economic and symbolic value. As we will
discuss later, this is also the case with Italian public hospitals.

The management board, so-called *Conseil Exécutif*, is constituted by
the hospital director and the team that the director decides to appoint.
As stated in the 2004 ministerial circular,[13] the role of the director is

strengthened.[14] The board's primary task is to elaborate the business plan, to organize and supervize the process of contractualization of services with the different medical divisions of the hospitals. One of the most significant powers of the director is to select the heads of the *poles d'activites*, which are the newly created cross-divisional groups of doctors in the hospital. Formally, the director's decision needs to be ratified by the *Conseil* and the Ministry. The director will exercise its management according to quality and performance indicators provided by the *poles*. In accordance with NPM, managerial devolution is advocated by the legislation. This implies that the director delegates managerial responsibilities to the heads of the *poles d`activites*.

The *Conseil Exécutif* is a new institution which is claimed to ensure an improved link between managerial and professional accountability by the contractualization of the relationships between the director and the doctors. The Conseil is composed of two constituencies in equal numbers: the management team and the *collège des praticiens*, namely the doctor's council. The director has discretion over the selection of the team. The Ministry of Health strongly recommends including the medical director of the hospital in the management team (Ministère de la Santé, 2007: 35). The legislation defines the maximum number of members of the Conseil as 16 in university hospitals and as 12 in all other public hospitals, consisting of six members from each category (six from the management team and six from the doctors' representatives). Thus, the Conseil can still be a large management structure and all members have equal voting power. The legislation establishes that, in the case of parity, the directors takes precedence.[15]

Potentially the hospital director has acquired important powers over the medical staff, thanks to the restructuring of traditionally insular departments into cross-functional medical groups. The hospital is now organized in *poles d`áctivites*, which are created by individual hospitals on the basis of their own business plan. Their heads respond to the director and they have to negotiate a service agreement with the director. It is outside the scope of this book to discuss in greater detail the reform of the medical structures in French hospitals.[16] Briefly, I have noticed that the creation of cross-functional units may offer opportunities for greater coordination and supervision by the hospital director, as predicted theoretically in Chapter 2.

Therefore, the hospital director is *'responsible mais pas patron'* (Assemblée Nationale, 2003: 45). The director is the centre of a wide web of relationships inside and outside the organization. This multi-centred structure is a potential obstacle for managerial accountability, as suggested by the Parliamentary Committee on health care. On the one hand, the central administration of the Ministry of Health, through its powerful *Direction generale de la santé* (DGS), the ministerial cabinet, the prefect, *le caisses*, the director of the regional hospital agency and the *Conseil d'Administration,* dominated by elected officials, are external accountability holders and constraints on the director's managerial discretion. The problem in France is an excess of accountability. I will return to this point in Chapter 5. On the other hand, internally the hospital director has to negotiate with the president of the medical council (*Commission Médicale d'Etablissement*), with the president of the *Conseil d'Administration* and with the professionals.

Despite the regionalization of the French health care system,[17] the centralized direction given to the hospital restructuring seems to suggest the contrary. Public hospitals do not enjoy the autonomy of German hospitals, as I will discuss in the next section, and British hospitals to design their own internal structures. The final decision-making power in relation to the appointment of managers rests with the Ministry, upon the recommendations of the *Conseil d'Administration* of hospitals. Thus, appointment is an important instrument for the central administration to control the process of managerialism and the reorganization of the hospital sector.

## Germany

The financial situation of German public hospitals is alarming, as the figures in the most recent Hospital Barometer 2007 clearly show (Krankenhaus Barometer, 2007). In the financial year 2006/2007, 28 per cent of all the hospitals were running deficits. The hospitals with the greatest losses are the ones with a capacity of over 600 beds, namely the largest units. The prediction for 2007 is that 42 per cent of public hospitals will experience a worsening of their financial condition. This is likely to add impetus to the plans for closing down approximately 30 per cent of hospitals due to overcapacity. Financial pressures are severe on the German hospital system.[18] The importance of hospitals in overall health care budgets makes them obvious targets for government's strategies to cut total spending. Upward pressure of health care expenditure has been a feature of all industrialized countries (Mossialos and Legrand, 1999). Countries with an insurance-based system, such as Germany and France, have been less successful at containing costs than tax-based health care systems, such as the United Kingdom and Italy. Therefore, it is not surprising that organizational reforms aimed at improving cost savings and efficiency have reached the top of the agenda in the German hospital system (Bundesministerium für Gesundheit, 1993; 1998). The national German association for hospitals has advocated changes in the management structures of hospitals as a necessary solution (Deutsches Krankenhaus Institut, 2007). The internal organizational structure of a hospital is a very important dimension of reforms for policymakers, though underresearched in the existing literature.

The history of health care reforms in Germany in the last 20 years has been one of cost-containment (Altenstetter and Busse, 2005). The 1993 Health Care Structure Act introduced competition between the sickness funds (*Krankenkassen*).[19] It was a critical juncture in German health care policy development. The 1999 Schroeder reform (Act to Strengthen Solidarity) also introduced cost-cutting measures. Reform proposals in 2005, which were part of the election manifesto for both the SPD and CDU, indicate the crumbling of the institutional stability of the neo-corporatist German health care system (Bundesministerium für Gesundheit, 2007). The administrative framework is frequently submerged under the study of the funding mechanisms or the major policy changes (Clasen, 2005), which have moved the German health care systems towards more market based and liberal systems (Hassenteufel and Palier, 2005). However, other scholars argue that the German system has remained immune to liberal approaches to health care organizations (Hacker, 2004). In this section I am concerned with administrative governance of hospitals in Germany, a topic which has been neglected in favour of studies exclusively and narrowly focusing on sickness funds and funding mechanisms.[20] However, had I analysed sickness funds' organizational changes, I would not have found a significant difference in relation to the introduction of managerialism. Sickness funds have changed their mode of governance and moved slowly away from corporatist boards towards a consumer-based model (Newman and Kuhlmann, 2007).[21] They function more as enterprises and, thus, marketing has become an important function of their activities, as interviews at the Ministry of Health have suggested. The management logic is not simply based on collective bargaining between social partners, but it is more centred around being successful at attracting 'clients' (Bode, 2006).

There is to date very scarce empirical research concerning the management boards of German hospitals and their new decision-making arrangements resulting from internal organizational restructuring distinct from privatization. Little attention, generally, has been given to the new governance system for public providers. Furthermore, the existing literature rarely frames the discussion of hospital management changes within the wider debate of administrative reforms of modernization, despite the increasing political salience of the paradigm of efficiency.[22] Public hospitals in Germany operate within a decentralized and highly fragmented system of governance, which is not the result of top-down devolution, as in the United Kingdom, but represents the historical path of the German health care system (Altenstetter and Busse, 2005). Competencies for hospital policy and legislation concerning the governance structures of German public hospitals are divided between the federal and the Länder governments. However, self-governance and subsidiarity remain the key legal and normative principles of the German system (Boedege and Schellberg, 2005; Merchel, 2003; Grunow, 1995). The most comprehensive piece of legislation which lays out the main stakeholders in the German health care sector is the *Sozialgesetzbuch* V (Fifth Social Code).

### Länder legislation, local government and the modernization of public hospitals

The regulation governing management and accountability regimes and processes of German public hospitals is very complex and detailed, and mainly entrenched in legal codes (Döhler, 1995). Hospital management and ownership arrangements fall within the competences of the Länder, which share responsibility for health care delivery with the federal government and with corporatist non-governmental institutions. Thus, hospitals are subject to Länder legislation. Public hospitals do not independently decide their management and governance arrangements, despite the widely accepted characterization of the health care system in Germany as corporatist self-governance (Schnapp, 1998; Merchel, 2003). On the contrary, laws prescribe which stakeholders are to be included in the planning process and their proportional representation in the relevant governing bodies. It is in the hospital field of Berlin and Hamburg that administrative reforms associated with NPM for public hospitals have gone furthest. Reforms have been radical in those cases, but the spread of the 'management gag' has been a widely acknowledged process in hospital care in Germany.[23]

The German health care sector is extremely diversified in terms of the internal organization of public hospitals (Kampe and Kracht, 1989). The majority of Länder make detailed provisions with regard to the composition of management boards for public hospitals, which have limited autonomy in so far as they must operate within rigidly set rules and frameworks. The most detailed provisions at the Länder level with respect to the roles and responsibilities of management boards and supervisory boards were found in Berlin. Berlin is an extreme case in which the Länder run their own hospitals with a considerable degree of tight administrative control. The dominant governance element in Berlin is the *Senatsverwaltung für Gesundheit, Soziales und Verbraucherschutz*, which has major responsibility for the planning and organization of the hospital system, among others.[24] As one interviewee suggested, the senate not only runs public hospitals, but it also plans the level of provision based on unclear measures of 'needs'. It also supervises the negotiations and bargaining between sickness funds and hospitals. At the regional level, thus, the City of Berlin represents a highly centralized system of hospital administration.

As one interviewee suggested, the institutional design of public hospitals and their directors is decided at the political level: 'It is the political community which decides on directors and managers of public hospital because ownership has always been local in Germany, in comparison to Britain'. In many cases Länder decide to devolve down to municipalities, which own the public hospitals, the regulation activities. In Germany, few public hospitals are owned by the Länder directly; more commonly they are owned by counties, cities and municipalities. As I did for the case of NHS Foundation Trusts, I will now look at the regulations underlying governance structures of public hospitals, the composition of boards, to which hospital managers are formally accountable, and how board members are selected. In comparison to the other three countries under investigation, the hospital sector in Germany is characterized by a wide variety of ownership and organizational forms. The federal government has limited competencies in the decentralized system of consensus-based collective bargaining. Expert interviewees have suggested that local government has been open to the reception of NPM ideas.

Municipalities and local government are at the forefront of administrative change related to managerialism in Germany, from the *Regelungskultur* (Jann, 2003) to cost efficiency. It is worth opening a brief parenthesis here, before going into the case study of hospital governance arrangements, as it has been widely accepted that there is a German version of NPM, known as the *Steuerungsmodell (New Steering Model)*. This was originally imported not from Britain, but in 1991 from the city of Tilburg in the Netherlands. It was promoted by a municipally funded non-profit consulting organization under its director Gerhard Banner,[25] the *Kommunale Gemeinschaftstelle für Verwaltungsvereinfachung (KGSt)*. The main elements of the New Steering Model included mainly microeconomic governance instruments, the clear-cut division of politics from administration, contract management, output emphasis, result oriented budgeting and decentralized resource responsibility *(Dezentrale Ressource nverantwortung)*, among others (Banner, 2001, 2005; KGSt, 2003).

German administrative scholars argue that Germany was a latecomer to the NPM reforms because many of its institutional features were already in place, such as decentralized management. Moreover, German local government contracted out personal social services, like kinder-gartens and homes for the elderly, to non-public and not-for-profit organizations (Wollmann, 2001). Welfare state provision in Germany has been predominantly organized through not-for-profit organizations (Leisering and Leibfried, 1999; Leisering, 2007).

However, in the 1990s Germany opened up to the NPM message. This shift was triggered by some contextual factors, including the public debts incurred by the financial burdens of German unification, and the pressure to meet the Treaty of Maastricht budgetary param-eters. The conservative government, led by Helmut Kohl, started to modernize its administrative structures. Kohl established in 1995 an independent expert committee, known as the 'Lean State' Advisory Council *(Sachverstaendigenrat Schlanker Staat)*. Later in 1999, the term *'Aktivierender Staat'* was coined to indicate the new red–green coalition's plans to modernize the state and innovate through results-oriented accountability. So far, the modernization has been closely directed in Germany toward cost-cutting (Bogumil et al., 2006). In contrast with the Anglo-Saxon original NPM, expert interviewees suggest that the separation between politics and administration 'was never bought in Germany'. Strong and politically legitimate local authorities, which characterize the German self-governance tradition, and their demo-cratic public accountability have been barriers to the marketization of public services (Wollmann, 2001). The *Rechtsstaat* tradition has also been viewed as an obstacle for the adoption of NPM.

The version of NPM introduced in Germany defends corporatist arrangements with the medical profession and federalism rather than replacing them with centralized control (Dent, 2004). Hospitals stand outside the institutional and legal framework of corporatism and, instead, negotiate directly with the sickness funds (Schwartz and Busse, 1997:107). This system has made controlling costs extremely difficult. The attempt to make sickness funds responsible for this has failed so far (Dent, 2005:631). However, despite all the predictions of resistance to NPM, public hospitals have undergone some radical restructuring from within, that is, without being privatized. The governance arrangements of public hospitals in Germany follow the main elements of the German corporate governance model (Hopt, 2000). Its main characteristic is the two-tier board system, consisting of a large supervisory board (*Aufsichtsrat*) and a management board (*Vorstand*). The supervisory board of a hospital consists of 17 members, on average. It is, then, much smaller in size than the average NHS supervisory board. The majority of members are representatives from the local government council, usually with clear partisan affiliations and representing the major parties. Frequently, they are local councillors elected directly by the district councils. There are also members representing the staff of the hospital.

Among publicly owned hospitals that have adopted new managerialism, *Landesbetrieb Krankenhauser Hamburg* (LBK) in Hamburg and *Charitè* and *Vivantes* public chains in Berlin stand out. They illustrate the most radical internal restructuring of public hospitals in Germany, and the adoption of private-sector management systems. LBK was privatized in 2005 after ten years of internal reorganization,[26] starting in the mid-1990s. Charitè and Vivantes are public corporations and remain wholly owned by the government. In 1995, the Hamburg executive cabinet (known as *Senat*) created a new semi-autonomous public corporation, called LBK, which took over the management of the public hospitals in Hamburg. Hence, public hospitals have been the target of government modernization plans since the mid-1990s.

In 2001 the SPD, which had been in office for a long time, was massively defeated. The new government sold LBK to a private group in 2005.[27] The pre-privatization reforms were carried out with the advice of the consulting firm Accenture, which was involved in designing the new business model for LBK. In 1996 a new corporate board was established. The management team was comprised of only three managers, and this is still the case today after privatization. The pre-privatization legislation in 2004 established that the supervisory board of LBK would be composed of 18 members appointed by the *Senat*. The chief executive of the board is a representative member of the *Senat*. One-third of the members of the *Aufsichtsrat* were elected from the staff of the hospitals. They all remained in office for four years. There was no provision for the participation of the public or citizens in the supervisory board. The *Senat* also appointed the members of the *Vorstand*, which was a slim structure composed of only two members.[28]

The case of the pre-privatization organizational reforms in Hamburg does not remain an isolated case in Germany. Another massive restructuring of the internal management and organization of public hospitals happened in Cologne. The transformation of the city's clinics started in 1996 in response to concerns about inefficiencies. In August 2002, the new conservative-dominated city council's health care committee hired a consultancy firm for organizational restructuring of its public hospitals, which were put in a public corporation (*Gesellschaft mit beschraenkter Haftung* (GmbH)). The *Kliniken der Stadt Köln* (the city's hospitals) are run by two managers and 13 members of the *Aufsichtsrat*. It is striking that the overwhelming majority of its members are elected local councillors, including the leader of the SPD party. The *Aufsichtsrat* also includes four members of the hospitals' staff. Again, as is the case in Hamburg, no representative of the public is included, unlike the British and French supervisory boards of public hospitals. Despite the reorganization inspired by NPM, the majority of members of the supervisory board are elected politicians.

### The Charité: Modernization without privatization

As one interviewee of the management team at the Charité said, 'at the end of the 1990s we introduced a new paradigm. We looked at the success story of private chains and we took them as a paradigm for our restructuring'. In the case of Berlin, the Charité case illustrates at best a reorganization along managerialism lines without privatization, at least not yet. I do not intend to introduce this case study as 'representative', but rather as an extreme case for which one would expect, theoretically, to see the greatest degree of challenge to political accountability and the greatest degree of change in terms of the relationship in the accountability regime (from political to managerial). Before I delve into the case study, I will provide an overview of the internal governance framework of the hospital system in Berlin. The supervisory boards are made of a member from the Berlin's local administration (the Senate for Health), the members of the hospitals' management board, a member of the workers' council, a doctor representative of ambulatory care physicians and a patient advocate. Clearly, the representatives of the public and patients are again in the minority. The strong political accountability of the supervisory board is also reinforced in Berlin by the fact that its term of office is the same as the duration of the legislative session, namely four years (Pugner, 2000).

The research findings here presented are drawn from extensive fieldwork interviews with and direct observation of members of the management team of one of Berlin's biggest public hospital network, the Charité, the largest hospital in Europe, which has nearly 15,000 employees, 3,240 beds, and 128 medical departments, and which treats roughly 123,000 inpatients and carrys out 900,000 outpatient consultations per year.[29] The Charité has been growing steadily in the course of its almost 30 years' history, but never as rapidly as in 2003, when the medical faculty of Humboldt University merged with the Free University of Berlin. This fusion created the largest medical school and university hospital system in Europe (Berliner Universitaetsmedizingesetz, 2005). It describes itself as 'a large business enterprise using state-of-the-art management and up-to-date processing technology in medicine and administration with a total budget of 1.02 billion Euro'.[30] The German Democratic Republic wanted to make the Charité a model state facility and reconstructed most of the buildings which were destroyed during the war. The Charité belongs to the Land Berlin.

Since 2003, the Charité has been headed by a full-time board of directors. The Charité is radically breaking the decades of tradition in hospital administration, in order to increase efficiency and transform the public delivery institution into an autonomous public 'enterprise' able to compete in the market. Interviews at the Ministry of Health have suggested that, together with hospitals in Hamburg, the Charité illustrates at best the new managerialism adopted in German public hospitals. Letting a public hospital adopt a deliberate commercial attitude is an extraordinary approach to health care services in Germany, as claimed by the members of the management team, the *Vorstand* of Charité.[31] As one interviewee stated, 'my credo is the enterprise-Charité. Why should we not earn money and compete with the private sector?'.[32]

The major organizational restructuring in 2005 has conferred all responsibilities for results to the *Vorstand*,[33] a rather slim management group made of the chief executive officer, the *Direktor des Klinikums* (director of the medical center) and the *Dekan* (dean of the medical school). The author has been told that the medical director has recently become a deputy member of the *Vorstand*, with the aim to strengthen the management position of the medical profession. The medical director is *primus inter pares* and is elected from among the staff physicians of the hospitals. The introduction of managerial experiments at the end of the 1990s in Hamburg and Berlin had changed the role of the medical director from *primus inter pares* to an assistant of the executive board. One interviewee has suggested that medical directors have direct access to politicians who may support them against the other members of the management team, if necessary. The members of the *Vorstand* are appointed by the *Aufsichtsrat*, namely the supervisory board, which is chaired by the Minister of Culture, Science and Research of Land Berlin. Interviews with senior managers in the public hospitals of Berlin have suggested that senior management posts are also highly political appointments. Managers are appointed on the basis of their competence and expertise, but it would be unthinkable not to be endorsed politically as well. Politicians, thus, are powerful players in the Berlin health care system.

In Germany there is a strong tradition of separate management and supervisory boards. In the case of most German public hospitals, supervisory boards include elected politicians, unlike the supervisory boards of British NHS Foundation Trusts. The Charité has a supervisory board of 12 members, including Berlin's Senator for Finance and Senator for Culture.[34] According to one interviewee, this creates a dual leadership structure about which the Charité has been worried. If the two belong to different parties, decision making becomes more difficult. For instance, in the past the Party of Democratic Socialism (PDS) encouraged a participatory governance model for Charité, whereas the SPD has supported a centralized and strong management with clear lines of responsibilities geared towards the Charité enterprise. Centralized management is very difficult to implement at the Charité because it has traditionally been a decentralized structure with autonomous hospital clinics. The 2003 merger has offered management the opportunity to exercise more centralized controls, such as clinical pathways, and to establish best practice, but 'all we can do is to ask doctors for *ex post* justifications, [...] we cannot impose clinical pathways', as one interviewee of the management team argued.

The hospital's supervisory board also consists of representatives from the local authorities, and scientists, not necessarily medical professionals. It has been suggested to the author that another clear indicator of the chain of political accountability running from the Berlin government down to the supervisory and to the managing board is represented by the concurrence of the duration of the legislative term and the length of office of each hospital's supervisory board. This would imply that a new government could dismiss and replace members of the supervisory board, effectively creating a spoils system.This illustrates that the hierarchical chain of political accountability remains strong, despite most radical restructuring. 'Who would not want more autonomy from the politicians?', noted the chief executive during an interview with the author in December 2006.

The supervisory board plays more than a symbolic and advisory role, as in NHS Trust. Indeed, it is entrusted with key decision-making power. The *Aufsichtsrat* of the Charité is not merely a consultative body, as it has emerged from site interviews. Its responsibilities include supervising the legality of rules and procedures, the cost efficiency of the public enterprise (*Wirtschaftlichkeit*), and the attainment of targets by the management board. As we mentioned earlier, the supervisory board has ample discretion over the appointment of the fixed-term members of the *Vorstand*, including approving the elected medical director. Another important role is promoting medical teaching and research to the management board. It is striking that the supervisory board has also control over the internal organization of the Charité. As such, it does call the *Vorstand* to account for changes in the organization of individual units and centres. Furthermore, it has a key role in investment decisions, together with the Berlin government.

From the formal responsibilities set out in the statute[35] it emerges that the management board is constrained in its autonomy, especially in so far as the internal organizational design is concerned. In practice, interviewees have suggested that indeed managerial coordination has been adopted, but the institutional autonomy is limited by two sources: the supervisory board and the administration of the Land Berlin. The supervisory board may interfere with decisions pertaining to outsourcing and buying shares of other companies. In general, autonomy on financial investment is very restricted, as many interviewees have suggested. Another interviewee presented to the author a picture in which the supervisory board exerts not only policy guidance, but also control over minor decisions. This is as much lamented as accepted, given the public ownership of the Charité. As far as the scope of local government intervention is concerned, this can be as invasive as to call into question the hospital's purchase of diagnostic equipment or inquiring about the number of employees working in outsourced companies. The Land administration also regulates the volume of service provided and is heavily involved in negotiations with sickness funds (Senatsverwaltung für Gesundheit, 2005). What is most resented by the management team, as interviewees suggested, is the scarce freedom in acquiring new companies and financial investment planning.

Although political accountability remains firmly entrenched in the internal governance structure of the Charité, and fundamentally unchallenged by the transformation of the hospital administration from a bureaucratic to an entrepreneurial provider of public services, this is not to say that political control includes the patronage practices found in the French or Italian cases, where members of the supervisory boards have a say in the appointment of heads of hospital departments (Mattei, 2006). The heads of departments of the Charité are appointed by the faculty and do not suffer from political interference, as suggested by the interviewees. They enjoy a contract similar to public servants, and the newly appointed heads of departments have been exposed to an element of performance-related pay. This is a small minority amounting to less than one per cent of all physicians, as the deputy medical director told the author.[36] In fact, junior doctors do not have a performance element built in their employment contracts. The new system of performance-related pay is not used as an incentive to monitor performance and output, but rather as a mechanism for conferring financial privileges on the senior physicians. This is also confirmed by a weak and unclear system of developing performance indicators. Among the indicators which were referred to during interviews, turnover generated by private consultancy was cited as the first one. 'How much money we generate is an important indicator', one interviewee suggested. When asked about quality indicators, an openly irritated interviewee responded, 'I prefer to be treated in a German than in a British hospital, although here patients do not have a voice'. Legal and formal controls carried out by the Land administration are still predominant over performance indicators.

The Charité has created one post specifically for the internal managerial reorganization, interviewed by the author. He summarized the situation of ongoing changes as 'we can smell the blood'.[37] Legal litigations are frequent, especially with the medical professors and doctors. The person responsible for supervising the internal restructuring of the Charité also emphasized the significance of reforms aimed at coordination between units, which is particularly challenging for a large group of traditionally independent hospitals. He described to the author the innovation of the *Zentren*, which are budget-holding independent units. It is the *Zentren* which then allocates funds to the divisions. This internal organizational restructuring is something that Charité's management team is very keen on.[38]

Although the form of political accountability reveals marked elements of continuity, its content has changed significantly. The supervisory board expects the new management team to create the conditions that make it possible for the Charité to compete with the private sector at market prices. 'The social function of the hospital is to provide employment in Berlin', was the response of one interviewee to my question concerning the changed institutional mission of the Charité as an enterprise. For instance, interviewees have mentioned the crucial project concerning the laboratories' reorganization. The private consultancy firm Roland Berger has been involved in external benchmarking and cost-effectiveness analysis of all laboratories. Fierce resistance to the reorganization plans at the Charité has been reported by interviewees, who speak of the affected units as 'victims'. There is organized resistance from doctors, especially junior ones, in the so-called *Aertzeinitiativen*. One interviewee said that 'junior doctors thought their profession was about something else'. These quotes illustrate the radical cultural changes at the hospital and how they are experienced by the actors involved. The deputy medical director suggested that one of the reasons for this fierce resistance is that change is happening at a very fast pace, and the social function of the hospital is changing too rapidly.

## Italy

The shift from a politico-representative to a technical–managerial type of health care administration in Italy was signalled by the 1992 reform of the health care system (Rebora, 1999). When the Italian national health care system was created in 1978, local health authorities became a fiefdom of 'notables' who would establish their power base by distributing social benefits. This practice was perpetrated through management structures composed of locally elected officials and trade union representatives (Ferrera, 1989; Hine, 1993). Since political parties used the governing bodies of hospitals and local health authorities as an arena for party competition in local electoral politics, they have generally opposed the introduction of general management and the creation of a new executive post at the head of public hospitals, claiming that the rise of powerful bureaucrats would undermine supposedly democratic representation (Mattei, 2007b). However, as political parties decreased their 'veto power' (Immergut, 1992), the fiscal and political crisis of 1992–94 created propitious conditions for pushing through a groundbreaking reform affecting the public management of health care (Ginsborg, 2001).

In the Italian case, as will become clear, welfare reforms embrace private sector managerialism in order to debureaucratize and depoliticize the health care administration. One of the deficiencies of the 1978 law[39] was the creation of a health care system which did not give clearly defined responsibilities to individual managers (Borgonovi, 1988). The preferred decision-making process was *ad hoc* collegial coordination. Article 3 of the 1992 decree creates the post of *direttore generale*, literally general manager, of public hospitals. The Minister of Health describes the introduction of general management in this way: 'Public hospitals and local health care authorities will become public firms. It will be possible to identify a person responsible for outputs. Management boards will disappear, so will all executive boards made up of politicians.

Finally local health care authorities and public hospitals will have a *direttore generale* who is not involved in politics.'[40]

The review of management arrangements had been debated since the introduction of law no. 111/1991, which first created the new post of *amministratore straordinario*, or special manager. This signalled the initial challenge to collegial management practice by introducing single executive posts. In addition to the *amministratore straordinario*, the 1991 law established an executive board invested with policy functions[41] and an accounting committee for internal auditing. Departing from past practice, the 1992 decree eliminated the executive board and all the residual mechanisms for collegial decision making.[42] This was an extremely radical and unprecedented move. It was claimed that the government's proposal to concentrate all management functions in one single post would improve the efficiency of decision making by reducing the democratic representation of local interests, and by diminishing the political control of local politicians over managers (Borgonovi, 1988; Rebora, 1999). Municipal councillors, trade unions and medical representatives made up the management committees in order to represent the demands and interests of the local community. But this wide representation of local interests compromised the efficiency of management and decisional mechanisms (Zanetta and Casalegno, 1999).

In order to give managerial discretion to the *direttore generale*, two preconditions were introduced: the 'privatisation' of the director's employment contract[43] and the introduction of the *aziendalizzazione*, literally enterprise formula, the transformation of public hospitals into 'public enterprises', independent from the municipal administration. With regard to the first precondition, the 'privatisation of public-sector employment contract',[44] the range of powers granted by a private contract[45] is wider than the more limited ones of public employment. For instance, administrative decisions by senior civil servants can always be overturned by any elected official (Papadia, 1993). Although general managers were to be employed with a fixed-term contract, under civil law, this new type of contractual hybrid may have been incompatible with public law. For instance, some jurists have highlighted the incompatibility of being appointed by an administrative act while being responsible for job specifications set out in a private contract.[46]

Although the objective of the 'privatisation' of the employment contract[47] was to increase managerial discretion and responsibilities, the appointment procedure appeared to weaken the autonomy of the *direttore generale*, who depended on the regional executive for the offer and renewal of the fixed-term contract, by means of a relationship of trust.[48] The Under Secretary of Health from 1992–3 claims that 'the debate about the appointment procedure of the *direttore generale* turned into a quarrel'.[49] The parliamentary debate reveals the concern of some MPs about what appears to be a great risk and perhaps an incentive for a new type of subordination of the administration (Mattei, 2007a). One MP expresses his fear in relation to this: 'How can we guarantee the autonomy of senior civil servants? Not with private contracts, I think. The 1980s scandals of corruption prove that we need a bureaucracy which is recruited according to its merits and not partisan appointments. The bureaucracy must be proud of serving the state and needs to be autonomous, loyal only to the laws of the Republic, and an effective counterweight to the power of political parties, which will end up controlling directly appointed public managers.'[50]

The 1992 decree opted for the so-called *intuitu personae* method of appointment.[51] The president of the region appoints the *direttore generale* by choosing from a national list of candidates drawn by an *ad hoc* committee of experts and senior civil servants at the Ministry of Health.[52] The decree does not specify the conditions for inclusion on the list. Alternative proposals for the appointment included a regional rather than national list of candidates, a ranking system, a public competition system, appointment by a committee made of doctors from the competent local health authority, and contracting out the recruitment process to private headhunting firms. Even the latter option, arguably the most depoliticized, disturbs the then president of the Health Care Committee in the Senate, who is convinced that, 'in Lombardy they use headhunters to recruit directors. I think this is a good idea that helps meritocracy. In truth, political control is still possible though.'[53]

The second precondition for bringing general management into effect in Italian public hospitals is the establishment of the 'enterprise formula', which in Italy means the change in the juridical status of public hospitals from public bodies to public firms.[54] The 1992 reform granted all local health care authorities and selected public hospitals juridical autonomy (Balduzzi and Di Gaspare, 2002). They were given organizational, administrative and accounting discretion from municipal administration.[55] The enterprise formula aims to shift the health care administration from a rigidly legalistic to a managerial, moving away from formal controls and introducing efficiency criteria. Public firms would plan their own activities according to local demands, allocate their budget without municipal participation and establish rigid accounting systems.

The significance of the introduction of the enterprise formula does not rest only in its juridical implications, but also in its underpinning model, characterized by a view of public administration based on the private sector. The paternalistic state (Cassese, 2001), from which citizens derive their social rights, such as health care,[56] is now challenged by the process of 'customerisation' (Self, 1993). The introduction of a new system of public management in health care inevitably led to the redefinition of the relationship between citizens and the administration by transforming them into 'clients'. This entails a radical change in the administrative culture of civil servants from self-referential to public service (Pipan, 1995).

To summarize, the central aspect of the restructuring of management arrangements in the Italian public hospitals was the replacement of management boards with a single executive post covered by a high status and powerful general manager. The representation of local interests was sacrificed in favour of the concentration of executive power into one post. This was claimed to speed up decision-making procedures and to ensure greater transparency, as only one person was responsible and accountable for performance. Thus, the general manager was granted considerable discretion and managerial autonomy by the legislation. However, there was some scepticism regarding the system of appointment. The relationship of political trust established between the manager and the regional executive caused some concern about the possibility of renewed politicization (Endrici, 2001). The departure from the traditional practice of political control depends on the commitment of regional executives and leaders to a reformed health care system. This is facilitated by the new role played by the regions in providing, organizing and financing health care services.

## Conclusions: Convergence towards the enterprise formula

Changes in the internal governance structures of public hospitals have raised scholarly interest insofar as they are instrumental to improving institutional performance. This is a question of primary significance for the functioning of health care systems. In contrast, this chapter has analysed the question from a rather different analytical perspective. I have set out to answer the following questions: How does managerial autonomy affect the existing accountability regimes of public hospitals? How is the interplay between political steering, strategic management and clinical management changing as a result of administrative reforms of the state of health care? The main empirical finding is that across countries, with different health care systems and state tradition, public hospitals are increasingly built upon a corporate management decision-making structure, which places chief executives at the centre of power relationships. Managerial accountability is the predominant mode of organizational legitimation, beyond policy symbolism. Internal restructuring of public hospitals aimed at strengthening the role and position of managers is clear and visible in Britain, Germany, France and Italy. Table 3.3 at the end summarizes this convergence of managerial accountability.

A common pattern emerges from the analysis of the internal reorganization of public hospitals in Britain, Germany, France and Italy in the 1990s. Reforms aimed at improving the efficiency and productivity of hospitals have strengthened influence of the management team in monitoring results and the process of medical care. Hence, a powerful new stratum of public 'managers' or 'directors' is located at the centre of the European health care systems' decision-making process. Across different countries and types of health care systems, it is possible to note a heightened delegation of responsibilities to the executive teams of public hospitals. As I have suggested in Chapter 2, public hospitals are among the most fragmented and specialized welfare institutions, and as such are prime targets for attempts to centralize and coordinate from the top. Therefore, one of the most striking similarities is the displacement of 'old' internal governance arrangements with managerial accountability as the 'new' administrative and normative framework within hospitals. Far from being simply a symbolic device, managerialism has radically changed management structures of European public hospitals, and raised managers to a central position of power. This is even more striking in countries like Italy or France, in light of the expectations from the literature about the 'bureaucratic phenomenon' (Crozier, 1964; 1970) and inertia (Hayward, 1976; Rose and Karran, 1984). The problem is not defining what change is and what it is not, but rather looking for it in the wrong place, namely in policy change or policy goals. Change is in the administrative nuances and it occurs at the organizational level of analysis. I will come back to this point in Chapter 5.

One of the consequences of the rise of this new caste of hospital managers is the disturbance caused in the traditional corporatism of the medical profession. This tension between managerial and professional accountability has been well documented in the literature and for this reason was not the central focus of this chapter. Conflict between managers and doctors has been widespread in every country. The introduction of general management, following the Griffiths model, heavily based on performance accountability, strengthened the hierarchical relationship between managers and doctors at the expense of the corporatist dimension and horizontal types of accountability. The traditional accommodation between the state and the medical profession in relation to the allocation of resources within budgetary limits has been challenged by the new monitoring and control powers of managers over doctors within hospitals. Horizontal accountability has not proven to be able to resist the new managerial hierarchies. Hence, in Britain, Germany, Italy and France, the relationship between managerial and professional accountability has moved similarly in one direction, namely towards greater managerial accountability. In this respect, public hospitals are converging.

The convergence of hospital care systems here analysed is less evident in the political accountability dimension. Who holds managers accountable and via what mechanisms? There are two models which have emerged from the empirical analysis in which the discriminating factor is the institutional role given to the supervisory board by the legislation. They are presented in Table 3.2. This in turn depends on the degree of structural autonomy that hospitals enjoy from central

*Table 3.2* The 'Buffer' the 'Agent' types of supervisory boards of public hospitals

|  | Role of supervisory board | |
|---|---|---|
|  | **Buffer model** (isolate management team from political direct interference) | **Agent model** (channel health authorities' decisions to management) |
| **Hospital structural autonomy from health authorities** | High autonomy of hospitals. | Limited autonomy of hospitals or no autonomy. |
| **Relationship between political and managerial accountability** | Accountability is via the supervisory board, with weak direct links between chief executive and central health authorities. Internally, managerial accountability is predominant. | Accountability is via a hierarchical chain, from chief executive to supervisory boards to health authorities and ministers. Political accountability is upward and hierarchical. |
| **Reference country** | • Britain (Foundation Trusts)<br>• Germany<br>• Italy | • France |

*Table 3.3*  New governance structures in European public hospitals

| Public hospitals | Appointment methods | Composition (local politicians) | Role | Public accountability relationships |
|---|---|---|---|---|
| **Britain**<br><br>*Board of Directors of NHS Foundation Trusts* | Chief executive appointed by the non-executive directors, subject to approval of the Board of Governors and Chair. Other executive directors appointed by the chief executive, together with non-executive directors. Non-executive directors appointed by Board of Governors at a general meeting from the public. | Ten to sixteen members: Executive directors (chief executive, financial officer, one practitioner, one nurse).<br><br>Non-executive Directors (public; politicians only in personal capacity). | Strategic (non-executive directors) Operational (executive directors) -Strong planning -Resources allocation -Staff remuneration -Internal organization of public hospitals -Investment plans. | Directly to the Board of Governors (local community), no longer to the Secretary of State for Health.<br><br>*Election* is the key method of selecting members on the Board of Governors. |
| **Germany**<br>Vorstand | Chief executive appointed by the *Aufsichtsrat*. Other members appointed by chief executive, approved by *Aufsichtsrat*. | Three members:<br>-Chief executive<br>-Medical Director<br>-Nurse. | -Operational -Day to day running of the hospital. | -Accountability to the *Aufsichtsrat* -Strong bureaucratic accountability to the Land administration. |
| **France**<br>Conseil éxecutif | Chief executive appointed by the Minister of Health, upon approval by the *Conseil d'Administration*. Other members appointed by the chief executive. | Twelve members:<br>-Six from the management team (including chief executive)<br>-Six members from the professions. | -Elaboration of the five-year business plan (*projet d'établissement*) -Internal contractualization with medical divisions -Appointment of directors of medical divisions -Performance monitoring. | Directly to: Minister and his cabinet, the newly established Regional Agency of Hospitalization, the prefect and the *Conseil d'Administration* of the hospital. |
| **Italy**<br>Direttore Generale | Appointed by the regional government. | Chief executive<br>-No politicians. | -All powerful. | Accountability to regional minister of health (direct relationship). |

government's control (Mattei, 2007). First, the supervisory board serves as a buffer, isolating the management team of a public hospital from the direct interference of politicians in government. This new role allegedly makes the hospital more autonomous and efficient. Secondly, the supervisory board operates as an agent of the level of government responsible for hospital planning. Accordingly, political accountability remains hierarchical and not much different from traditional accountability. These public hospitals do not enjoy as much autonomy as the ones in which the supervisory board's aim is to create a buffer from political interference.

From an organizational perspective, as Table 3.2 suggested, the buffer model is predominant in European hospitals. In the British case the supervisory board was reorganized as an institutional buffer to protect the internal structures from central government and politicians' interference. The Board of Governors of NHS Trusts is composed mainly of elected representatives from the public and the staff. There is no politician, unlike in France, Germany and Italy, and elected officials are not members of the supervisory boards. On the other hand, in Germany and France local politicians are the 'owners' of public hospitals, not the lay public. They play a very important role in the decision-making process through planning and supervising managers. In the case of German hospitals, the board is sometimes appointed concurrently with local elections. Thus, political accountability of the most traditional type does not seem to be replaced by new types of 'outward' accountability, directly to citizens (Sinclair, 1995). French hospitals likewise have not witnessed any major transformation of political accountability as a result of managerialism. With the exception of Britain, political accountability has not changed significantly, despite the radical and deep transformation of management behaviour and structures within hospitals.

As far as the formal shift from 'old' electoral types of political accountability towards the new customer-oriented types, I argue that this phenomenon can be confined only to the British NHS Foundation Trusts. As discussed in great detail in this chapter, the new modes of governance which allow direct participation by citizens seem to produce meagre results and I have cast doubts on their effectiveness, in the light of empirical evidence. Paradoxically, most studies on new modes of governance focus on the extreme case, Britain, which is rather the exception, and, alas, which does not prove the rule. Having said this, I do not suggest that the relationship between managerial and political accountability remains the same in public hospitals on the continent.

Conversely, the accountability regime has changed. As I will discuss in Chapter 5, it is more the content of accountability and less the formal relationships which signal the most important departure from the past. I develop this concluding argument further in Chapter 5. For now, I turn to the case of another crucial sector for the welfare service state, public schooling, to verify whether similar patterns are visible or cross-sectoral differences emerge.

"convocare" is rather formal (strengthening of directors) but interpretation makes a lot of it (for which no additional evidence is provided)

# 4
# Patterns of Convergence in Educational Accountability in State Schools in Europe

Public schooling in Europe is one of the areas of the service welfare state which one would least expect to introduce new managerialism (Taylor-Gooby and Lawson, 1993; Clarke et al., 2000). A patient in a hospital and a child in a compulsory school do not have the same anthropological status in society (Demailly and Dembinski, 2002). Whereas health care is viewed as a burdensome 'cost', the debate about education is not as often couched merely in financial terms. Education policy is framed in public debate as an investment for the future and for the country's productivity. Introduction of reforms aimed at 'cutting costs' in public schooling is perceived as less legitimate than in health care (Demailly and Dembinski, 2002: 58). This is not to suggest that governments are not concerned about the level of public expenditure in schooling. Yet the reforms strategy is to maintain the financial austerity imperatives covert. For this reason, managerialism provided an apparently neutral solution to the tougher language of marketization. It also permitted politicians to push through unpopular decisions, challenging the professional and bureaucratic consensus on state education, and representing them as technical matters. Managerialism does not necessarily imply spending cuts. Thus, I hereby continue to keep managerialism and market-oriented reforms clearly separated, focusing on the former.

In most European countries, the state has been the main provider of public schooling (primary and secondary schools) for a long time. State involvement in education pre-dates the development of other services like health care. Mass education came to Britain later than in France, Germany and Italy, nor was public expenditure on education conspicuously generous in Britain by international standards in the 1970s (Glennerster and Midgley, 1991).[1] On the contrary, in France, Italy and Germany the historical development of state education, as a field of social policy (Leibfried and Pierson, 1995),[2] is interwoven with the institutional formation and consolidation of the nation state. Beyond providing a narrow view of the economic benefits of education, the institutional mission of schools in France has traditionally been to strengthen republican values. In Italy, education and schools have served the interest of the state elites in unifying a relatively young and fragile unitary state since 1861 (Sepe, 1995; Melis, 1996). Hence, education is not perceived as a financial problem as such because its administrative salience has been historically inseparable from the creation of the nation state in many European countries.

Educational accountability has been historically rooted mainly in bureaucratic and professional legitimation (Bacon, 1978; Becher et al., 1981). Bureaucratic channels of accountability vary in Britain, France, Germany and Italy, depending on the degree of central government's involvement in the definition of national curricula, allocation of financial resources, legal regulations and assessment practice. Governments exert control on schools in many of these areas. However, bureaucratic accountability pertaining to state education is counterbalanced by the professional norms of teachers (Dale, 1980; Broadfoot, 1985: 278). For instance, the notion of 'standards' in education implies assessment criteria which have been, until recently, defined mainly by the teaching profession. The school self-evaluation movement has allowed teachers themselves a greater voice in the identification of these assessment criteria. Professionals have traditionally been one of the major sources of influence on the normative climate of state education in Europe.

The relationship between managerialism and the changing patterns of educational accountability in a comparative perspective is still under-researched. The purpose of this chapter is to discuss whether public schooling in Britain, France, Germany and Italy has been affected by reforms inspired by new managerialism, and what the implications of such reforms are for the traditional accountability regime and balance between bureaucratic and professional accountability. The focus here is on public secondary schools and on the relationship between heads/managers, governors, teachers and users, for this illustrates the degree of change in decision making and shift of power in schools. The analysis concentrates on whether decisions concerning the allocation of pupils or resources are made on technical/bureaucratic and professional grounds or are left to the interplay of political pressures.

In particular, echoing the research question in the previous chapter, I will analyse the change of educational accountability as a result of organizational autonomy aimed at the transformation from bureaucratic to managerial types of organizational arrangements. The first section of the chapter will discuss how the role of the head teacher has changed recently and whether the structure of school leadership has become more hierarchical and increasingly defined by performance accountability. Broadly defined, performance accountability refers to output measured against goals, which are defined increasingly by central governments and regulators, rather than professionals (Murphy and Seashore, 1999). Head teachers may serve as pedagogic leaders, line managers or bureaucratic administrators. This may vary across different educational systems. Their authority may rest upon professional judgement or managerial accountability, as I will discuss in greater detail in the analysis of four cases – Britain, France, Germany and Italy.

As set out in Chapter 2, capacity, specialization and coordination are the three main structural characteristics, which differently influence the relationships between actors within a hospital or a school. The central question of this chapter, entirely devoted to reforms of state secondary public schools, is whether the new regime of performance accountability (National Commission on Excellence, 1983) and autonomy of schools (OECD, 2007) have changed the power and influence of heads, teachers, governors and users. Differently to the growing field of educational management studies in the Anglo-Saxon world, I do not approach these questions by an operational angle. On the contrary, I analyse the different types of accountability and how they contribute to creating a predominant organizational accountability regime within schools (Handy, 1986; Bennett, 1974; Westoby, 1988; Tyler, 1988; Caldwell, 1988). I am concerned with the power relations between the governors of public secondary schools and the head teachers within the new framework of school autonomy and performance assessment in Britain, Germany, France and Italy. This chapter contributes to furthering empirically our understanding of the central question of this book, namely the effects of managerialism on democratic accountability and the relationship between managers and other actors. Before I discuss the four cases, I will offer an overview in the next section of the reforms introduced and the new methods of performance evaluation, accountability and measurement.

## From bureaucratic to managerial accountability through performance regimes: The changing role of the school head

The recent changes in educational accountability, from bureaucratic controls to managerial accountability for performance of individual schools against standards, make educational leadership the central element of reforms and organizational change at the level of the organization of a school. Educational leadership is an instrument for goals and priorities setting (Grace, 1993; Dale, 1989) and more generally an essential instrument to move from bureaucratic accountability and legal sanctions towards managerial accountability regimes. This radical transformation creates organizational turbulence to the embedded structures of power and influence of actors. It also creates opposition and tension between managerial and professional norms, as teachers are increasingly marginalized from standards setting and the definition of education criteria. The evaluation of schools based on outputs and exam results, associated with a blurring of the public–private finance and delivery (West and Currie, 2008), increases the demand for organizational leadership. Is the traditional school organization, whereby the head was a *primus inter pares*, being revisited by the demand for single-headed chief executive of schools? What does this change imply for education accountability more widely? This chapter will explore the new internal organizational arrangements of secondary schools in Britain, France, Germany and Italy to analyse the shift in role and influence of heads of schools, in relation to teachers, governors and users. It will also draw more general conclusions concerning converging patterns of education accountability in Europe. As I emphasized in Chapter 2, this study analyses the changes at the organizational level foremost, but it also discusses the alignment of individual schools at the systemic level.

Schools in Europe have been subject to a common trend towards greater autonomy from external governments controls (Eurydice, 2007). There has been a shift from focus on systemic performance and goals to individual schools. For instance, as I will discuss for the case of French schools, the change represents a significant innovation from the past consensus of the education system, namely uniformity of teaching activities, curricula constraints on teachers, administrative control through heavy financial and legal sanctions, among others. Autonomy implies the establishment of the individual school as a crucial player in the system and as an actor in its own right. The trend is most visible in centralized education systems, such as the French and Italian ones. The 2005 report by Eurydice (*Key Data on Education in Europe*) shows that schools are increasingly autonomous in education provision, that is, the way subjects are timetabled over the school week, teaching methods, choice of textbooks and pupils' continuous assessment. The same report also indicates that European countries vary the most with regard to the level of autonomy in the management of human resources and hiring of teachers. This indicates the prominent impact of the national administrative settings. For the countries under investigation here (Britain, France, Germany and Italy), the degree of autonomy with respect to the five dimensions identified by Eurydice (educational provision, teaching content and processes, schools regulations, budgeting and staffing) is summarized in Table 4.1.

Accounts of educational reforms have commonly been framed in national terms (Green, 1990; Tomlinson, 2001; van Zanten, 2000; Ventura, 1998; Wolf, 2007; Wössmann, 2007). A series of publications in the 1970s and 1980s pursued a line of inquiry that emphasized political and bureaucratic structures as significant determinants of the different educational models which evolved in Western Europe. This work is best exemplified by Margaret Archer's (1979) seminal work on the origins of four educational systems (France, England, Denmark and USSR). She used the concept of decentralized and centralized educational system as the focus for a historical appraisal and also to predict how they might evolve in the future. France more than any other country is seen as characterizing the centralized and highly bureaucratic model of educational control, whereas England exemplifies the decentralized educational system. Since the beginning of the 1990s, however, a degree of convergence has emerged in public schooling in Europe, especially insofar as new accountability structures and governance are concerned.

Most of the empirical reports on education focus on social and political factors as explanatory variables for differences between educational systems (OECD, 2007). Hence, there is a tendency to downplay the organizational dynamics of change as they unfold at the level of analysis of individual schools. The problem is that the two levels of analysis are kept isolated and not linked in any systematic way. In the study of education accountability, it is increasingly essential to discuss the interplay between processes occurring at the two different levels of governance, the systemic and the organizational one. The power relationship between the teachers, managers, governors and users is indicative not only of systemic and external determinants but also of endogenously induced processes (March and Olsen, 1989), which are of great significance in the analysis of new accountability regimes, as pointed out in Chapter 2. The new role of heads of schools, as chief executives, is linked to the wider reforms aimed at transforming the performance accountability of education, increasingly measured by quantitative figures. I argue that the new performance regimes provide

*Table 4.1*    Schools' autonomy in five areas of decision making

| | Educational provision (timetabling of subjects, number of days per year, start and end of lessons) | Teaching content and processes (textbooks, subjects methods, subjects offered as options, content of teaching programmes) | School regulations and organizations (school rules) | Budgeting (allocation of the overall school budget) | Staffing (recruitment for teaching vacancies and appointment of school head) |
|---|---|---|---|---|---|
| **Britain** | Full autonomy | Full autonomy | Full autonomy | Limited autonomy | Full autonomy |
| **Germany** | Limited autonomy | Limited autonomy | No autonomy | No autonomy | No autonomy |
| **France** | Limited autonomy (full autonomy for timetabling of subjects, but limited autonomy for number of hours per year) | Full autonomy | Full autonomy | No autonomy | No autonomy |
| **Italy** | Limited autonomy | Full autonomy | Full autonomy | No autonomy | No autonomy |

Source: Author's elaboration from Eurydice 2005 (Brussels: Eurostat).

a facilitating terrain for the consolidation of managerial accountability in schools, for they offer heads a new role in performance and evaluation of schools and of teachers (Besley and Machin, 2006).

As part of the *Programme for International Student Assessment* (PISA) 2003 survey, school heads were asked to identify their main responsibilities in a number of areas.[3] Interviews and qualitative content analysis of national legislation, provided in this chapter, are necessary to analyse trends at national levels based on actual enactment of reforms by central governments. Interviews also reveal how actors experience the change, which is a dimension not captured by statistics. Table 4.2 presents the results of the PISA survey and focuses on three main areas of decision making in Germany and Italy: (1) selecting teachers; (2) establishing pupil assessment policies; (3) decisions on school enrolments. In France in 2003 the school questionnaire was not completed by school heads, and in the United Kingdom the response rate was considered too low to guarantee comparability of data. It is clear that the recruitment of teachers is still the main responsibility of local authorities or central governments. Teachers or the heads of teaching departments are reported to have the main responsibility for choosing textbooks and an important role also in establishing pupil assessment policies. In Italy this is the case to a great extent. School heads suggest having the main responsibility in the enrolment of pupils, which is shared with the board and teachers.

One of the most prominent changes in educational accountability in developed countries has been the issue of 'standards' and 'performance' in the provision of education (OECD, 2007). Teaching is a

*Table 4.2*  Areas of decision making and responsibilities in schools

|  | Germany | Italy | UK | France |
|---|---|---|---|---|
| **Selecting teachers** | Not a responsibility of the school, but of external educational authorities | Not a responsibility of the school, but of external educational authorities | NA | NA |
| **Establishing pupil assessment policies** | Main responsibility of teachers or heads of teaching departments | Main responsibility of teachers | NA | NA |
| **Decisions on schools enrolment** | Main responsibility of school head | Shared responsibility of school head, board and teachers | NA | NA |

*Source*: PISA 2003 Survey of school heads (Paris: OECD).

process which has been increasingly quantified and infused by the logic of efficiency and 'value for money'. Beginning in the 1980s, the underpinning assumption about the quality of an educational system was its capacity to meet targets and raise standards. The rising salience of the concern for quality came to drive educational expectations and policy ideas, equally in Britain, Germany, France and Italy (only most recently). Secondary schools in Europe are experimenting with new methods to improve their accountability mechanisms, through performance indicators, management by objectives, business plans, quality and teachers' review and so on (Adams and Kirst, 1999). League tables have been published in almost every country, and measurement has become one of the key methods to assess the quality of an educational system (Koretz, 2008). There seems to be a new political consensus about performance-based accountability, built upon the value of technical administration and efficiency. Who better than head teachers to become the agents of the new managerial model and encourage teachers to comply with centralized new forms of accountability and controls?

Mapping schools which have introduced new systems of accountability has been rather more problematic than in health care, given their smaller size, low relevance in national political debate and lack of reliable data on the implementation of this performance measurement. Policymakers have made piecemeal progress, and most systems represent vast experiments, rather than clear-cut reform strategies, with the significant exception of Britain. The strengthening of the role of head teachers and the transformation of their relationship with teachers into manager-managed, rather than peers, has transformed the distribution of power within schools and has created political and organizational turbulence. Moreover, external standards, often imposed upon professionals from the central government, have met with some resistance at the level of the individual school. Different countries vary in their relationship between internally and externally designed systems of accountability. In Germany, for instance, as I will discuss, schools have been encouraged to pursue self-evaluation, whereas in other countries like Britain, the heavy centralized performance regime directed by the regulator Office for Standards in Education, Children's Services and Skills (OFSTED) does not leave much room for local experimentation in self-evaluation and performance assessment.

Bureaucratic accountability was the main structure of relationship between individual schools and the competent administrative level, be it the Land in Germany or the Ministry of Education in France or the

Local Education Authority in Britain. The role of the head teacher was that of an administrator and agent of centrally set rules and uniform standards. In all the countries under investigation, secondary schools are part of a complex and continually evolving administrative system, made of central and local educational agencies, local offices of the central ministries and regional administration. Therefore, schools have been traditionally administered through hierarchical decision making, standardized programmes, national curriculum, centralized textbook selection and course offering.[4]

As far as political accountability in public secondary schooling is concerned, the traditional mechanism of representation of local communities is the school governing body, predominantly composed of elected councillors or bureaucrats of the relevant local or regional authorities and staff. It is only very recently that members have been drawn increasingly from parents. They are also represented in administrative councils and management bodies within schools. Their influence varies considerably across a range of areas. They may have decision-making powers or exercise consultative functions. Overall, school-level bodies which include parents are least likely to have decision-making powers in the area of teacher recruitment, the termination of teaching contracts and in matters regarding teaching content. They are most likely to be involved in deciding upon the school plan and drawing up rules for everyday school activity. The institutional structure of a school governing body is the main institutional mechanism of public accountability. These bodies used to be very large and dominated by the local educational authorities. Recent reforms have changed their role and structure considerably, as this chapter will show. From the latest PISA exercise, it emerges that schools in most European countries have gained a significant degree of autonomy in the areas of appointment of teachers, setting budgets and determining the course content (OECD, 2007). As Table 4.3 shows, at least 95 per cent of students attend schools where heads reported that the school had the main responsibility of teachers' appointment. Hence, according to the OECD data and 2006 survey of heads of schools, the responsibilities of schools have changed dramatically in the last five years.

By comparing the results of Table 4.1 with Table 4.3, which refer to data respectively for 2002–3 and 2006, the most significant changes for that period are apparent in schools in Germany, France and Italy. British schools continue to be the most autonomous, in comparative terms, concerning budgetary areas of responsibilities and even more so for staffing policy. British schools have lost some of their autonomy in

*Table 4.3*   Stakeholders and decision making in secondary schools

Percentage of students in secondary schools where the head reported direct influence on decision making for Governing Board, Educational Authorities and Teachers Groups.

| | Instructional Content | Budgeting | Staffing | Assessment Practices |
|---|---|---|---|---|
| **Britain** | 72.4 *External Examination Board*<br>62.1 Educational authorities<br>21.2 Teachers<br>18.9 Governing Board | 90.8 *Governing Board*<br>59.1 Educational Authorities | 88.4 *Governing Board*<br>29.1 Educational Authorities | 60.9 *Educational Authorities*<br>30 Teachers<br>21.2 Governing Board |
| **Germany** | 76.1 *Educational authorities*<br><br>72.3 Teachers<br><br>33.0 Governing Body<br>6 External Board | 60.1 *Governing Board*<br><br>23.9 Educational Authorities | 93.6 *Educational Authorities*<br>9.4 Governing Board | 76.2 *Teachers*<br><br>53.6 Educational Authorities<br><br>39.7 Governing Board |
| **France** | NA | NA | NA | NA |
| **Italy** | 76.2 *Teachers*<br><br>44.1 Educational authorities<br><br>9.9 Governing Board<br>5.5 External Board | 88.3 *Governing Body*<br>24 Educational Authorities | 90.2 *Educational Authorities*<br>2.9 Governing Body | 78.4 *Teachers*<br><br>16.6 Educational Authorities<br><br>12.3 Governing Board |

Source: Author's elaboration from PISA, 2006 (OECD, 2007).
Note: Data from France are not available (NA).

defining the teaching content and processes, lost to external examination boards and central government. Only 18.9 per cent of pupils go to schools where the governing body is responsible for the definition of the instructional content, as Table 4.3 shows. German schools are acquiring significant budgetary autonomy, with only 23.9 per cent of pupils reported as going to schools where educational authorities interfere directly with budgetary matters. This is a prominent departure from the traditional governance system, as I will discuss later in great detail in the section devoted to Germany. In contrast to British schools, German schools' staffing policy is heavily controlled by the educational authorities. The same pattern is found in Italy. Italian secondary schools have also acquired budgetary autonomy, although they had none until 2002–3. Staffing is also managed by central educational authorities. Similarly to Germany, and in marked contrast to British schools, in Italian schools teachers play a very influential role in determining the instructional content. Whereas in German and Italian schools, respectively, 72.3 and 76.2 per cent of pupils attend schools where teachers have a direct role in deciding teaching content, in British schools this area of decision making is primarily in the hands of external examination boards and educational authorities. Teachers in continental school systems remain important actors in decision making, unlike in British schools, where the teaching profession has lost ground in many areas of decision making.

## Britain

Firstly, education occupies a peculiar place in the restructuring of welfare delivery in Britain, for it has been the largest share of the budget for local authorities and a source of perennial conflict between them and the central state. Secondly, schooling has been one of the sectors of welfare provision which has been most vulnerable to the introduction of NPM in the last 20 years, from the 1988 Thatcher reform (Department of Education, 1988) to the most recent changes adopted by New Labour's managerialism. Here I will analyse how the relationship between head teachers, teachers and governors has changed as a result of administrative reforms associated with the introduction of new managerialism in schools. In particular, I will discuss how the role of the head teachers has changed in relation to a shift from bureaucratic to managerial accountability regimes, as discussed in Chapter 2. From the nineteenth century to the early twentieth century, managers and governors were in general active as school leaders. In a hierarchical and class stratified society, a head teacher was not expected to have much institutional leadership in schools, with the exception of independent public schools (fee paying). What was expected from a head teacher in state-funded schools was moral and pedagogical, but not institutional management, which was the responsibility of schools' governors (Anderson, 2001). As it emerges from the analysis later, the head teachers are the winners from the reforms of English schooling in the 1980s and 1990s. I also argue that there has been no discontinuity from Thatcher to New Labour's trends of reforms.

The Thatcher government's objectives of educational reforms (Department of Education, 1988) were not much different from other policy sectors: to curtail provider's power, to restructure the welfare provision by the creation of competitive markets, to establish the rights of consumers and offer them freedom of 'choice' and to pursue efficiency (Vickerstaff, 2003). Managerialism was viewed as one of the most important means to achieve these goals, by making managers the agents of broader political reforms. However, the creation of managerialist systems and organizations took a life on its own and became an end in itself. As Fergusson argues, managerialism became as essential as substantive reforms themselves (Fergusson, 1994: 96).

One of the most radical educational reforms in British secondary schooling, which left long-lasting results on the social relationship of actors involved, was the 1988 Educational Reform Act. The thrust of this reform was to grant individual secondary schools budgetary autonomy, allocating central funding directly to them according to the numbers on roll. The Local Management of Schools introduced delegated responsibility for the budget, formula funding, in which most of the school's budget is based on the number of pupils; devolved responsibilities for staffing matters; and performance indicators in the form of league tables of pupil performance (Thomas and Bullock, 1994: 4). Prior to the reform, Local Education Authorities (LEAs) had the responsibility to allocate funds and to control schools. The centralist policy of the 1988 reforms offered schools financial incentives to opt out from LEA control over staffing, finance and the curriculum. A majority of parents could vote to take schools out of LEA control and, as such, to be directly funded by the central government as Grant Maintained (GM) schools.

In an attempt to empower consumers, the 1988 reform transformed the role and composition of the Governing bodies of schools. Parents acquired a major role as members of governing bodies, together with other lay people. Beforehand, local councillors used to be members of the governing bodies as well as representatives of LEA, who were experts in educational matters. Most of the controls over finance, staffing and even promotion of teachers were transferred from the LEA to the governing bodies. Thus, they acquired a crucial role in replacing the hierarchical bureaucratic accountability structures. Elected parents and lay members hold managers accountable, and they are important actors in the internal governance systems, replacing accountability to local councillors.

However, the effectiveness of parents' control of head teachers is arguable and certainly varies significantly across schools. The head teachers, who were interviewed by the author from January to April 2007,[5] suggested that the Governing Body mainly approves decisions they have already taken. For instance, teachers are selected and appointed by the head teacher, after only formal consultation with governors. At Cherwell School in Oxford, for instance, the Governing Body is composed of 21 members. It meets four times a year, and it works with subcommittees: a Finance Committee, a Curriculum, a Personnel and a Wellbeing/Pastoral one. The head teacher describes her relationship with the governors in the following way: 'I provide the governors with the necessary information and I present them with the schools' objectives which I have prioritised ... the strategic management of the school rests with the management team'.[6] She also reports multiple accountability relationships, beyond the governing body, such as to OFSTED and the central Department of Education. However, she suggests that 'also the reverse has happened: parents and students are less accountable to teachers'.

In the new system of budgetary autonomy and ample room of manoeuvring from local authorities and local politicians, head teachers have acquired a key role as agents of centralist policies. Some scholars have argued that they have become 'autocratic' managers, especially in relation to the teaching profession (Fergusson, 1994: 101). As far as their new role is concerned, head teachers have gained unprecedented budgetary powers, including personnel and equipments. Moreover, they are responsible for teachers compliance with the central regulations regarding the curriculum. The 1988 reform introduced the national curriculum and standardized testing across British secondary schooling. This has revolutionized the relationship between managers and teachers, from horizontal to vertical accountability regimes. For instance, interviews suggest that the head teacher has become the 'line manager' for all teachers. They make the final decisions over teachers pay and employment conditions, a prerogative that head teachers in no other European countries enjoy.

The management team of a school receives financial information from the local education authority. Teachers or governors may not have information to fully understand the financial implications of current spending patterns. Teachers are unlikely to know whether the budget is not too small to maintain current staffing levels, nor will they know how decisions on redundancy will be made. This information deficit creates asymmetry of power between the management and the professions (Halsey, 1993: 54). The head teacher is fully responsible for budgetary issues and since staffing costs often represent more than 80 per cent of a school's non-capital budget, has ample discretion in hiring decisions. The head teacher's power over the profession is also significant in relation to performance-related pay. In fact, the local school management has no longer bound schools rigidly by the national pay rates. This has created a further distance between the management team and teachers in British schools. Budgetary autonomy has created a wedge between management and teachers, deteriorated further by the need to compete with other schools in the local area for income based on the number of enrolled pupils, as one interviewee suggested.

The relationship between head teachers and governors is formally one of direct accountability to stakeholders. However, in practice parents and lay members do not have the expertise, and sometimes the information, to challenge the head's authority or policy decisions. Beforehand, LEA's members of the governing bodies had educational expertise and were generally appointed from among the ranks of teachers, so that they could supervise competently the work of the head teacher. Therefore, managerialism, as framed by the 1988 Thatcher policy change and subsequent reforms, dilutes the professional and public opposition to the managerial power of the head teacher. In the name of compliance with central departmental regulations, they have acquired a top-down accountability approach to educational leadership in schools, facilitated by the truncation of the intermediary administrative layers of the LEA. As one head teacher suggested, 'once, local educational authorities did everything. Now, they are much less influential and less powerful. The central hand is descending upon schools through OFSTED.'

The centralization of the national curriculum and standardized testing have provided a key incentive for the consolidation of a hierarchical relationship between head teachers and teachers. The 1993 Audit

Commission has reported managerial abuses in the excessive financial management of head teachers and lack of accountability. Head teachers are reported to withhold information from governors and not to consult them before taking decisions.[7] Managerialism, thus, has become the means to deliver centralist policy objectives at the expense of teachers' professional autonomy. Once these institutionalized management structures were introduced in schools at the end of the 1980s, they were about to remain for a long time. Managerialism has been a creeping feature of New Labour too, which has pursued similar objectives to the previous Conservative governments.

The novelty of British New Labour's reform programme, centred on decentralization and autonomy, thus, should be assessed against the historical legacy.[8] The British education system, in comparison to the French and Italian one, has traditionally been decentralized and has suffered from the late development of a state public administration (Heidenheimer, 1993). Prime Minister Tony Blair has announced the 2005 White Paper as 'a pivotal moment to ensure fair funding and fair admissions' and vindicates the 1997 pledge that education would be at the core of New Labour's reform programmes.[9] Indeed, key elements of the White Paper have antecedents in past reforms, including the *2004 Five Year Strategy for Children and Learners*,[10] and, most significantly for the issue of organizational structure and governance, to the 1998 *School Standards and Framework Act*. The *2005 White Paper* raised most concerns in relation to an allegedly new type of school organization, the Trust school.[11]

Through the creation and support of Trust schools, the Blair government has sought to promote this type of organization as a way forward for the future. The main objectives were to 'create independent self-governing state schools', as the then Secretary of State announced to the House of Commons.[12] This plan was also introduced one year earlier when the Blair government aimed to provide 'freedom for all secondary schools to own their land and buildings, manage their assets, employ their staff, improve their governing bodies and forge partnership with outside sponsors and educational foundations'.[13] Therefore, the independence of schools was at the heart of the Government's proposals for change in the administration of education.

The reform trajectory of autonomy for secondary schools reveals a high degree of continuity, since 1998, when the School Standards and Framework Act, the first of the then new Labour Government, appeared to sanction definitely the demise of GM schools, which had been the epitome of individual schools' autonomy from local authorities' control.

The 1998 Act marked the end of the opportunity for schools to become grant-maintained, thus eliminating the controversial opportunity for opting out of LEAs control, introduced as part of the *1988 Education Reform Act* by a previous Conservative Government (Fitz, Halpin and Power, 1997). A detailed analysis of the 1998 Act reveals that the existing GM schools were submerged into a new category, so-called Foundation schools. This category included governors' responsibility for the employment of staff and ownership of assets and ensued the retention of key elements of the structure associated with GM schools (Whitty et al., 1998).

The 2005 White Paper, while allegedly creating 'new' Trust schools, in reality represents another rebranding exercise. In fact, Trust schools will enjoy the freedoms of Foundation schools and are designed to resemble their organizational and self-governing structures: 'Trust schools will have the freedoms and flexibilities that self-governing (Foundation) schools currently enjoy. They will employ their own staff, control their own assets and set their own admission arrangements.'[14] Trusts will be not-for-profit organizations able to appoint governors to the school. The governing body will include elected parents, staff governors and representatives from the local authority and local communities.[15]

To sum up, head teachers in Britain have significantly changed their managerial role in the last 30 years. They have increasingly distanced themselves from classroom purposes (Grace, 1993). From pedagogical and moral leadership, they have developed into powerful leaders of institutional change and champions of institutional autonomy of schools. The leadership role of head teachers has been advocated by the educational management gurus (Chubb and Moe, 1990). It is especially the self-governing school that sustains a heavy top down approach and strong managerial responsibilities of head teachers. Collegiality is more symbolic than substantive in autonomous schools in England. As one head teacher suggested, 'the predominant organisational culture in schools nowadays is more individualistic than in the past. The positive aspect of managerialism is that I can subvert the rules in a very individualistic way.'

Therefore, there has been a consistent consolidation of a managerial structure with a heavily vertical and hierarchical governance system within schools. Head teachers are at the interface of central state policy framework and local market pressures to attract pupils for income and develop innovative and specialist curricula. Not shielded by the local administration, managers of schools are exposed directly to the blame of school failures (Hood, 2007). Their accountability for results and raising standards is highly personalized (Power, Halpin and Whitty et al., 1997) and no longer mediated through institutional mechanisms. Most of the interviews with head teachers suggest that they are very concerned with 'reputation', especially in the local community and local media. As one head teacher framed it: 'parents want to send their pupils to schools which are safe and trustworthy'.

In practice, head teachers are accountable to the Department of Education, though according to statutory provision they operate within governance arrangements that make them directly accountable to schools' governingbodies, which represent in theory the voice of users. However, the buffer structure of the school governing body does not make head teachers autonomous from central control. In the case of British schools, managerialism has enhanced centralized political control of public schooling. One head teacher has referred to the intrusive 'guidance' received by the central department of education about how to deal with snowfall. She reported a specific instance in relation to the snowfall in January 2007: 'the central department of education dictates when we have to close or keep our school open, in the case of snowfall. My school is located up hill and it is not safe to keep it open in the case of snowfall, but I shall abide with the central regulations for all schools, and keep it open'.

Among the main areas of concerns reported by parents' governors, the relationship with the head teacher figured prominently as one which deserves closer attention. According to a study carried out in the Greater Manchester area, parents' governors are frustrated because they claim to be alienated from financial decisions and staff appointment (Diamond, 1993). It was also reported that governors were self-elected, namely they decided to stand for election at the invitation of the head teacher, because it was difficult to secure the participation and interest of parents. This problem emerged also in the case of hospitals, as discussed in Chapter 3. However, head teachers interviewed for this project suggest that the pressure from parents is much greater than that of local authorities and local councillors nowadays. Although this is perhaps not channelled through the institutional structures of accountability at the school level, like the governing bodies, it is indeed a public pressure enhanced by the publication of league tables and performance.

## France

The French and Italian administration of education is highly centralized and more institutionalized than in Britain or the United States

(Heidenheimer, 1983; OECD, 1995), as illustrated by the omnipresent and powerful field services of the central Ministry of Education, which exercises a tight supervision over schools at the local level (Cole and Peter, 2001; Cole and Jones, 2005). Both systems have their origins in state intervention in the area of education, by which the state has to provide public education in the general interest of the nation. In France education has been perceived as operating within a hierarchal system which has left very little room for organizational autonomy at the bottom (Archer, 1979). The French notion of public service provides the foundation for the administrative framework of the French educational system and the rights and obligations of its employees (Cole, 2001). The reform of the state introduced by Alain Juppé's government in July 1995[16] viewed the ministerial field services as constituting the main impetus to change.

Centralization, uniformity and neocorporatism are traditionally identified as the fundamental traits of the French educational system (Archer, 1979; Ambler, 1985; Cole, 2001). The central government until the mid-1980s was responsible for the organization of the educational services throughout the country, the regulation of national examinations, the definition of the content of the national curriculum, the training and recruitment of teachers and the control of teaching methods. Not much was left to the sub national level of government or individual schools as far as educational policymaking was concerned. The highly centralized state was contrasted frequently with the educational system in Britain (Broadfoot et al., 1985). Contrasting State traditions in France and Britain were exemplified in the field of education.

The modern *école* was built upon a dual power structure: on the one hand the state setting rules, and on the other hand the teaching profession, largely autonomous with regard to their pedagogic activity. From its historical origins, the public school has always excluded users and parents. The long tradition of educational centralization and the independence of the professions have been mutually reinforcing and have made the system not open to external influences (notably parents). Nothing was more alien to the republican school than the idea of external partnership (Zay, 1994: 35). The historical development of secondary schools has created tensions between the bureaucracy and the autonomy claimed by teachers. The state and professional powers have balanced each other through a '*compromis bureaucratique*', namely a governing system through bureaucratic rules and professional norms.

It was only in the midst of the economic crisis of the mid-1980s that a new actor was institutionalized and created between the state and the teachers, that is the '*établissement*' (the school organization). The *établissement public local d'enseignement* (EPLE) was a new organization indicative of an attempt to reorganize state education by debureaucratization (Demailly, 1993: 28).[17] The reform of schools, announced in 1975, and only enacted in 1985, with a series of decrees and laws, conferred upon them for the first time in the history of the French Republic responsibilities and new autonomy. The public debate of autonomy has been informed by the need for differentiations between schools and diversification in the teaching offer. In the case of France this meant a break from the uniformity of the system. Most importantly, the creation of the EPLE has triggered three processes (Demailly, 1993). First, it has modified the relationship between teachers and head teachers by conferring upon the latter an unprecedented right to interfere with the formers' professional decisions. Secondly, the autonomy of schools has created a demand for transparency about what actions they take to fulfil their new responsibilities. Thirdly, the creation of the EPLE has enhanced a process of professionalization of the head teacher, encouraged to develop new skills, beyond a merely bureaucratic role.

## Changing role of head teachers and anti-autonomy forces

The French Education Ministry is one of the most impressive bureaucratic organizations of the French state, dating back to the Napoleonic period. France was divided into 22 Academia, each headed by a rector. The first *lycées* were also established by Napoleon. A rector is the minister's direct representative in the regions. It is a political position, nominated by the Council of Ministers. The rectorate is a complex organizational structure with major service delivery responsibilities. The rectorates represent, thus, the field services of the Education Ministry. Reforms in the 1990s have introduced global budgets and cost centres status for rectorates, which have greater financial flexibility and autonomy in setting targets and allocating resources. Successive measures of decentralization have also strengthened the regional-level field services of the Education Ministry. As Cole argues, this was perceived partially in terms of internal bureaucratic rivalries within the French state because the regional educational services would be able to stand up to the new prefectures (Cole, 1997: 140). The new responsibilities of rectorates included the allocation of staff.

Even the minimal decentralization of secondary education met with fierce resistance from an anti-local coalition, made of teachers and central bureaucrats at the Education Ministry (Hatzfeld, 1991). Teachers, in particular, have resented strongly any kind of decentralization of staff management to the regional authorities. Secondary school teachers are public servants in France. They are recruited by public competition and are attached to their academic discipline, not so much the institution by which they are employed. Although the traditional neocorporatist style of public management of education in France has weakened, due to internal division between the unions, teachers and their associations remain committed to the republican values and beliefs that education is concerned with providing equality of opportunities and uniform services. Thus, among the centralizing forces of French education the teaching union *Syndicat national de l' Enseignement Secondaire* (SNES) plays a central role. The teachers' unions participate in national policy-making, especially in relation to matters of personnel management (pay, promotion and transfers). The union members take part in ministerial advisory parity committees to propose appointments, transfers and promotions.

Therefore, there is a deep reluctance of school autonomy on behalf of schoolteachers who insist on the respect of national rules and public service ethos. Ministers who have tried to challenge the teaching profession had to withdraw their plans, after public action, or had to resign. Minister Allegre has become the symbol and the victim of the forces which resist change. Under the Jospin government (1997–2002), Allegre introduced reforms to empower the directors of primary schools and decentralize the recruitment of new staff. His reforms failed and he had to revert his policy, and eventually resign.

The leadership style of French schools is based on consensus and negotiation between a plurality of actors and interests. No fundamental change to the structures and values of collegial decision making has been implemented (Dutercq, 2007; Legrand, 2005). The symbolic institutions for the negotiation of educational interests are the schools' *Conseil d'Administration* (MEN, 2006). Governing bodies have become slightly more influential, but they are far from exercising any strategic management function. A head teacher has defined them as 'symbolic places of participation' (Desagnat, 2005: 39). The *Conseil d'Administration* of a school is the only institutionalized structure of management and locus of responsibility in French secondary schools. It is usually composed of 30 members belonging to three different constituencies in equal parts. First, members of the regional councils are represented, the so-called *collectivité territoriale*. In the case of the *lycée*, this is the *Conseil Régional*. This group also includes representatives from the municipalities and the intercommunal organizations. The head teacher, deputy and the financial director are also members of this first category. Secondly, the constituency is made of delegates of the teaching staff, the administrative staff and the trade unions' representatives. Thirdly, the *Conseil d'Administration* is composed of students and parent representatives (MEN, 2006). The total number of parent members on the governing body is five.

Differently from British and German schools, local elected politicians are members of the *Conseil d'Administration* of schools. They are present at meetings and are frequently consulted by the head teacher for minor matters as naming a new school (Desagnat, 2005). The 1982 Law Deferre-Mauroy had implications for the local elected members of schools. For the first time, regional elected councillors could become members of the school boards (*élus régionaux*). The Conseil, as described by Desagnat, is an arena for competition of different social and political interests. Political conflict penetrates within the institutional structure of schools. For instance, if the local elected representative is from the Opposition, he or she is in a weaker position than the other members of the Conseil and is subject to the pressure of parents and staff. When the local councillor, on the contrary, belongs to the majority, which controls the local or regional councils, he or she enjoys a greater authority within the Conseil. In all cases, the head teacher has to play a very important role of neutrality and has to mediate between different and conflicting partisan interests in the Conseil.

Whereas the function of the Conseil is to represent the *collectivité territoriale*, the head teacher represents the French state in the school. The head teacher is responsible for the elaboration of the *projet d'établissement* (MEN, 2002; Blanchet et al., 1999), the organization of the teaching (but not the content of teaching), the implementation of laws and day-to-day running of the school. He or she is also the President of the Conseil d' Administration. The head teacher is supported by a financial administrator (*gestionnaire*). The head teacher has a fixed term employment contract which lasts for nine years. However, until 2001 this was a permanent contract. The career development of a head teacher starts with the position of deputy director. It is a springboard for an administrative career. After being head teacher, the ambition is to be appointed at the rectorate or at the Education Ministry and climb up the ladder of the state bureaucracy. The role has been traditionally administrative. However, as Demailly argues, the new *organisational modernisme* has prompted a holistic view of education, namely a less rigid separation between administrative and teaching roles, among other things by developing a pedagogic culture in head teachers. This is a new key development to which I shall return to in Chapter 5.

Head teachers have acquired greater resources at their disposal. They are able to apportion 10 to 20 per cent of their schools' budget to non-curriculum activities and subjects. This has offered some leeway for schools to diversify their educational offer. In this way, schools may attract very good pupils beyond their catchment areas. The *chef d'établissement* is also responsible for the elaboration and implementation of a school plan (*projet d' établissement*) which contains three-year objectives (Blanchet et al., 1999; MEN, 2006). As in the case of hospitals, these instruments are introduced to enhance individual schools' autonomy. As far as the head teacher's discretionary power is concerned, in large schools the head teacher tends to have a more hierarchical relationship with teachers than in small ones (Cole, 2001: 718). In general, there is nothing like the British experience with local management of schools, and there is no delegation of main budget and staffing decisions to schools governing bodies or head teachers. French schools have little financial autonomy and no control at all over staff management, which remains the responsibility of the academies.

Areas of professional life have opened to the new managerial logic of evaluation, like in the German case. In the French public debate, the association of the *chef d'établissement* with a *patron* is recurrent. In fact it is the inspectors of the academies that are perceived as 'managers', rather then the head teacher, as they carry out the 'evaluation' of the teachers. Traditionally, evaluation is carried out entirely by the subject-based inspectors of the Education Ministry, not by the organization of the school. In the old system there was a clear-cut separation between administrative controls and pedagogic ones. The latter were not managed by the head teacher but by state inspectors, who would offer direct feedback to teachers. In the new managerial system, however, new quantitative performance indicators are designed at the Education Ministry as instruments for head teachers to assess the performance of the school (MEN, 2000).

An extremely insightful study of how performance indicators affect the management of French high schools was carried out in 1992 and 1993 by Fixari and Kletz (1996). Their empirical findings suggest that head teachers are provided by the *Direction de l'Evaluation et de la Prospective* (DEP) of the French Ministry of Education with new quantitative indicators to inform their strategic management. However, only 15 per cent of schools use them, still preferring qualitative judgements, for they are still more interested in the pedagogic effectiveness of the teaching process. The slow implementation of the new performance indicators is a missed opportunity for the full realization of autonomy of schools, according to Fixari and Kletz (1996). Some structural constraints are identified for the incomplete success of self-evaluation. First, the head teachers find themselves isolated in their responsibilities for the elaboration of the *projet d'établissement* (Law 10/07/1990). Secondly, head teachers lack the power to recruit teachers. In general, teachers do not have collective system of mobilization and they are individualistic and only loyal to their subject, and less to the organization. This is a fundamental trait of French schooling: teachers of different subjects are not inclined to coordinate and mobilize upon issues of organization, management, etc. The tendency for individualism in the French teaching profession means that all responsibility for initiatives of a managerial nature, including the introduction of innovative actions, new programmes and new performance instruments falls on the shoulders of head teachers.

## Germany

The German Länder have considerable centralized control over secondary schooling. Recent reforms at the end of the 1990s, however, have opened up the possibility of granting individual schools some autonomy over their teaching programmes. In selected Länder, including North Rhine–Westphalia, Hessen and Berlin, pilot projects and experimentations have introduced some degree of autonomy from centralized controls by encouraging individual schools to design self-evaluation mechanisms and processes.

### Self-governing schools

Education and cultural affairs are, in Germany, a policy domain of sole responsibility for the Länder (states). Their jurisdiction is constitutionally guaranteed (Art. 31 of the 1949 Basic Law), so that the Federal state and the government have no formal power to interfere with the Länder's policies on determining the curricula, staff and resources allocation, and, generally, the organizational structure of schools. At the federal level the coordinating body for educational policy is the Standing Conference of Ministers of Education, created in 1949. Since the start, the decision-making process of such coordinating institutions has been veto driven, for unanimity is required. Despite the existence of this coordinating mechanism, education is off-limits for the federal government (Allmendinger and Leibfried, 2003). With respect to the autonomy of individual schools, it has traditionally been very contained in Germany, given the strong hold of regional bureaucracies on the education system. Thus, federalism has two main effects on the introduction of reforms aimed at the autonomy of schools. Firstly, it reinforces the dependence of all secondary schools on the Ministry of Education of each Land for school personnel and finance, and on local counties for other resources. Thus, centralized control operates at the Land level. Inspection and supervision of individual schools is quite heavy in Germany, compared with other decentralized educational systems, such as the British or the American one. Secondly, education federalism does encourage policy experimentation and variety of organizational systems and provisions (Manow, 2004). Although federalism makes structural reforms difficult, Manow (2004: 33) argues that outside social insurance we should expect high policy experimentation in the field of education.

For the purpose of this chapter, I focus on the case of *Selbständige Schule* in North Rhine–Westphalia, and the case of Berlin school system, which stand out from the rest in terms of legislative and administrative impetus to introduce autonomous and self-governing schools. Before considering these cases in some detail, I will briefly offer an overview of the differentiated degree of enthusiasm towards organizational autonomy in different Länder, from Bavaria to Hessen. Bavaria belongs to a group of Länder which are the most conservative in terms of departure from the tradition of secondary education, whereas the states of Hessen (Hessisches Kultusministerium, 2005) and North Rhine–Westphalia have been the most dynamic in terms of embracing innovation and experimentations. The last one in particular is of special significance.

In Bavaria, the educational system remains firmly entrenched in a hierarchical bureaucratic system. School management is centralized at the Land level.[18] The Ministry of Education establishes the details of the curriculum for all schools. The choice of books has to be approved by the Ministry, which also provides rigid guidelines for centralized examinations and students' assessment exercises. Training of teachers is also a matter of sole responsibility of the Land, rather than individual schools. The head teacher is nominated by the Ministry of Education after public competition, as it is common in most German Länder.[19] Thus, staff policy is highly centralized and not much discretion is left to individual schools. The post of head teacher in Bavaria is for five years, and it is renewable. A school council, made of representatives of teachers, pupils and parents, offers advice to the head teacher, but it is mainly a consultative body.

In the state of Hessen, autonomy has been slowly developed through legislation. Each school is allowed to develop its own teaching programme within the frame of the law and the curriculum. Schools have been increasingly encouraged to develop self-assessment methods within the search for quality assurance. A new pilot project has been recently launched, to run from 2005 until 2008, aimed at reorganizing the internal structure of schools, and improving the quality of the service. An important element of the *Modellprojekt Selbstverantwortung plus* is the organizational autonomy granted to schools, and the creation of new regional coordinating mechanisms.[20] Within the framework of the general curriculum prescribed by the Ministry, schools are allowed to define their goals and priorities in self-developed school programmes. They must also submit themselves to internal and external evaluations.

In 1992, North Rhine–Westphalia introduced a new experimental project for quality development and quality assurance, so-called QUESS. The central idea was the decentralization of the school system by providing greater autonomy to individual schools. The project was concluded in 1997, with 19 schools participating. They developed individual programmes, although they had to remain within the scope of existing curricula established by the Regional Ministry. The schools were responsible for self-evaluation, followed by external evaluations conducted by the school boards, which maintained a double function of supervising and providing advice to the schools. From 1997 to 2002 the Ministry for Education of North Rhine-Westphalia launched a project aimed at improving the quality of learning and the efficiency of schools (*Stärkung von Schulen im kommunalen und regionalen Umfeld*). This trajectory of reforms geared towards granting freedoms to individual schools has continued until recently with the 2002–8 ambitious project called *Selbständige Schule* (Ministerium für Schule, 2001; 2002; 2003). So far 270 schools have been involved and have witnessed internal management changes, such as the strengthening of the head teacher's responsibility.[21]

Through recent projects, the Land (North Rhine–Westphalia) has continued to remodel its relationship with public sector schools, along the theme of '*Qualitätsorientierte Selbststeuerung von Schulen*', namely quality-oriented steering in schools, and '*Regionaler Bildungslandschaften*', namely the regional education area. Their activities fall into two major categories. Under labels like 'new steering', of which the *Regionale*

*Steuerungsgruppe* is an illustration, the first type of activity is the development of IT-based new systems *(Lernen mit Medien)*. Accordingly, schools are encouraged to implement innovative teaching systems and collaborate more closely with parents and form partnerships with voluntary and private sector organizations *(zivilgesellschaftliches Engagement)*.[22] Secondly, performance standards and comparisons are being developed, together with new organizational models, as interviews have confirmed.

The Land Berlin has introduced in 2004 a landmark reform of the public school system (Schulgesetz für das Land Berlin, 2004), which contains as its *Leitidee* the 'autonomy' of individual schools, known as 'self-responsibility' in German *(Eigenverantwortung)*.[23] The main purpose of the law, as presented in its preamble, is to debureaucratize the schools' administration *(Entbuerokratisierungsoffensive)*. This is consistent with the wider administrative reforms in Germany to streamline the bureaucratic machinery (Bogumil, Jann, and Nuellmeier, 2006), as I have discussed at some length in Chapter 3. The reform goes one step further in granting schools devolved budgetary autonomy concerning personnel. This is a remarkable break from the German schools' administrative tradition of heavily centralized staff recruitment. Schools in Berlin have greater freedoms and devolved responsibilities. A pilot project was launched in 2001 for the duration of fours years, so-called *Modellvorhaben eigenverantwortliche Schule* (MES). A total of 31 secondary schools in Berlin took part in the project, sponsored by the Land Berlin. The central idea has been to make schools self-governing and introduce an organizational culture based on service provisions and contracts *(Dienstleistungs- und Kontraktcultur)*.

The extremely detailed regulatory framework contained in the 2004 law casts some doubts over the genuine intentions of the reformers concerning the adoption of managerial accountability. Clearly schools are not free to choose their own internal organizational design and management structures. It is all prescribed in great detail in the law. The sixth section concerns the legal form of schools, known as *Schulverfassung*. Article 69 establishes the responsibilities and powers of the school director *(Schulleiter/in)*. Traditionally, in Germany, the head teacher has had an authoritative role in public schools, since Prussian times. The school administration is still part of the public administration, according to Article 7(1) of the German Constitution. During Prussian times, the head teacher was a school monarch with a weak counterweight by other internal bodies, although there has always been a *Lehrerkonferez* that is a teaching council. It was only during the time of the Weimar Republic that collegiality increased in schools.

Unfortunately, the Nazi regime reinstituted a highly hierarchical governance system within schools.

The 2004 law in Berlin places the head teacher in a powerful position, not only in relation to teachers, but also to parents. However, there are plenty of internal committees and councils which function as consultative bodies, like the *Klassenkonferenzen*, the *Schulkonferenzen*, the *Lehrerkonferezen* and many others. Article 69 states that the *Schulleiter* 'has to inform the representatives of parents', which is indicative of their weakness in the decision-making process, at least formally. Moreover, the law confers upon head teachers the power of hiring and transferring teachers, which is a radical change from the past. The management of personnel has been one of the areas in which schools in Berlin, and Germany generally, have received no organizational autonomy. Another important role of the head teacher remains that of compliance with the many acts and regulations issued by the Land administration. As interviewees suggested, the new legislation is strengthening the position of the head teacher against the teachers.

Despite the growing autonomy, or self-responsibility, as it is known in Germany, the regional administration keeps a very heavy centralized control through the *Schulaufsicht*, the school governing board. It is responsible for the organization of teaching, for instance. This is the real strategic body of schools, responsible for setting policy goals. The *Schulaufsicht* remains an integral part of the Land's administration (*Schulverwaltung*) and is composed of members of local authorities and civil servants of the Land, but not parents nor the public. This is a marked difference in comparison to British schools' governing bodies.

Despite these few instances of experimentation in some Länder, the educational system of Germany remains firmly entrenched in the tradition of stabilization rather than change. Educational federalism seems to facilitate 'experimentations', but institutional re-engineering is not sufficient to defeat the historical legacy of an educational system (Phillips, 1987). Continuity prevails over change, though reform attempts and windows of opportunities have been present, not least when the shocking negative results of the 2003 OECD PISA of competences of 15-year-olds were published. This created a deep legitimacy crisis in Germany (Allmendinger and Leibfried, 2003: 67), for it seemed that Germany may have been overtaken by other industrialized countries. Unlike Britain, German schools are reluctant to publish their individual school's data on results. This increases the difficulty in assessing the impact of the PISA shock on re-legitimizing reforms. The intensity of the public debate did not necessarily translate into radical reforms which would have been possible elsewhere. Strong federalism clearly is a hurdle for introducing reorganization reforms. However, in the wake of PISA 2003, new or modified procedures of performance evaluations were demanded. Cost-cutting proposals, such as reducing the variety of a number of courses, were made (Lingens, 2003).

Policy stability is not only attributed to institutional factors, such as federalism, but most importantly to path dependency in policy developments. Decentralization to individual schools was part of the education reform plans that the Allies had proposed in the immediate post-war reconstruction (Ertl and Philipps, 2000). Yet, the German authorities opted to look back to the reforming years of the Weimar Republic and to readopt a system which seemed to have worked, the principle of 'On from Weimar' (Phillips, 1987: 228). Stabilization was the main concern for the first 20 years of the young Republic, ensuing from an inherited distrust of reforms after so much upheaval. The opportunity was missed to reform the old tripartite schooling system.[24] The deep conservatism of German educationalists was successful in preventing major organizational restructuring of this system from the post-war to recent days. The strong historical tradition explains the ultra conservative secondary school system and 'non-reforms' (Robinson and Kuhlman, 1967).

The distrust of new beginning and experiments, and the desire for social stability, was again confirmed by the missed opportunity to reform secondary education generated by the process of reunification. As Wilde (2002) argues, East Germany's educational system was highly restructured and transformed on the model of West Germany, rather than triggering a reform of the old tripartite system. Reunification created a momentum for reflecting upon the modernization that the secondary education system required. Yet, the opportunity to introduce greater autonomous decision making was missed again, which makes for a learning environment which can adapt to local needs, as in the British school system. Again, education federalism did not seem to enhance policy innovation, but rather acted as a brake on experimentation.

## Italy

The reform of public schooling has been one of the fiercest terrains of partisan competition in the 1990s in Italy (Ferratini, 2002: 259), with distant ideological positions in defence of the role of the state (centre-left governments) and in favour of consumerism and marketization of education, summarized in the slogan *scuola-azienda* (school enterprise).

The ideological underlying dimension of the political process of reforms is remarkably similar to the British one. However, some issues have been consistent across partisan positions during the 1990s waves of legislative output on public schooling. Autonomy of individual schools is one of them. It is claimed to be a necessary condition to improve the efficiency of the educational system.

The major theme of the reform of education in the 1990s in Italy has been the organizational autonomy of schools in the wider context of the decentralization of the state (Mattei, 1999). The most recent amendment of the Italian Constitution has made education a shared responsibility of the central state and of regional governments (law no. 3/2001). The educational reforms in Italy in the 1990s have been inserted into the wider administrative and institutional landscape of the reform of the state. Therefore, organizational issues have figured prominently in the public debate and in the legislative output. The reform of education has been primarily that of its bureaucratic administration, concerning the redistribution of responsibilities at different levels of government and within schools between different actors (a vertical and horizontal reconfiguration of authority). The landmark reform, which transformed the role of schools as agents of the state into autonomous entities, was law no. 59/1997, which transferred to individual school's budgetary, policy and organizational autonomy (with the exception of staff management). Thereafter, the Prodi government issued a decree to implement the autonomy of schools (D.p.R. no. 275/1999): 'Schools are free to adopt the organisational structure they deem appropriate to their needs as indicative of their planning autonomy. In each school the allocation of teachers and organisation of classes and schedules can be autonomously decided on the basis of the teaching programmes.'

Therefore by 'autonomy' the 1990s reforms refer to devolved responsibility for the organizational, educational and budgetary management of individual high schools from the central administration of the Ministry of Education and its field services, the *Provveditorati agli Studi* to individual schools. This process is in line with NPM ideas of decentralization of managerial responsibilities (Pollitt et al., 2000). However, the confusion deliberately created between territorial decentralization of state functions to regions and provinces and granting organizational autonomy directly to individual schools has hindered the internal effects of the reform of education in Italy.

Following the British example of local financial management, successive reforms in the 1990s have radically and consistently transformed the highly centralized and bureaucratic Italian educational system into a decentralized system of local school management (Ministero dell'Istruzione, 2002; 2003). The change enacted is profound and unfortunately has not yet raised the necessary attention by the international community of education scholars. My concern here is to discuss the main innovations with regard to the internal governance of schools and how these relate to the wider context of the reform of the state in the 1990s, which has witnessed decentralization and autonomization of individual public organizations as one of its main trajectories. The traditional educational system confers upon the Ministry of Education the undisputed role of directing, organizing and financing the national educational system. In order to guarantee national standards and national management of staff and resources, the Ministry operates with powerful field services, called *Provveditorati agli Studi*. The Italian system is designed along the French one, in terms of its bureaucratic and administrative framework.

In Italy, the autonomy of individual schools has been misapplied. Decentralization has created a duplication of administrative control over what were supposed to be emerging autonomous schools. The Italian experimentation with autonomy of schools has distorted the rationale of decentralization of responsibilities to smaller and independent units, as advanced by NPM. For instance, a clear inconsistency with NPM can be revealed in the reform of the head teacher's employment contract. The head teacher was granted managerial responsibilities and greater discretion over the budget and administration. As the 'manager' of a public service, the head teacher is in theory responsible for the achievement of specific targets and operates under the logic of private sector management, the maximization of profits and cost-benefit assessments. However, even though the head teacher of an Italian school has acquired new responsibilities, both organizational and administrative, he or she remains a civil servant. The head teacher is selected through a public competition (*Concorso*) and has a permanent job, regardless of performance. The contract of employment is the one established by law no. 29 of 1993 regarding the *dirigenza pubblica* (public sector managerial group of senior civil servants). The idea of managerialism, borrowed from NPM, is entrapped in the rigidly determined and legally bound Italian system of pay and conditions of employment (Wright and Cassese, 1996).

The main objectives of managerialism in Italian education, as stated by Minister Berlinguer,[25] Minister of Education under the 1996 Prodi government, and as found in the Charter for the Service of Education,[26] include: the autonomy of schools and the decentralization of responsibilities from the centre to the periphery;[27] attribution of managerial responsibilities to the head teacher; a change of administrative culture; and improved quality of service (Ministero della Funzione Pubblica, 1996). The head teacher would have the same contract as a director general (*dirigente*) in the public sector. This means a higher salary and greater budget and management responsibilities. This is all in principle.

Autonomy of schools is the subject of a long-lasting debate that has brought concrete results only in recent years. The aim is to reduce the *dirigiste* and 'centralist hypertrophy'.[28] A wide range of formal procedures limits the freedom of manoeuvre of schools that wish to respond to different local needs. Moreover, the head teacher is not free to hire any personnel. Rather, the local field administration of the Ministry, the *Provveditorato*, allocates teachers to different schools and has the responsibility of staff management and recruitment. The distribution of teachers does not always respond to objective criteria, such as number of pupils or schools in the local area. In most instances, the only concern is to maintain the existing public employment level. Granting autonomy gives the head teacher responsibility for the management of the factors of production (teachers and infrastructures). Budgetary autonomy seems to be particularly important because, under the old system, the allocation of public money to schools depended on covering personnel costs. It was not based on output, that is, on the number of students or the number of classes. The rigid system of public money allocation and its management did not allow schools that offered a better service to continue improving. By contrast, the aim of the new system of autonomy provides for individual schools to control directly their budget and the quality and efficiency of service.

As far as the internal governance of individual high schools is concerned, a major break with the past bureaucratic administration has been introduced by the 2002 guidelines for the internal management of schools, the *Norme concernenti il governo delle istituzioni scolastiche*.[29] It shifted away management responsibilities from the School Council (*Consiglio della Scuola*) to the director (*Dirigente Scolastico*), contrary to 30 years of participatory management established in the 1970s. The law, which originated from parliamentary bills in the permanent Committee for Education, rather than from the Executive, established that the head teacher or *Dirigente Scolastico* has the sole responsibility for the management of the school, whereas the *Collegio* contributes only to the process of defining the priorities and strategic objectives of the school. Clearly the legislation follows the NPM prescription to divide policy from management (Art. 1 section 5).

Within the frame of the new autonomy granted to schools regarding the definition of their internal organizations and structures, the national legislator has intervened to strengthen unambiguously the role of the head teacher, by upsetting a long-established power structure which benefited traditional trade unions, teachers and participatory mechanisms, like committees and collegial structures. The new *Dirigente Scolastico* is responsible for the financial management of resources and for the achievement of results, presiding not only on the School Council, but also the Teachers' Council. He or she controls the agenda of their meetings and the issues to be discussed, and has a permanent employment contract, whereas the School Council remains in office only for three years. The head teacher is recruited through national public competition and appointed by the Ministry of Education in Rome.

The School Council used to be a highly participatory and powerful management structure. After the 2002 reform, however, it lost most of its influence in the day-to-day running of the school. It is made of 11 members, established by national legislation (Article 4): the head teacher, three elected representatives of parents, two students, three teachers, the administrative director of the school and one representative of the local authority. Thus, the Council is slim and composed primarily of users (5 out of 11). The school has full discretion in deciding the methods of election of the members of the School Council. This body approves the teaching programmes, as developed by the Teachers' Council. It also adopts the annual budget and the school's overall plan. Each school can also autonomously establish new structures for the participation and representation of parents and users (Corriere della Sera, 2007; Ferroni, 1997).

The allocation of clear responsibilities for results to individual schools and head teachers is a major breakthrough in the Italian public education system, given the historical legacy of an unresponsive ministerial bureaucracy which administered the Italian education system with laws, circulars, deliberations, suffocating any individual school initiative and attribution of clear responsibilities (Brachetta, 2002; Brocca, 1995; Brocca and Frabboni, 2004; Capano, 2003). The decentralization of responsibilities has led in Italy, differently to in France, to a profound change at the microlevel of education provision, transforming the 'management by committees' into personalized management. Education reforms have a dual impact on accountability: first, to reconfigure the relationship between different levels of government, and secondly, to improve the efficiency of the administration of schools. As I have argued elsewhere (Mattei, 2007b), the analysis of the reforms of both health care and education in France and Italy benefits from being located in the wider frame of the reforms of the state. This partially explains why reforms in Italy have not been triggered by the publication of PISA results, as in Germany. The relatively low score of Italy in the PISA report did not generate a public debate of the same intensity as in Germany (Cavalli and Ferratini, 2003; Bottani, 2002; Martini, 2002).

## Conclusions: The fragility of the managerial model in European schools and the British anomaly

Empirical findings suggest that only in Britain at the school level heads of schools have gained such a prominent role in the governance systems of schools as to challenge the traditional accountability regime based on professional and bureaucratic types of legitimation. Unlike the OECD findings, which do not disaggregate data at the level of individual schools (OECD, 2007), instead accounting for leadership structures as one unified collective actor, this chapter, based also on interviews and the qualitative assessment of comparative legislation, suggests that heads of British schools have acquired influence against parents, teachers and governors in the management of schools. They have ample budgetary and recruiting powers, unmatched by their colleagues in continental Europe. In the case of French schools, the role of the head has changed over time, though less dramatically than in Britain. Heads of schools have acquired greater autonomy in relation to the teaching profession, but still a limited one in the area of financial management. Unlike in England, this process has not been associated with top-down managerial accountability, but rather a professionalization of heads. This is a remarkable development, considering how they used to be bureaucratic agents of the state. With the emergence of organizational autonomy, French heads of schools have acquired managerial responsibilities, but not at the expense of teachers. Elected politicians continue to have a great influence in the governing bodies of French schools, and the local field services of the state, such as the academies, remain the ultimate source of accountability. Bureaucratic accountability has not been replaced in French schools by managerial accountability, but a process of sedimentation prevails, namely a layering of new practices over old ones.

The German education system is characterized by federalism (Allmendinger and Leibfried, 2003) with ongoing trials of autonomous schools and pilot projects in Berlin, North Rhine–Westphalia and Hessen, among others. In comparative terms, Germany still represents the most reluctant education system to introduce autonomy and alter the traditional accountability regimes based on bureaucratic and professional accountability. In comparative terms with Britain, for instance, German teachers play an influential role in the internal governance of secondary schools. They are in control of the teaching methods and instructional content, and they are highly involved in defining assessment criteria and practices. The managerial challenge to professionals by heads of schools has not been a prominent phenomenon on continental European schools. The pattern is similar in German, French and Italian schools. Therefore, in Germany, France and Italy, educational accountability is still based on the consensus of the main political goals of state education, which is legitimated strongly by professional codes and norms. Table 4.4 below captures the empirical findings of this chapter.

The study of managerialism in the secondary public school systems in Britain, France, Germany and Italy reveals the marked scholarly limitation of relegating to the margins the debate about administrative reforms in the welfare state. The negligence in the transformation of democratic accountability, as a result of administrative changes inspired by managerial accountability in the 1980s and 1990s, represents a major scholarly omission. This criticism is not only applicable to the study of state educational administrations in continental Europe. Likewise, in Scandinavia scholars have lamented the lack of research on welfare states and NPM (Green-Pedersen, 2002: 287). This is even more lamentable in light of the wider implications of the changes in the welfare administrative framework of educational administration in Europe for the welfare state. What is at stake is not a technical problem, but the redefinition of professional and organizational identities (Demailly, 1993), as a result of the 'managerial' transformation of state educational systems. Thus, we need much more steady research in future years on this theme of primary relevance for the future of the welfare state.

Despite the existing limited scholarly research in the area of educational policy studies, the international reform trend suggests that individual schools are gaining significant organizational autonomy, as far as the level of decision making is concerned (Eurydice, 2007). The devolution of new budgetary powers and structural autonomy shows patterns of convergence, making the application of Esping-Andersen's (1990) regimes typology quite questionable to educational systems. The most recent PISA and Eurydice studies indicate increased autonomy over many aspects of school management, with countries aiming to improve performance levels and responsiveness by devolving responsibilities

Table 4.4 New governance systems of schools

| State secondary schools | Organizational autonomy of schools | Managerial autonomy of head in relation to governing board and teachers | Staffing autonomy of schools | Instructional content and policy autonomy | Accountability of schools |
|---|---|---|---|---|---|
| **Britain** | School has ample budgetary, financial, delivery autonomy from educational authorities. Decentralized financial management. | Head is accountable to central educational authority via performance regimes. Teachers and governors are consulted, but do not have power in practice. Democratic accountability not effective via the governing board. | Head recruits teachers, after formal consultation with governing board. Governors lose influence. | Increasingly decided by central educational authorities. Teachers have a marginal role in defining teaching process and curricula. | Head teacher to central government. |
| **Germany** | Limited autonomy, but on-going trials in selected Länder. Most schools have acquired budgetary autonomy. | Teachers continue to play a key role. Assessment practices are entirely done by teachers. Slow introduction of high stakes testing. Governing board is only a consultative body, and head has mainly administrative responsibilities. | No autonomy by schools. Recruitment is extremely centralized and via the regional education authority. | Teachers play a role to define content of teaching and methods. Schools have limited autonomy in selection of textbooks, but teaching offer is more autonomous for optional courses. | Heads and governing bodies to regional educational authority. |

*(Continued)*

*Table 4.4  Continued*

| State secondary schools | Organizational autonomy of schools | Managerial autonomy of head in relation to governing board and teachers | Staffing autonomy of schools | Instructional content and policy autonomy | Accountability of schools |
|---|---|---|---|---|---|
| **France** | New autonomy with the creation of the *établissement public local d'enseignement.* No decentralized financial management to schools. | Professionalization of heads. Governing boards continue to play central role. Local politicians highly involved in the governing body. | No autonomy. Centralized recruitment via Ministry of Education. | Teachers continue to play key role, and resist centralized attempts to exert direct influence in this area. Inspectors of the Academies play also role in this. | Governing bodies and local politicians to local communities and central government. |
| **Italy** | Limited autonomy and misapplied. No decentralized financial management. | Heads gain power against governors and parents, but not teachers. | No autonomy. Centralized recruitment through open competition at national level. | Teachers and educational authorities decide. Parents, students and governors are minimally involved. | Head teacher to central educational authorities. |

(OECD, 2007). The centralized–decentralized dichotomy proposed by Archer is useful in explaining the different degree of administrative resistance to the introduction of managerialism in France and Italy on the one hand and Britain on the other. However, it is not as useful in explaining the convergence of different educational systems on the dimension of change pertaining to the autonomization of individual schools from central government controls, which cuts across centralized and decentralized systems.

Contrasting state tradition was exemplified in the field of state education (Archer, 1979). This is still generally valid. However, convergence of changing patterns of autonomy of state schools in Europe causes this identification between diverging education systems and different state tradition to be revisited. Empirical evidence reveals convergence in the direction of administrative restructuring towards a less rule-bound, less uniform, and more differentiated, flexible and decentralized system of public secondary education in Europe. As countries depart from very different starting points, clearly the British system appears to be disproportionately different to continental ones. Nowhere in Europe do schools have such an ample discretion over their budgets, their staffing policy as in Britain. As far as autonomy is concerned, British schools enjoy the greatest in Europe. However, schools in France, Italy and Germany are slowly moving towards the British system.[30] This applies to the organizational level foremost. Thus, I argue that convergence is applicable to the 'direction' of the process of change, with countries still diverging if we take misleadingly a short-term perspective.

By emphasizing the empirical findings of convergence, I do not wish to suggest that welfare service reforms are easy to implement and one-dimensional. The degree of convergence *towards* the organizational autonomization of schools is not paralleled by a similar pattern of direction and intensity in the managerial aspect of autonomy. Divergence and national variations dominate as far as the role of heads of schools, and their main responsibilities are concerned. Likewise, this empirical study has found enduring differences in the role of the other governance bodies within schools, such as boards. Therefore, empirical evidence of greater organizational autonomy affecting Germany, France and Italy remains unmatched by managerial autonomy, here referred to as the adoption of an internal corporate management decision-making system. The new managerial model has been extremely difficult to implement in France and Italy. Its fate is still uncertain, as there is widespread reluctance to implement performance and efficiency-driven measures.

The managerial model is thus a fragile revolution on the Continent. Managerial accountability is far from replacing both bureaucratic and traditional political accountability mechanisms. Head teachers are far from being the line managers into which they have evolved in British schools. Although head teachers have become pivotal levers of change, in the structure of decision making in France, Germany and Italy, their bureaucratic leadership is still a greater source of legitimation than their managerial aspirations. In France, for instance, their professionalization is much more pronounced than their managerialization. While the state bureaucracy and its field services in France and Italy are resisting the new managerial model, its normative power is very persuasive at times of a deep professional crisis of the teaching profession in those countries, and the weakening political and social consensus about the goals of state education, which in the 1960s and 1970s was forged upon enhancing social equality via a strong state.

This chapter concludes that one of the most striking institutional developments of the 1980s and 1990s has been the centrality that schools have acquired as separate and autonomous 'organisations' within their national educational systems (Thoenig, 2003; Mintzberg, 1979). Change has occurred at this level of analysis, despite the systematic scarce attention that scholars have drawn upon it. The target of much modernization of educational bureaucracies in Britain, Germany, France and Italy has been the organization *per se*, and only to a lesser extent the teaching content or activities. The new actor on the rise is the Organization of the school, an independent collective actor in a changing educational system, pressured by new demands from globalization and governance reforms, and the transformations of the state (Leibfried and Zürn, 2005). This dimension of convergence is a pattern which has emerged from all the cases analysed here. This institutional change pertaining to the organizational modernization of educational bureaucracies is supported by the fusion of the old administrative–professional divide, exemplary in France, into a new accountability regime whereby bureaucratic and professional accountabilities are less demarcated. The head teacher is both a pedagogical leader and an administrative authority, who can supervise teachers' performance, monitor the outcome of their teaching and meanwhile expand his policy scope into areas which used to be the autonomous realm of the teaching profession. The outcome in Britain is indicative of an outlier case, as far as the effects of managerialism on old accountability regimes are concerned.

As far as the 'old' political accountability is concerned, the only educational system which remains quite unchallenged by organizational autonomy of schools is France. Elected representatives and local councillors are active members of the schools' governing bodies, and they are influential actors in the local education system. Whereas accountability of schools in France mainly relies on politicians as accountors, in Britain, Germany and Italy public accountability is also achieved by means of renewed parents' involvement in decision making. The participation of parents and interest groups into the schools' decision-making governance system is much more extensive in Britain, Italy and Germany, than in France. Direct participation of parents has been one of the main objectives of New Labour's education reforms. It is worth noticing that in Italy and Germany, parents have always been central actors in the educational system. Thus, in principle 'outward' accountability is strong.

Despite the reform trends to strengthen the position and role of users and parents in the internal governance system of schools (Eurydice, 2005; Davies, 1990), recent reports have shown that parents are showing increasing apathy and disaffection for participation in school's councils and meetings (Corriere della Sera, 2007).[31] In the case of Britain, where the model of quasi-markets (West and Pennell, 2005) and parental choice has been most predominant, interviews have suggested that governing bodies of schools are merely consultative bodies, which approve decisions by the head teacher. Considering the doubtful effectiveness of new participatory experiments in British schools and the fact that only in France elected politicians continue to play a major role in the decision-making process of secondary schools, and that in Germany and Italy, local politicians are not members of school governing bodies, overall in Europe public accountability is in crisis. Prizes for excellence, league tables and performance indicators, mainly quantitative, continue to attract European media coverage, but political accountability is rarely acknowledged as a problem by those who are content with the claimed transparency provided by the media or by the efforts of international organizations. In the next chapters, I will draw conclusions on the cross-sectoral dimension of the restructuring of the welfare state, drawing comparative insights from the empirical analysis of chapters 3 (hospitals) and 4 (schools). Moving beyond a narrow definition of sectoral boundaries, I will explore the external validity of the argument of convergence *towards* patterns of autonomy and managerialism in the core social policy areas.

# Part III  Welfare Democracy and Managerialism

# 5
# Towards the Managerial Welfare State: The Mechanism of a Silent Revolution

*The insular path could become a continental passage.*
(Leibfried, 1994: 22)

We have learnt from the empirical analysis of health care and education, respectively in chapters 3 and 4, that individual organizations of service delivery in Germany, Britain, Italy and France are increasingly framed upon the 'autonomous enterprise formula'. Organizational restructuring of delivery institutions is an empirically observable phenomenon particularly in those areas of the welfare state committed to the provision of services in kind, such as hospitals and schools. Although organizational changes may be dismissed as merely formal and legalistic, they are not inconsequential for the future transformations of the welfare state and need greater attention in the social policy debate about European welfare states. The empirical investigation of organizational changes of the welfare state in four European countries in the last 20 years has indicated a convergent process of homogenization. This chapter's purpose is to explain convergence drawing upon institutional theories of organizational theory, in particular institutional isomorphism (DiMaggio and Powell, 1983: 148).

The welfare state has been frequently assessed in terms of the amount of benefits and the politics of redistribution, and less often in terms of the transformations of modern democratic institutions, including bureaucratic organizations. 'Organising' welfare influences the formation of preferences, norms and opinions and, thus, the institutional framework for future welfare activities. In this chapter the conventional rankings of welfare states by macroeconomic indicators takes less relevance, and more emphasis is placed on the process of organizational adaptation leading to convergence of 'organisational fields' (DiMaggio and Powell, 1983)[1] pertaining to the welfare state. The main purpose of this chapter is to explain convergence in the administrative structures of service delivery across sectors. Homogenization refers to the process of narrowing the variance between organizations, as similar innovations and change are adopted across different sectors and over time. Organizational change affects the structure, processes and behaviour of actors. This is the most visible measurement of convergence. As Egeberg argues (Egeberg, 1999), organizational structure affects agenda setting and actors' preferences, influences the decision on behaviour and has a lasting impact on actors' interests.

Here in this chapter I am most interested in how organizations of welfare delivery are becoming more similar in their internal account-ability arrangements. Empirical findings presented in chapters 3 and 4 suggest that welfare administration in Europe is converging towards a similar accountability regime type, namely managerial accountability, independently from different programme areas of social policy and welfare regimes (Esping-Andersen, 1990). I argue in this chapter that this convergence of the institutional structure of welfare administra-tion is not directly driven by globalization or justification of efficiency gains but rather by the need for organizational survival and legitimacy (Powell and DiMaggio, 1991). For such purposes, organizations endorse the models which are perceived to be most innovative or 'modern'. When the empirical link between managerialism and performance is inconclusive, sociological concepts such as mimetic isomorphism are useful. Why do different organizations adopt formal structures, pro-cedures and values that are so identical? As the discussions of public hospitals and state schools have emphasized throughout the analytic narrative in chapters 3 and 4, convergence is not only the result of policy diffusion of ideas, but also, and more importantly, a process of structural transformations to the institutional structure of European welfare states.

On the basis of the empirical data exposed already in chapters 3 and 4, here I develop further the argument that the organizations of service delivery are becoming more similar, without necessarily making them more efficient. An important question for convergence is not only the one of narrowing variance, but also that of motivational drivers and causal mechanisms. Why would different organizational fields across countries adopt similar structures, in light of weak supporting evidence of efficiency gains? In the first part, the chapter discusses the reach of managerialism and the main empirical conclusions from the cases of health care and education in Britain, Germany, France and Italy. In the second part, it focuses on explaining the patterns of convergence. In the concluding session, I return to the theoretical expectations set out in Chapter 2 and discuss them in light of what we have learnt from the empirical findings.

## Cross-sectoral reform patterns

'Autonomy' has risen to the top of the agenda of restructuring the service welfare state mainly for two different reasons: democratization and decentralization. First, autonomous hospitals and schools from centralized controls are better equipped to respond to their users, that is to patients, parents, students and the local communities at large. Such autonomy is an instrument of democratization of welfare bureaucracies. Secondly, individual units of welfare delivery have become autonomous in the wider frame of administrative reforms of the state to fight against bureaucratic inefficiencies. Autonomy, thus, is an instrument both of enhanced local representation and democratization and of organizational 'modernisation' of the state.

Therefore, autonomy of public schools and hospitals is the organizational side both of a territorial political conflict between different levels of government and of an administrative struggle to improve public services and their quality. In this first section of the chapter, I will identify the main patterns that emerged from the analysis in chapters 3 and 4 of two sectors at the core of the welfare state, health care and education.

### Public hospital sector

Let us first identify the main changing patterns concerning the relationship between managerial and political accountability in the hospital sector. In Britain, France and Italy the legislative impetus has been directed not only towards strategies of cost-containment, but most remarkably towards the reshaping of established accountability regimes, which we have defined as a systemic component of welfare organizations. In these three countries, managerialism has been pursued with reform efforts aimed at strengthening the management of hospitals in order to mobilize consent around performance-oriented objectives. There is no evidence in Germany of reforms strategies to adopt general management à la Griffiths.

British NHS Foundation Trusts are among the most autonomous public hospitals in Europe, at least in comparative terms. They are the most autonomous in determining their own internal governance structure, a possibility which is very limited for French, German and Italian hospitals. Foundation Trusts are not dependent upon local authorities' decisions concerning planning or the organization of services, unlike the predominant 'localism' in Germany, France and Italy. They are also protected, in theory, from central controls by the creation of institutional buffers between the central Department of Health and the management of the hospitals. This is, among other things, the role of newly reformed Boards of Governors, which are supposed to protect the management team from centralized political pressures. The objective to isolate Trusts from political control has been relatively ambitious, in comparison with the hospitals in Germany, France and Italy. This aspect deserved special attention because it is crucial for an understanding of the changing relationship between managerial and political accountability.

The analysis of the role of the Boards of Governors in public hospitals in Britain, France, Germany and Italy has revealed how the most radical departure from the past in relation to political accountability occurred in Britain, with no parallels on the same scale in any other European countries. Traditional accountability regimes, characterized by the direct and hierarchical relationship between the management team of a public hospital and the Minister of Health, have been replaced in Britain by new ones focused on users' representation in the Boards of Governors. The lay public and users become the holders of 'political' accountability. The only electoral dimension of this new type of accountability rests in the election of the members of the Board by the constituents of local citizens, staff and so on. However, electoral and partisan politics do not feature in the organization of NHS Foundation Trusts.

The Board of Directors is a fairly large body, in comparison with its continental European counterpart. This is primarily because it is composed not only of executive directors, responsible for the running of the hospital, but also of an equal number of non-executive directors, who serve as a delegated branch of the governors. It is not surprising that areas of tension are reported in the different objectives of governors and non-executive directors on the one hand, and the management team on the other. Therefore, the new accountability regime of the British NHS at the system level replaces centralized political control with local accountability to users and to the governors at the level of the organization. Without wishing to evaluate this new system, I cast some doubt on the representation of the members of the Board of Governors and, more importantly, on the apathy which seems to be predominant among members (Klein, 2004). This apathy is most likely the response to what was intended as a democratic experiment (Dorf and Sabel, 1998) and turned out to be a decorative element of public accountability.

On the contrary, German, French and Italian hospitals have decided not to challenge the old hierarchical accountability regimes. This was not because of ineffectual political systems inept at adopting radical reforms or innovation as predicted from the literature. It was a deliberate preference for political accountability in its original electoral form. Thus, in France, Germany and Italy, local and regional councils remain influential actors in hospital care. They supervise the management teams of public hospitals. For instance, in German public hospitals the *Aufsichtsrat* (the Supervisory Board), composed of politicians, has ample power of appointment, supervision of managers and input in the decision-making process, especially in relation to financial investment matters. Local politicians are also members of the supervisory boards in French public hospitals. Their role is not merely a formal and consultative one, but political parties do play out their different policy positions in the hospitals' internal governance structures. Electoral politics do indeed continue to matter, contrary to the widely accepted view that hospital care is a technical practice, which should respond only to economic imperatives. Therefore, the empirical findings presented in Chapter 3 suggest that managerialism has not challenged the established political accountability regime in Germany, France and Italy.

However, what has changed in Germany, France and Italy has been the 'content' of managerial accountability, rather than 'to whom' the account is to be rendered (Bovens, 1998). In all three continental countries, managers are increasingly held accountable for performance and ex post results, rather than legality or procedures. This is clearly observable outside Britain as well. It is a remarkable and fully surprising change especially in countries where the administrative tradition is very different than in Britain.

The case of French hospitals is emblematic of the possibility to strengthen new management systems while preserving the old political accountability regimes which ensure democratic control. The reforms of the hospital sector in France supports Klein's point that managerialism can be put to the service of political accountability (Day and Klein, 1987). The management function has been strongly reinforced by the creation of a new *Conseil Executif*, by the autonomization of public hospitals, and more generally by the attribution of clear responsibilities and authority to the director, who has acquired, for instance, the power of appointing the heads of hospitals' departments. The director's power in relation to the medical profession within the hospitals has increased hugely, as I discussed in detail in Chapter 3. However, the reforms have ensured that medical staff from the start was part of the management structures of the hospitals. As the director was gaining authority, doctors were not excluded from the decision-making process.

The peculiar problem of the new French system of accountability of hospital care is the 'excessive' number of actors to whom the director has to render account. The problem would be significantly reduced if these accountability holders were part of a coordinated system, but it is well known that the French administrative system does not excel in administrative coordination (Meny and Wright, 1994). The directors and the *Conseil Executif* are accountable to the *Conseil d'Administration* of the hospital, made of local politicians, among other members, and also to the Minister of Health, who has appointed the director, and to the newly created Regional Hospital Agency. The director of the hospital is also bureaucratically and directly accountable to the Ministry of Health.

In Italy, the traditional methods of political accountability persist, despite the regionalization of the health care system (Mattei, 2006). Hospital directors are appointed directly by the regional minister of health, and these are widely recognized as 'political' appointments. The system of political accountability in the case of Italian hospitals, and more generally health care services, approximates a spoils system (Mattei, 2007b). The intended policy objective of NPM to 'depoliticise' the management structures of public hospitals has not yielded the expected results. The introduction of a radical and scientific form of new managerialism in the 1992 health care reform, the closest one to scientific management, has transformed the internal governance and organizational culture of hospital insofar as the content, not the form, of managerial accountability is concerned. Managers are no longer expected to gather votes for their political patrons, but rather deliver public services. As I have argued in other venues, there is a great regional variance in Italy in terms of the implementation of the 1992 landmark reform and introduction of managerialism (Mattei, 2007b). Contrary to health care policy experts' expectations that hospital care would be only touched marginally by entrepreneurialism (Mossialos et al., 2002), the new organizational modernization driven by managerial accountability has affected the internal governance arrangements of public hospitals beyond the core Anglo-Saxon countries. From the empirical findings in Chapter 3, it is also clear that reforms have affected public organization beyond the rhetoric and symbolic level.

The most significant change across different health care systems and different European countries resulting from the transfer of new managerialism into welfare institutions is the transformation of the 'content' of accountability, rather than the formal relationships between actors involved, be they 'web' or 'chain' type. With the exception of Britain, in most continental European countries the traditional hierarchical modes of political accountability in education and health care have not changed, not at least to suggest a radical and clear-cut move from government to governance (Jann, 2003). Local politicians continue to have a prominent role in the representative bodies of public hospitals, and their power of appointment seems to penetrate deeply enough to influence the heads of hospitals' divisions. The transformations of governing bodies will be discussed in greater detail in Chapter 6, in the frame of the question of welfare democracy. Despite the opening up of supervisory boards to users and the public, it is only in the British NHS Foundation hospitals that direct participation has been given more organizational relevance than political representation. In fact, in most other European countries elected representatives continue to be the undisputable accountability holders and locus of authority.

## State secondary schools

Similarly to the restructuring of public hospital care, state schools in Britain, Germany, France and Italy have been reformed so as to ensure performance-based educational accountability, moving away from mainly an input-based system. This theme has dominated the public debate and the policy agenda in all four countries, despite being rather under-researched outside American and British educational scholarship. In Britain, Germany, France and Italy the issue of educational leadership has become more prominent due to the excellence and standards movement. In order to achieve the expected results and educational outcomes, the management role of head teachers was strengthened in all four countries, with Britain and Italy as frontrunners of a new manager-managed relationship between head teachers and teachers. In Germany, professional and political accountability appears to be stronger than the new managerial accountability of head teachers. However, inevitably the new performance-oriented accountability has made educational leadership a favourite target of school reforms. Unfortunately, in most scholarly communities on the continent the organizational instruments to increase educational competencies do not receive the attention this topic deserves.

The case of public secondary schooling is particularly interesting for one central paradox. On the one hand, centralized controls have traditionally dominated most of the aspects concerned with the provision of education, from setting uniform teaching standards to designing the curriculum, to decide on management systems. The only exception was Britain, where a national curriculum was introduced with the 1988 Education Reform Act. Most of the transformations of accountability structures analysed in Chapter 4 have shown that there is a greater heterogeneity within the organizational field of public schools than the one found in hospitals. One explanation I have offered was that experimentalism with new arrangements has been implemented in a diffuse way, with intense professional resistance of teachers and their unions, and difficulties of head teachers in reinventing themselves as 'managers' rather than their traditional role as 'administrators'. Incentives have been created by central governments for head teachers to acquire greater power, but change has been overall much slower in education than in hospital care.

The new managerial role of the head teacher depends on the historical development of educational leadership within each system. As I have emphasized in Chapter 4, in France and Italy head teachers of high schools have been chiefly responsible for the compliance of individual schools with centralized standards and regulations. They have been the major agents of the state in schools rather than the representatives of local communities. In the French system the organization itself of the school has always been secondary to the autonomous professionalism of teachers who are obliged only to their subject specialism. Teachers have traditionally had a weak allegiance to individual schools. Thus, the weight of the traditional modes of educational leadership and how they are translated organizationally, especially with reference to central government interference on autonomy, has a great influence on the vulnerability to the transformations towards performance accountability regime.

A significant emerging pattern of convergence across different educational systems in Europe is the attempt to strengthen the role of head teachers in relation to the teaching staff, conferring upon them powers of performance evaluation, and closing the traditional gap between the administrative and the pedagogic evaluation. Therefore, empirical findings presented in Chapter 4 reveal that in all countries teachers are challenged by the encroachment of head teachers in their professional life. The intensity of the phenomenon varies across countries, with France being the case where head teachers most reluctantly decide to transform their role from peer to line manager. In the Italian and German educational systems there is a slightly more enthusiastic response by head teachers to their new managerial role, though they remain extremely constrained in staff management and budgetary issues.

As Table 5.1 shows, the French and Italian accountability regimes in education continue to reflect a bureaucratic compromise, only marginally changed by the new systems of performance-based evaluation. This accountability system is based on juridical and bureaucratic rules which the central ministries of education establish and expect to be implemented by their field services. In both countries, schools have gained legal and juridical autonomy and the head teachers have been strengthened, but reforms have witnessed resistance from the teachers' unions. In both countries, the reforms of schools' internal governance have progressed hand in hand with the decentralization of state responsibilities to the regional administrations. In territorial terms, Italy and France are becoming similar to the highly decentralized educational system of Germany, where regional administrations effectively control individual schools. For instance, the new rectorates in France have important new responsibilities in transferring staff from one school to the other. In Italy, as I have discussed in Chapter 4, the autonomy of schools has been always blocked by making administrative controls closer to schools through the field offices of the Ministry of Education. In France and Italy, the central state has always found a powerful ally in the teachers' unions, and only timid supporters of autonomy in the head teachers. However, even in the case of France and Italy the separation between the state and the teaching profession has become less rigid than in the past.

As far as political accountability and the role of governing bodies are concerned, there is a great variance between the different educational systems in Europe. In France, governing bodies are mainly political. They are large, usually composed of 30 members, with a majority coming from the regional or municipal councils and only a minority (a maximum of five) being parents. Local elected officials are powerful actors in French schools, and this remains an exception in Europe. The representation of parents is given a much greater voice in Germany, Britain and Italy. Electoral politics plays a central role only in France, to the extent that head teachers have reported that partisanship makes a huge difference in the role that local elected members of the *Conseil d'Administration* play. Local councillors had been members of governing bodies of British schools, but this has changed radically in the 1980s with the Thatcher reforms.

Conversely, in British schools in theory the role of parents as governors is less symbolic and more operational than in other countries. Parents are often consulted by head teachers with regard to priorities

*Table 5.1* Changes in accountability regimes

| | Hospitals | | | |
|---|---|---|---|---|
| | Britain | Germany | France | Italy |
| **Managerial accountability** | General management à la Griffiths | No general management à la Griffiths | Management function reinforced | À la Griffiths with single-headed executive |
| **Political accountability** | New types include Board of Governors (users) and local ownership | Old types with supervisory boards controlled by politicians | Old type with politicians on supervisory boards (as Germany) | Patronage type of political accountability |
| **Trade off** | Managerialism challenges democratic accountability | Old political electoral accountability remains predominant | Excess of accountability (highest number of accountability holders) | Old system of patronage. Change in content of accountability |

| | Schools | | | |
|---|---|---|---|---|
| | Britain | Germany | France | Italy |
| **Managerial accountability** | Head teachers are managers and challenge professionals. | Bureaucratic accountability predominant. Head teachers adapt slowly to managerialism. | Bureaucratic compromise. Head teachers are agents of the state. Professionalization of head teachers. | Head teachers, are agents of the state. Management function strengthened. |
| **Political accountability** | Enhanced role of parents and new types of public accountability. | No significant change. Direct accountability to State Minister. | Local politicians are powerful actors in governing bodies. | Crisis of representation of parents on governing boards. |
| **Trade off** | Strong managerial accountability has replaced political one. | Bureaucratic accountability is predominant, with ongoing trials of autonomy. | Strong local political accountability through schools' councils. | Managerial accountability is stronger. Direct accountability to the Minister of Education. |

and strategic management. Governing bodies formally approve staff appointments, for instance. However, interviews have suggested that in practice head teachers in British schools are autocratic managers and they perceive their role no differently to 'line managers' of teachers. Their scope of decision making is very ample and there is no effective counterweight within the internal governance structure to the power of the head teacher. Local educational authorities are effectively no longer a source of authority in terms of accountability relationships.

In Britain, Germany, France and Italy, empirical findings suggest that convergence along the managerial logic has entered the educational administration through the process of autonomization of state high schools and the strengthening of the management functions of head teachers. This is a pattern which is visible across the different educational systems, both in the most centralized and decentralized ones. Reformers have claimed that self-governing schools operating with autonomy from the administrative controls of the 'centre' are the essential pre-condition for the success of new types of political and managerial accountabilities. British schools are the ones in Europe with the greatest autonomy from central government, in relation to budget and staff recruitment and management. Despite the widely held belief that state schools are the bastion of the *dirigiste* state in continental Europe, findings suggest that reforms aimed at devolving down to individual schools greater powers of self-governance are now emerging in France, Italy and also Germany. The strategy of diffuse, piecemeal and incremental reform making should not mislead the researcher in downplaying the change occurring in educational administration and accountability also in continental countries.

## Mimetic isomorphism as a mechanism of cross-sectoral convergence

Financial uncertainty is one of the most important problem pressure and precipitating factors for the adoption of organizational models inspired by the private 'enterprise'. The efficient management of welfare services has gained a prominent position on the agenda of European governments, not only because it is claimed to gain popular support in the run-up to national elections, but also because it promises to solve the overriding financial pressures on mature welfare states. As DiMaggio and Powell (1983: 151) argue in their seminal work, 'modelling is a response to uncertainty and ambiguity about goals'. Organizational models are very useful for politicians because structural changes are visible to all, citizens and policymakers, whereas changes in processes are less apparent. For the survival and legitimacy of institutions it is essential to be perceived to be innovative, even in the absence of strong concrete evidence that the adopted models enhance efficiency.

Welfare organizations do often adapt to their institutional context, but they often play an active role in shaping those contexts (Parsons and Smelser, 1956). Interviews have suggested that national governments find it increasingly difficult to control welfare bureaucracies because the organizational source of legitimacy of hospitals and schools has changed. Welfare organizations show considerable ability to survive, precisely because they incorporate powerful myths and 'institutionalised rules' (Meyer and Rowan, 1977). I argue that entrepreneurialism and 'good' management have become in the last two decades part of the new institutionalized myth of welfare administration. Thus, organizational success depends not only on matching the demands of internal efficiency, but also on conformity with the prevailing normative obligations (DiMaggio and Powell, 1983). These myths are binding on organizations, for they create the necessity to redefine their internal organizational structures accordingly. External institutionalized rules are a legitimate source of organizational structure, which is not only the result of apolitical engineering. Entrepreneurialism is, then, the new myth for welfare organizations, and its high institutionalization in advanced democracies implies that there are ongoing deep transformations to the post-golden age welfare state (Zürn and Leibfried, 2005).

According to Powell and DiMaggio, there are two important organizational preconditions for processes of mimetic isomorphism. First, they argue that uncertainty in the relationship between means and ends will create incentives for organizations to model themselves after those they perceive to be successful. Secondly, they hypothesise that conflicting goals of an organization, as is the case in public hospitals and schools, will make organizations increasingly dependent upon appearances of legitimacy (Powell and DiMaggio, 1983: 155). These preconditions are particularly pronounced in the case of organizations responsible for welfare service delivery, which are constantly struggling to meet conflicting demands of performance and equity.

The process of mimetic isomorphism leads to increasing similarities between different organizational fields. The recent definition by Holzinger and Knill of policy convergence also refers to decreasing variance between characteristics of a certain policy across a given set of political jurisdictions over a long period of time (Holzinger and Knill, 2005). The units of comparison in this book are the organizational fields, not countries though, as I have explained in the methodological section of Chapter 1. The process conceptualized by Powell and DiMaggio unfolds at the organizational level. Thus, it leads to institutional changes and does not stop at the level of 'transnational communication' or travelling of policy ideas (Holzinger and Knill, 2005). Such recent approaches explain convergence in social policy highlighting policy learning through international organizations and transnational networks. The OECD and the World Bank have a central role in diffusing ideas about measuring performance and comparative assessment of education and health care standards. These are indeed actors and mechanisms facilitating convergence. However, mimetic isomorphism refers to the motives underpinning reform strategies and actors' behaviour.

Let us briefly consider what the 'myth' of organizational autonomy promises to welfare bureaucracies. Among the various alleged benefits of autonomy, disaggregation of the organizations in smaller units makes it possible to put the experts in charge of the decision-making process. This results in a more efficient use of human resources, for there is no point in employing highly qualified managers and then interfering in their daily operations. Autonomy from the central government's direct control allegedly unleashes the entrepreneurial skills of public managers, liberating them from the political 'burden' of the interference of their political masters. Decisions over resource allocation at the level of the delivery unit are made on technical grounds, or professional, without being left to the interplay of partisan pressures. The nature of allocation decision may change over time or differ between countries. Generally, it is likely to be more technical when it takes places at the periphery, whereas it is more open, recognized and 'political' when it is a matter of central concern (Glennerster, 1975: 39).

Another benefit of organizational unit autonomy is greater responsiveness to local needs and local communities in line with the 'participatory state' (Peters, 1996). This appears attractive to welfare states with a high degree of functional centralization, for example the National Health Service in Britain. Autonomy enhances the responsiveness of the organization to local communities. They establish priorities according to locally determined needs, for a uniform service would lead to inappropriate use of resources. Autonomy underpins the shift from a political to technical decision making, shifting the balance of responsibility for performance from central politicians to local managers.

Despite these alleged benefits, granting autonomy to public hospitals and schools has proved highly problematic and contested. Constructing a structural barrier between central political leadership and local management of service delivery has decreased the capacity of politicians to exert democratic political control over schools and hospitals. On the one hand, this was the intended effect of granting autonomy to delivery units, namely the possibility of liberating managers from political interference. On the other hand, this generates a dilemma between effective democratic control by politically elected representatives, and the rise of functionally and technically legitimated policymaking. As Christensen and Laegreid have suggested, structural devolution associated with NPM means 'a decrease in the central capacity and authority of control and less attention to political considerations in the subordinate units' (Christensen and Laegreid, 2001a: 81).

NPM reforms are based on a rather misleading view of the state and any promise of enhanced political control is based on a quite simplistic view of political processes. I doubt that party appointment, a formal mechanism of control, is effective in practice. The reassertion of politics within welfare organizations could be effective in practice if these organizations incorporate externally legitimated structures fundamentally different from the myth of entrepreneurialism. To the extent that parties are unable to reaffirm their partisan and representative function, they may not succeed in enforcing environmentally institutionalized rules of electoral accountability and democratic legitimacy. Hence, organizations struggling for survival and resources will depend on alternative legitimating rules, especially in highly institutionalized context such as mature welfare states. The reassertion of politics based on party appointment and formal control, without the necessary reaffirmation of the traditional legitimating framework of representative and electoral democracy, is deemed to fail, for organizational legitimacy is shaped increasingly by the external myth of entrepreneurialism and managerialism. These myths create the necessity for profound changes to organizational structures and internal redefinition of political and administrative accountabilities (March and Simon, 1958).

To sum up, reforms centred on granting autonomy to public hospitals or schools have created confusion and tension, especially in visible cases of maladministration and professional misconduct. When things go wrong and Parliament calls ministers to account for inefficiencies, they will displace blame on public managers, while intervening in that public body's internal affairs to make sure that criticism is addressed. Therefore, the trade-off between autonomy and accountability becomes a dilemma in cases of maladministration and professional misconducts.

Autonomy is politically difficult to sustain when things go wrong, and this problem is particularly acute for those systems in which the managerial model has been adopted with greatest enthusiasm. Ministers fall back on the rhetoric of autonomous public managers responsible for inefficiencies. This should not be surprising as the public and Parliament are inclined to attribute blame rather than assess the real causes of a crisis. The strategy of blame avoidance, which is equally employed by ministers and public managers in the policymaking process, challenges all mechanisms of political accountability, displacing responsibility from one level to the other and leaving no one clearly accountable for results. Autonomy, thus, has the unintended potential of enhancing the possibilities for activating this type of strategy and diminishing accountability.

## Conclusions

Despite the differences between the sectors of education and health care, and the organization of hospitals and schools, similar responses to the challenge of managerialism constitute the most significant reforms pattern. Public hospitals and public schools are complex welfare institutions designed to deliver very different services. They differ not only functionally but also structurally for their peculiar administrative and political framework of the intergovernmental structure of decision making, from the level of individual schools and hospitals to local authorities and to central ministries and agencies of coordination. Similarly, they are public institutions which deliver welfare services to citizens or users within a politico-administrative framework relentlessly posing conflicting demands of efficiency and representation. They are far from being technical organizations separated from political conflict and the mobilization of interests.

The cross-sectoral analysis of differences and similarities in this chapter has suggested that schools and hospitals have been equally subject to profound transformations of their administrative framework of coordination, as a result of the introduction of managerialism in both sectors. The external pressures on hospital care and schools originate from different domestic and external social-economic determinants, the financial one being particularly pressing in the case of hospitals. However, the response has been stunningly similar. In all countries investigated here, governments have adopted in secondary schools and public hospitals the necessary administrative arrangements to make them 'autonomous' from central or local government controls and from political intervention. Autonomy has been introduced as an instrument to allegedly improve the delivery and quality of welfare services. This has meant the adoption of new decision-making instruments and structures at the level of the organization, and greater managerial discretion.

Therefore, public hospitals and schools in Europe have been transformed in the direction of autonomous and flexible public institutions, inspired by NPM prescriptions. As far as this organizational dimension of welfare state change is concerned, there is increasing homogenization and institutional isomorphism across sectors and countries, despite different welfare regimes. Managerialism is not a dimension of social administration which is exclusively linked to liberal welfare states, like the United Kingdom or United States. There is noticeable convergence in the direction of reforms, although the pace of implementation is still significantly slower in secondary schooling than in hospital care, for reasons which have been discussed earlier.

Institutional isomorphism which has driven convergence towards the managerial welfare state is not only a result of a process of indiscriminate diffusion of similar policy ideas in OECD countries, for continental European welfare service bureaucracies are moving in the direction of the organizational arrangements found in Britain, and not vice versa. The phenomenon is rather more similar to hegemonization of an administrative model over the others. Although the effects produced by the introduction of managerialism on new types of public accountability single Britain out, for it is the only country in Europe in which welfare service bureaucracies have been 'liberated' by the 'burden' of politicians, schools and hospitals on the continent are becoming increasingly similar to the predominant model of the 'welfare enterprise'. Convergence is, thus, towards an Anglo-American hegemonial model. As Leibfried suggested in the debate of the Europeanization of social policy, 'the insular path could become a continental passage' (Leibfried, 1994: 22). In Chapter 6, I will return to the democratic question as set out in Chapter 1 in order to illuminate the implications of this predominant new model of welfare administration for the democratic governance of the welfare state.

In light of the theoretical expectations discussed in Chapter 2, structural capacity has proven to be a key facilitating condition for the realization of autonomy from centralized controls. Hospitals are usually large organizations, with a high level of internal fragmentation. They mobilize a wide range of interests and financial resources. On the contrary, individual schools tend to have fewer administrative resources.

Structural capacity of public hospitals has created the condition for autonomy by enhancing the role of the supervisory board as an institutional buffer between the internal management team of the hospitals and external public authority. Schools, conversely, are much more permeable organizations due to their smaller size.

Cross-sectoral analysis has also revealed that structural capacity, however, is not necessarily a facilitating condition for the representation of citizens in the decision-making process, and ultimately for democratic accountability. On the contrary, large bureaucratic resources do not necessarily ensure a more democratic welfare organization. In most European public hospitals, the voices of patients, users and citizens are often unheard. Some members of the new rising caste of managers, interviewed by the author, dismissed the concern for democratic control by defining the rights of patients as such: 'it is already enough if they are admitted to the hospitals. They should consider themselves lucky.' Although elected politicians are members of the supervisory boards of public hospitals in Germany, France and Italy, it is not clear how this mechanism of representation increases democratic governance, for politicians may be more interested in political control through appointment than representing and channelling the social needs of citizens. Therefore, I conclude that structural capacity is a necessary condition for the full realization of autonomous and flexible welfare bureaucracies, but it is not a sufficient condition for the democratic governance of schools and hospitals. Representation of citizens is thus not proportionate to financial resources. The case of public schooling is a clear indication of this point. As I argued in this chapter, schools perform overall better than hospitals as far as public accountability is concerned.

Besides structural capacity, the predominant mechanism of coordination in hospitals and schools is the second most important administrative variable which influences the different effects of the introduction of managerialism on welfare bureaucracies. As Chapter 2 suggested, a collegial style of coordination offers greater scope for bargaining between managers and professionals. In such an institutional context, it is more likely that legislative efforts to transform directors of schools and hospitals find higher resistance. As emphasized in this chapter, head teachers in German, French and Italian schools have been reluctant to fully implement managerialism and to transform their relationship with teachers into manager-managed one. Hospital executives, however, have not been equally prudent in exercising their new powers against the medical profession. Therefore, a collegial style of coordination, as found in schools, enhances a consensual relationship between managers and professionals and reduces conflict and fragmented decision making induced by NPM. Moreover, collegiality has been traditionally linked to wider representative functions of supervisory bodies and committees. Despite their smaller size and limited bureaucratic capacity, schools have traditionally been governed by a multitude of committees and consultative bodies which have improved their public accountability, especially in Germany, France and Italy.

# 6

# European Welfare States and Democracy: Marching to the Same Tune?

Broadly defined, the role of social policymaking is to link intentions with actions. The predicament of the sick and of the poor is addressed by taking actions with the objective of relieving their conditions. The aim of the welfare state is to improve the quality of life of the sick and the knowledge of pupils and society, among others. Policy objectives are debated and defined in the political arena, mainly by political parties, and in the legislatures at national and local levels of government. The definition of the aims is a crucial part of the political process of social policy change. It is also important as the aims provide the standards for the evaluation of policies. The elaboration of evaluative frameworks, increasingly dominated by economists and quantitative targets, in itself reflects the objectives to be achieved.

However, there are two noticeable problems with the current debate about the administrative reforms of welfare state bureaucracies. The first one is the displacement of means and ends. The second one is the sidelining of the contrast between managerial and political accountability, with a research agenda exclusively focused on the former. The attention drawn to ranking tables of educational achievements, or hospitals' success at meeting targets, suggests that standards of welfare services are increasingly defined by performance accountability rather than political consensus. Managing social policy and welfare institutions as private enterprises, with the creation of similar incentives and opportunities to managers, has become the objective of policymakers not only in Britain and the United States, but also in Germany, France and Italy. What was initially introduced as an instrument of cost containment, and pursued as such throughout the 1980s, has become one of the central aims of the welfare state to be achieved in the twenty-first century. This is an inappropriate and harmful objective, for as such it disguises the final

161

aim of a social policy, namely the improvement of the predicament of the sick and poor. It is harmful because the objective of managerialism defines in turn the standards upon which welfares services are assessed and it shapes the system of public expectations.

The second problem with the debate about the administrative restructuring of the welfare state is the sidelining of the question of the democratic dilemma between managerial and political accountability.[1] In this book, I have decided to address this upfront. Chapter 5 has argued that the introduction of managerialism in social policy has not altered the formal arrangements of political accountability in Germany, France and Italy, but its substantive content. The most noteworthy change has been in the substantive content of the accountability relationships between actors. Hospital managers are accountable to supervisory boards for balancing the budget, and generally for cost-driven objectives, for health care is primarily conceptualized as a 'financial burden'. Good management is rewarded with higher salaries and more discretion independently from medical expertise and citizens' needs.

If there is a significant ongoing threat to European welfare states, this is in the new substantive content of public accountability of welfare services. As I suggested in Chapter 5, the relationship between managerial and political accountability has not altered in terms of formal power relationships, but in terms of its content. Politicians in continental Europe remain firmly 'involved' in welfare state bureaucracies, at all levels of decision making. However, managers and politicians alike are becoming entrapped in the same legitimating organizational paradigm of managerialism, which underpins the new content of accountability. For instance, directors and, more generally, the management team of public hospitals have been empowered with new governance instruments, such as the *projet d'établissement* in France. These new instruments for strategic planning force managers to direct their actions towards short-term outcomes rather than long-term processes.

Managerial accountability has been elevated in many European countries to a *deus ex machina*, not only the solution for inefficient delivery of welfare services, but also a new organizational legitimacy based on politically neutral 'results', as argued in Chapter 5. The reforms of managerialism in welfare services offer two sets of clear alternatives: first, between privatization and managerialism as a way to make public organizations run better and more efficiently, and secondly, between 'good' management and politics (Mattei, 2007b). If service organizations are liberated from the burden of negotiations, bargaining and political representation, this will trigger a virtuous bureaucratic cycle. Large and collegial committees, aimed at representing the interest of the public, are often opposed to 'efficient' and small executive teams, made of managers responsible for running welfare 'enterprises' efficiently. As the empirical analysis in this book has suggested, managerial accountability is not only part of a symbolic process. Against the scholarly expectation that managerialism is mainly a rhetorical tool, we have learnt from the analysis of the administrative reforms of public schools and hospitals in four European countries that managerialism has triggered radical transformation of welfare democracy.

In no other areas of governmental activities has managerialism transformed the substantive 'content' of accountability as in the welfare state. This is so because expertise and technical advice are nowhere more legitimized means of professional accountability as in the delivery of health care and education services. This concluding chapter presents the central argument of the book. Managerialism is the new silent revolution transforming the administration of the service welfare state in the era of permanent austerity. The significance of this new challenge rests not simply in the legalistic changes of internal administrative arrangements *per se*, but in unsettling the link between democratic governance and the welfare state (Rieger and Leibfried, 2003), a link which has been forged with struggles, conflicts and scars.

The new threat that managerialism poses to the welfare state is the subject of the first section of this chapter. It is a very serious challenge, not confined to liberal welfare state regimes. The risk equally affects conservative welfare states with a remarkable trajectory of convergence, as I suggested in Chapter 5. The most significant factor which amplifies the potential threat to the welfare state is the nature of solutions sought to counterweight managerialism, namely the design of 'new' types of outward democratic accountability. The uncertainty of the solution is the subject of the second section of this chapter. The new internal governance arrangements, with the changes concerning the appointment and composition of supervisory boards, is a response to consumerism and consequently to the new expectations that 'democratic accountability' is not much different to 'responsiveness' to clients. Finally, in the third and concluding section I propose to return to the social administration question. I suggest that we may have looked for 'crisis' of the welfare state in the wrong place, namely in specific policy and programmatic changes, and in public expenditure trends, but not in the administration of the welfare state.

## The enterprise formula and the welfare state: System and organizational levels

The use of the analytical tool developed in Chapter 2 concerning the relationship between formal accountability arrangements and substantive issues of welfare programmes has allowed us in this book to distinguish between the rhetorical and symbolic use of managerialism and its operationalization through organizational autonomy of welfare delivery institutions. For once, the gap between reality and rhetoric is smaller than expected, insofar as different countries and different welfare regimes are converging in the direction of the British model of managerialism of welfare bureaucracies. The core findings of this project have revealed that the democratic foundations of the welfare state are challenged by the relentless expansion of the 'enterprise' formula into welfare administration in Germany, France and Italy, countries once thought to be less vulnerable to NPM.

New managerialism has provided managers with a central coordinating role, which has included the definition of 'needs' of customers. The new conflict of the welfare state is endogenous, mainly unfolding within organizations of delivery. The politics of this increased tension and conflict relates to power distribution among professionals, managers and politicians. As I have argued, politicians are increasingly abdicating their representative function. Professionals, who used to represent their client's interests, because they know better, are increasingly sidelined by managers. As a way to increase control on their staff, managers claim a central role in defining their customer's needs.

For managerialism is an instrumental logic (Laval, 2007), its rationale is to instil flexibility and an entrepreneurial spirit into welfare bureaucracies. The modern welfare service state should be the entrepreneurial state, or so it is claimed. As the empirical mapping of the phenomenon has suggested, the enterprise formula has a clear relevance at the system level, for it has spread across different sectors, in public schools and hospitals, and different countries. On the one hand, it has been a contested process which has generated resistance, as the case of schools in France and Italy has shown. On the other, the 'enterprise' has been a rather attractive alternative to the bureaucratic–professional compromise, typical of welfare organizations. The discourse is based on 'liberating' managers and users from the bureaucracy. In France and Italy, where the administrative tradition is different to Britain, the enterprise formula has been associated with the weakening of the public authority tradition of the state and the transformation into a 'public service' culture (Page, 1992). As Lise Demailly and Olivier Dembinski (2002) have perceptively argued, the new emerging actor of the entrepreneurial welfare state is the organization *per se*, oriented towards economic efficiency and measurable results. The bureaucratic and professional compromise, typical of state education (Mintzberg, 1990), is being supplanted by the organizational logic.

The entrepreneurial welfare state is not a universal phenomenon transforming welfare bureaucracies in a one-dimensional direction, along a clear developmental pattern. Forces of continuity are also at work. Chapters 3 and 4 have presented the stories of change in hospitals and schools, mapping the spread of managerialism at the level of the individual organization, but also the bureaucratic and professional resistance against the new models. Overall, the greatest difficulties in implementing convergence on Anglo-Saxon managerialism were found in French schools and hospitals, where representation of needs through institutional mechanisms is still predominant over active and direct public engagement and participation. France is the most diverging system from the homogenization process described in Chapter 5. It is widely accepted that what the French perceive as most menacing in globalization is the forces at work to move France towards an Anglo-Saxon model (Berger, 2006: 288). Managerialism in France has been to the advantage not of users, but of intermediate levels of government, such as the rectorates, and generally the meso level of the administrative system. The client-based accountability model has been weak in France, in comparison to Britain. I leave it to the reader to decide whether this represents a democratic deficit of French schools and hospitals or the resilience of 'old' political accountability and democratic governance. In the next subsection, I will argue that schools overall score better than hospitals on public accountability, on the basis of an analysis of their internal governance system and the trade-off between efficiency and representation.

## Representative versus efficient decision making

Similar reform trajectories cut across both education and health care, such as strengthening the role of managers of welfare delivery institutions and bridging the gap between managerial and professional accountability by harnessing the latter to the former. In both schools and hospitals, managerialism has been adopted not only at a symbolic level, but by transforming the internal organizational structures and power relationship between the various governance institutions, mainly strengthening efficient decision making over representative bodies. A new stratum of public managers has emerged in the European welfare administration. They are located at the centre of a web of accountability relationships, as suggested in Chapter 5.

However, one key difference between schools and hospitals emerged from the empirical findings. It concerns the role of governing bodies as (1) new instruments of political accountability and representation and (2) tools for making 'autonomy' effective at the level of the individual welfare institutions by isolating management structures from direct political interference from central government. These dual goals, namely providing a democratic control of management structure and strengthening autonomy and efficiency of welfare provision, are intrinsically conflicting. As far as the first role is concerned, namely the representation of public interest, chapters 3 and 4 suggest that the new types of users' engagement have not produced the intended results, at least as far as their impact on the decision-making process is concerned. Where this 'new' type of political accountability has gone furthest, in Britain, apathy and indifference are reported (Klein, 2004; Robinson, 2002). What is most worrying is the self-election of governors, who are frequently invited to stand for elections by managers. Table 6.1 summarizes the dual role of governing boards as it applies to schools and hospitals.

There is a longer tradition of parents' engagement in public schools and responsiveness to local communities than is the case for patients

*Table 6.1*   Trade-off between representation and efficiency in governing boards

| Role of governing Boards | Schools | Hospitals |
|---|---|---|
| Representation of interests | Strong parents and users engagement. Their role is highly institutionalized in internal bodies and committees. | Patients' groups and users are marginal actors in internal decision-making bodies. |
| Efficient decision making | Large collegial and consultative bodies are influential governance structures. Concentration of power of head teachers is fully balanced by strong mechanisms of representation of needs. | Strong executive functions concentrated in small management team. Directors of hospitals are often autocratic and powerful actors, defining needs. |

in public hospitals. Across sectors, the representative role is still more effective in schools than in hospitals. Management by committees and collegial coordination of activities have been more institutionally embedded in schooling than in hospital care. In public hospitals overall, governing bodies have fulfilled the second role better than in schools, namely to serve as institutional buffers between hierarchical and centralized controls and the hospital's management team. Therefore hospitals perform 'better', as far as internal autonomy is concerned, and schools conversely score higher in relation to public accountability.

In order to explain this key cross-sectoral fundamental difference in the policy outcome of similar reform trajectories, as they hit the organizational systems of hospitals and schools, one could claim that the nature of the service provided is totally different. Teaching a pupil how to derive the square root of a number is intrinsically different to prescribing antibiotics for an infection. More precisely, one could argue that the technical expertise provided by the medical profession produces a greater power asymmetry between doctors and patients than is the case between teachers and parents. Therefore, governors of public schools are more likely to provide an input to the decision making about the organization of teaching and classes scheduled, whereas members of supervisory boards of hospitals are likely to have more difficulties in dealing with technical issues. Accordingly, governing bodies of schools function properly in terms of the input that governors can make to the decision-making process. They are more capable, if not willing, to represent the demands of lay people and users. This argument is persuasive insofar as it explains why schools and hospitals score differently in terms of effective representation of needs within their governance structures.

I maintained in Chapter 5 that structural capacity, namely an endogenous factor of these organizations, is a key variable to explain the different outcome of governing bodies in schools and hospitals. The latter have, generally, great financial and organizational resources to create and sustain governing bodies which serve as institutional buffer in protecting the institution from external political interference and strengthening organizational autonomy. Many public hospitals operate across different territorial areas of responsibilities and they are intercommunal and regional, diluting the veto power of any single level of government (Mattei, 2004). Public schools are small, in terms of public resources they use, and internally less specialized than hospitals. Their structural capacity is thus more limited, so that governing bodies cannot serve adequately as buffer to external influences. The permeability of schools' governing bodies to political pressure remains high. This explains why hospitals score better and schools worse on organizational autonomy, but the situation is reversed on the dimension of political accountability.

Drawing a balance between managerial and political accountability, I argued that representation, which is the underpinning criteria of traditional political accountability, is still the basis of educational governance, unlike hospital care. As discussed in Chapter 2, one of the main differences between schools and hospitals as organizations of welfare service delivery is the method of decision making and coordination, chiefly collegial for the former and hierarchal for the latter. Traditionally, the function of management committees, councils and governing bodies in schools has been to represent the interests of teachers, pupils, parents and the local authorities in a collegial way, by means of negotiation, bargaining and debating. The relationship between different actors within schools has not been entirely based on hierarchal methods of coordination. Collegiality is a facilitating condition for the representation of demands and interests.

In sum, the cross-sectoral difference concerning the function and effectiveness of governing bodies suggests that different organizational traits are important in determining the relationship between managerial and democratic accountability. The structural capacity of hospitals enhances their realization of autonomy, but schools' predominant method of internal coordination by collegiality ensures their high score in terms of political accountability. This book shows that the relationship between managerial and political accountability is indeed determined by the endogenous conditions at the level of individual welfare institutions, and not only by contextual system variables.

## The representation of citizens' needs in trouble

The managerial regime in social policy is transforming the democratic foundations of the welfare state. This is the core argument of the book. Managerialism operates *through* the existing social, political and administrative system of welfare services. For this reason, Chapter 1 has set out the expectations concerning the challenge of the new managerial restructuring of welfare bureaucracies to representative democracy. As I argued in Chapter 1, the welfare state is not only a response to social needs, but also the outcome of an institutional developmental process embedded in the political institutions of Western European democracies. As such, it continues to pose peculiar challenges and pressures to existing institutions and administrative arrangements of the state, especially under the new managerial accountability regime.

How do politicians respond overall? As I have concluded in Chapter 5, managerialism of social policy has enabled politicians to divest themselves of responsibility for the provision of welfare services. I have indicated how the role of elected officials on supervisory boards of public hospitals and schools does not necessarily respond to a representative function, but rather to a patronage use of organizational resources. The real indicator for effective political accountability, thus, is not whether politicians are present in the upper echelons of organizations or not, but what conflicts they are interested in.[2] As the empirical chapters of the book have suggested, traditional political methods of control are still used by politicians, such as appointment of heads of hospitals divisions or head teachers. However, political control is a different question than democratic accountability (McCubbins et al., 1987). As managerialism has evolved, the essential link between the citizens and elected (national or local) officials has severed. Citizens are less able to hold their representatives to account for welfare service delivery, which is increasingly rendered faceless by being confined to the anonymous force of technical expertise and technocracy.

What is problematic about the managerial revolution as applied to social policy is the assumption that the client's demand, not the citizen's need, is the 'voice' to be heard (Leys, 2001; Pollock, 2004). Nowhere better than in Britain the reforms of welfare delivery arrangements have been marked by the claim of direct participation of the public and local citizens to the internal governance structures of hospitals and schools. Supervisory boards have been enlarged to include local members of the lay public, in the hope to increase 'local ownership' and citizens' engagement in the decision-making process of welfare bureaucracies. However, chapters 3 and 4 have emphasized the problematic outcome of these experimentations, including self-selection of representatives and often the invitation to stand for election on the supervisory boards by managers. Parents on school boards have also lamented the difficulties in negotiating with the head teacher in relation to staff hiring, for instance. More empirical research is needed in the future to assess the performance of the 'new' types of 'outward' accountability, as far as representation of needs is concerned, but the first evaluations are not encouraging.

Among the various reasons for the disappointing experiments of new types of public accountability, based on direct participation of users, the assumption of equal resources and power of representatives on governing boards is most worrying. It is not clear how managerialism and the new governance arrangements improve 'outward' accountability under conditions of existing and continuing inequality of information between actors. Whether the new mechanisms of local ownership increase accountability depends on the capacities of citizens to exercise their power. As Lukes (2004) argues, political rights depend on supplying the preconditions for core citizenship by enabling citizens to acquire and maintain the capacities needed for its equal exercise.

People who are ill are concerned the least about organizational models. Their first hope is to return home as soon as possible, healthy and restored in their strength and opportunity to continue their daily life. The second most important preference is to have a voice and to be able to decide as much as possible upon the choice of therapies. Not only patients but also their families are frequently involved in very difficult choices. Why should they have a voice in the first place, one may ask? Would it be not sufficient to be admitted to a public hospital and receive medical attention? Is not a hospital like any other enterprise, namely a production centre delivering commodities to its users? What is the difference between a 'client' and a citizen who is suffering from sickness and poverty?

The significance of managerialism for the welfare state is not only the managerial challenge to the existing power structure. It does not stop at the power struggle between managers on the one hand and doctors and teachers on the other.[3] The conflict between managerialism and professionalism, as emerged from the cases of hospital and school reforms, is only one subset of a wider cluster of processes associated with new managerial restructuring of the welfare state. As I argued in Chapter 5, managerialism in social policy is the most worrying and potentially unravelling change for other reasons than diminishing power of professionals. Already in the 1960s and 1970s, technicism and professional expertise of professionals had started to replace bureaucratic methods of delivery. However, the new challenge that managerialism poses to the welfare state in the twenty-first century is more profound and destabilizing because it is accompanied by the weakening of instruments of citizens' democratic controls of institutions. The evidence presented in this book indicates that the public interest is represented on school governing bodies and hospitals' boards in a contestable way. It is likely that inequalities of resources between actors are reproduced in these bodies, rather than resolved.

Although this book does not come under the field of normative political theory, it offers comparative insights into the value system underpinning managerialism. Representative democracy, thus, sits uneasily with both the discourse of managerial views of consumerism, with the professionals' definition of clients and with direct participation mechanisms of citizens' engagement. Although managerialism is composed of various discourses, and different strands, its effect on the welfare state is to question the normative systems upon which universal provision of public services is based in a social democratic consensus. The intellectual home of managerialism is the 'corporate' and business world, whereby managers are flexible and free to manage. Managers are claimed to be more modern and flexible than professionals and politicians, and as such they are elevated to guardians of users' demands. Chapter 5 has argued that the emphasis of new types of accountability on responsiveness and consultation effectively undermines the traditional role of local politicians. The old structure of representative democracy is replaced by more personalized responsiveness to clients.

The managerial model of 'responsiveness' differs profoundly from the traditional one of electoral politics, based on the notion of 'representation' in a liberal democracy. Participation has traditionally been via the electoral process, through which citizens exercise their political right to elect individuals to represent their interests and needs (Dahl, 1989). The 'new politics' of the welfare state (Pierson, 1996) not only brings party competition towards centrist positions (Pierson, 2001), but it goes much further than this. I maintain that the new politics of the welfare state praises non-partisanship, the technical, and the politically neutral 'responsiveness' to clients. It is not surprising that new types of public accountability are contested in France and Italy, where elected politicians play a larger role in the governance structures of welfare provision than in Britain. In France, the new model of client-based participation is still at an embryonic stage. Representative democracy is the predominant method of giving voice to citizens. However, the entrepreneurial formula and its commercial values create a great threat to the old notions of solidarity and 'old' representation of needs. Given any model of democracy, citizens need to know roughly how decisions are taken. Publicity is a fundamental element of the socialization of political conflict and democratic governance (Schattschneider, 1975). Any meaningful accountability model of democracy in the welfare state should entail that citizens know how policies are produced and whether politicians are effectively representing their social needs so that social rights can be exercised (Titmuss, 1958).

There is no reason to be alarmed because pressures on the welfare state have never had cataclysmic effects, at least in the short term.

Organizational regimes are stabilizing factors and the new forms of accountability mix, as identified in Chapter 2, are the product of long adjustment processes, not a burst of policy episodes. Organizations are independent collective actors with their own internal governance rules. Perhaps, managerialism may be reverted by governments. As I argued in Chapter 5 though, convergence is not through hybridization but rather hegemonic dominance of one model, the managerial and entrepreneurial one, over the bureaucratic and professional compromise, which was at the basis of the welfare state. Thus, reversal to old accountability regimes is quite unrealistic. Moreover, we are not simply dealing with policy change, but transformational forces of the structural and administrative terrain of welfare politics. Managerialism has been a rather consistent trend in the last 30 years. The problem is that in most places where it has been adopted, it has broken the link between input and output, by exclusively focusing on the latter. And once the link is broken it is hard to restore it, though not impossible.

## The future challenges for social administration

The welfare state is under pressure from a transformational force which is distinct from marketization and privatization, the most studied challenges in the social policy debate. The new threat is the silent managerial revolution substantiated by the enterprise formula, which has been transferred from the reforms of the civil service to the welfare state. The ideas, instruments and reform patterns associated with managerialism in social policy do not originate from the design of programmes, but are part of the wider package of the administrative modernization of the state. As such, policy change in specific programmes is not the most suitable indicator of the institutional change of welfare bureaucracies. Given the focus of the research agenda on governance, primarily intended as the blurring division between public and private spheres, managerialism in health care and education, the core sectors of the welfare state (Marshall, 1950) have remained under-researched. Moreover, the lack of visible effects of managerialism on public expenditure has not made it an attractive topic of welfare state studies. The empirical findings of this book have clearly established that managerialism is an empirically prominent phenomenon in most different sectors of social policy such as public schooling and hospital care, and in different European political and administrative systems, including Britain, Germany, France and Italy. Managerialism is also the most consistent reform trajectories in the last two decades, in contrast with other market-type mechanisms, which have shifted continually without clearly identifiable patterns of change.

The risk that managerialism poses to the welfare state through the transformations of its administrative deep-seated arrangements, as far as service delivery is concerned, is directly proportionate to how much we downplay its significance for the transformations of the welfare state. This is a very powerful paradigm associated with specific reform programmes. The alternative to its non-adoption is claimed to be the non-sustainability of welfare services provided by the state. Despite the implications of managerialism for the welfare state, it has received scarce attention from social policy scholars, only to be dismissed as a technical matter. It is clearly much more than this. The introduction of quasi-market mechanisms, the development of contract relationships between government agencies and service providers, public expenditure cutbacks, to mention just a few reform strategies, have received much more scholarly attention in understanding the welfare state in the era of permanent austerity. These reforms have visible distributional effects, whereas managerialism has hidden costs.

This book has studied the effects of managerialism on social policy change through the lens of institutionalism in organizational theory, emphasizing the new organizational settlement of the welfare state at the meso and micro level of analysis. Managerialism is clearly not reducible to a policy fashion, or simply to a paradigm (Hall, 1993). It is a pragmatic alternative to retrenchment and, as such, it is a reform strategy based on pragmatic instruments of institutional change pertaining to accountability regimes in the welfare state administration. It is not a result of fortuitous and contextual circumstances, but a deliberate strategy of reforms to improve organizational legitimacy (Powell and DiMaggio, 1983). Managerialism is adopted in most different social policy areas and countries by mimetic processes of isomorphism, rather than evidence-based indicators of efficiency gains.

Paradoxically, management as a reform strategy is not a technical subject matter. Rather, it entails new configurations of power distribution between welfare actors and deep institutional change. The effects of reforms associated with managerialism in social policy are related to two dimensions of welfare state bureaucracies, an internal and an external ones. As far as the internal dimension of change is concerned, managerialism has caused a reconfiguration of power relationships between actors in schools and hospitals, including politicians, managers, professionals and users. Overall, the winners of the managerial silent revolution are not users, but instead directors of schools and hospitals. Managerial accountability has been elevated to the predominant normative framework of welfare provision, and has severely challenged democratic controls, despite the efforts to foster outward accountability to users. A new collective actor has also gained unprecedented centrality in social policy, namely the 'organisation' *per se*, independently from external system variables. As far as the external dimension of the institutional change caused by managerialism is concerned, the fundamental structures of political accountability are resilient in Germany, France and Italy, whereas they are changing dramatically in Britain.

Regarding the managerial dimension of social policy change, I argue that convergence is a sufficiently prominent phenomenon to revisit the mainstream argument about the characteristically Anglo-American scope of the phenomenon. The level of adoption of managerialism is still more enthusiastic in Britain, but this is not a sufficiently strong claim to dismiss the thesis of convergence. The direction of change in which most different systems are moving is the same. Even in those institutional contexts where political accountability operates according to conventional formal mechanisms, mainly through elected representatives sitting in supervisory boards of large hospitals and schools, managers are accountable for matters which are decided by themselves and not by politicians after a process of political negotiation. Although formal accountability arrangements remain stable within and outside organizations, managers are accountable for self-originated responsibilities. This distortive accountability finds its source of authority in the substantive content of the relationship between managers and politicians, with the latter alienated by the language, techniques and instruments of management sciences and gurus. This has been made possible by the fundamentally instrumental logic of managerialism, and the deliberately hidden nature of this new conflict for the welfare state.

The political neutrality of managerialism and suchlike reforms is a rhetorical instrument to conceal the deep-seated institutional transformation of European welfare states. As Paul Pierson (1994) argues, resilience is the result of avoiding the unpopularity and high political costs of visible retrenchment. Social policy change in this book follows exactly the reverse dynamics: welfare state restructuring is the result of the popularity of policy instruments which have low political costs and hidden consequences. Political elites prefer to elevate managerial accountability to the best pragmatic solution to the financial unsustainability of the welfare state. Rather than creating hostility among welfare recipients and electoral clienteles, politicians propose solutions which are apparently 'neutral', legitimized by values of 'modernity' and efficiency (Scharpf, 1999). By so doing, politicians divest themselves of their primary role of representing citizens' needs and offering a voice to citizens, not clients. Managerialism of social policy has the potential to leave citizens without meaningful democratic control of welfare institutions. Can the problem of voiceless citizens be effectively counterweighted by faceless bureaucrats, whose public accountability is determined by their own norms? Public accountability is becoming increasingly internalized, losing its most fundamental democratic character, namely its external dimension.

Whether the welfare state is resilient or not depends on where we look for change and whether we accept 'silence' as a resourceful and deliberate reform strategy. The evidence of an internally induced restructuring of welfare bureaucracies in Europe does not leave much scope to escape the empirical reality of convergence of a predominant model of welfare service provision, which reconfigures the welfare state as an 'enterprise' and citizens as its clients. It remains to be seen in future years how European citizens will respond to this transformational force, if their voice will be heard. Popular sovereignty is at the heart of democracy and 'choice' is not real until the public participates in the decision-making process in a meaningful way. The resilience of the welfare state is increasingly complicated in its core services by the transformational force of managerial accountabilities and by its effects on the relationship between the state and its citizens. The future of the welfare state is linked to the structures of democracy, but whether they will march to the same tune remains an open question.

# Appendix

## List of Interviews

Alan Lane, Birmingham, UK.
Aldo Taroni, Bologna, Italy.
Alis Oancea, Oxford, UK.
Anne Wheatley, Oxford, UK.
Bärbel Jäschke-Werthmann, Berlin, Germany.
Catherine Ryan, Oxford, UK.
Christiane Wenner, Cologne, Germany.
David Nägler, Berlin, Germany.
Detlef Ganten, Berlin, Germany.
Enrico Rossi, Florence, Italy.
Ferdinand Rau, Bonn, Germany.
Fiona Caldicott, Oxford, UK.
Franz Knieps, Berlin, Germany.
Gerard Banner, Cologne, Germany.
Jill Judson, Oxford, UK.
Lutz Fritsche, Berlin, Germany.
Lutz Leisering, Bielefeld, Germany.
Maria Pia Marconi, Rome, Italy.
Marian Döhler, Potsdam, Germany.
Nicola Falcitelli, Rome, Italy.
Philip Kraeger, Oxford, UK.
Renato Botti, Milan, Italy.
Rolf Zettl, Berlin, Germany.
Rosy Bindi, Rome, Italy.
Shanon Moore, Birmingham, UK.
Werner Jann, Potsdam, Germany.

# Notes

## Introduction

1. Hood (1991) defines NPM as 'a shorthand name for the set of broadly similar administrative doctrines which dominated the bureaucratic reform agenda in many OECD countries from the late 1970s. 'Entrepreneurial state' refers to the doctrinal component of NPM linked to stress on private-sector styles of management practice, exemplified by greater flexibility in hiring and rewards, discretionary control of organizations from named persons at the top 'free to manage'. The prescriptions of NPM, as articulated in *Reinventing Government* by Osborne and Gaebler (1992), include: the separation of the purchaser role of public services from the provider role; the growth of contractual or semi-contractual arrangements; accountability for performance; flexibility of pay and conditions; the separation of the political process from the management process; the creation of internal markets or quasi-markets; an emphasis on the public as customer; the reconsideration of the regulatory role of the state; and a change in the general intellectual climate.
2. In his *Administrative Behaviour*, Herbert Simon (1945: 272) provides the following definition of efficiency: 'the concept of efficiency allows us to identify among different alternatives, the option which can produce the maximum outcome in light of a given amount of resources'.

## 1 The New Administrative Settlement of the Welfare State

1. The assumption of the *solidarité sociale* can be traced back to the French Revolution. The more advanced social legislation dates back to the Third Republic and the *Bloc de Gauche*, whose values were social harmony and protection. These values were concurrently part of the French democracy. The French republicans saw a direct link between social harmony and democracy.
2. The 'reinventing government' debate in the United States (Osborne and Gaebler 1992) has several notions in common with NPM, a loose term referring to the recent paradigm change in how the public sector is to be governed.
3. Territorial State, Rule of Law, Democratic State, Intervention State (TRUDI) is the acronym indicative of a conceptual mapping of the modern nation state as unfolding on four interlocking dimensions: the resource, the legal, the legitimacy and welfare dimension (Leibfried and Zürn, 2005). In the 1960s and 1970s, during the golden age of the state, the four functions constitutive of the four dimensions all merged at the nation state level, where the Territorial state, the Rule of Law, the Democratic state and the Intervention state were combined in one. Within this conceptual framework, the organizational change is defined on the 'horizontal' axis, and comprises a shift of the

state capacity to act in terms of the public–private divide (Rothgang, Obinger and Leibfried, 2006: 251).

4.  One of the major pressures leading to the 'state withdrawal', arguably, has been the ideological shift in the 1980s from the macroeconomic paradigm of Keynesianism and full employment to monetarism and neoliberalism. The ideological shift has been from *dirigisme* to market-driven politics (Leys, 2001). The market has been inherently seen as more efficient than the state.

5.  For a discussion of the conditions which must hold for quasi-markets to be successful, see Bartlett and Le Grand (1993). One important condition has been to put in place a market structure by splitting the insurance/third-party payer function from the provision and management of services and making providers compete for contracts.

6.  As discussed in more detail in Christensen, Laegreid and Wise (2002: 154), the *transformative* perspective assumes that administrative and political leaders operate under unique conditions that may facilitate or limit the extent to which they are able to pursue an active administrative policy. Thus, rather than using the comparative method to identify universal principles that transcend national cases, they employ the transformative approach to increase understanding of how shared administrative reform policies are transformed by case-specific contextual factors. The transformative approach perspective draws heavily on the broad institutional approach by March and Olsen, but it is refined by its application to comparative public administration.

7.  The classic welfare state typology was formulated by Esping Andersen in 1990. First, the 'liberal regime' is based on need, and social welfare is selective and aimed at providing a minimal safety net. This model is represented by Britain. Secondly, the 'conservative type' is based on social insurance schemes, and benefits are tied to employment. This model is found in Germany and France. Thirdly, the 'social democratic regime', represented by Scandinavian welfare states, is based on tax-financed and citizenship-based public income transfer and social services schemes. Leibfried also develops a fourth category, which is the 'Latin rim' type, exemplified by Italy and other Southern European countries (Leibfried, 1994).

8.  Interviews were semi-structured. They were audio taped whenever feasible. I have transcribed each interview to increase validity and accurate coding during the analysis. Moreover, for the case of Germany I have also used member checking as a method of validity. Some of the transcripts were shown to respondents to check whether their views were being reported accurately. Interviews lasted from 60 to 90 minutes on average. However, with some key policymakers they lasted more than two hours. Thus, the data generated from interviews was very rich. I conducted all interviews myself, in English, German and Italian. I offered the respondents their favourite language. Only in one of the interviews the respondent found it difficult to talk openly and was extremely defensive.

9.  Hospitals and schools were chosen for interviews both in Britain and Germany as to maximize variance in relation to the adoption of new managerial ideas and systems. Initial interviews with actors involved in the policymaking process at the macro level, as well as the assessment of legislation, helped the author to identify cases of extreme managerialism and 'negative cases', where adoption was slow or absent. In federal systems, like Germany, the case

selection of schools and hospitals reflects the different vulnerability of states to managerialism. In Germany, not only the case of Berlin was analysed, for this represents an extreme case of managerial ideas, given the financial pressure on Berlin's government, but also the cases of Hamburg and Cologne, in relation to hospital restructuring were studied. The educational legislation in Bavaria for instance was also analysed, as a case in which reformers have been less enthusiastic about managerialism. Likewise, in Britain and Italy case selection has maximized variance, including cases in which traditional structures were deemed to be resilient. Generally, the method of selection was not based on sampling, or 'representative' or 'typical' cases. The process of selection unfolded from the snowball effect of initial interviews, where the author was directed towards 'critical' cases of significance for the specific questions addressed in the book.

# 3  Enduring Managerialism in the Internal Governance of Public Hospitals

1. *Griffiths Report, NHS Management Inquiry,* 1983, Department of Health and Social Security, London.
2. *De la réforme de la gouvernance hospitaliere,* 2007, (*Ministère de la Santé*) Ministry of Health, Paris.
3. The logic behind the internal market is to separate strategy, planning and purchasing functions from execution, administration and provision. The internal market transforms the public integrated health care system in three ways: granting hospitals autonomy from local health authorities' planning and management; introducing contractualism and competitive tendering, which are practices outside public law; and mobilizing private providers. With respect to the first aspect, an important precondition for the successful implementation of the internal market was to correct the distorting collusion between local health authorities and their public hospitals, which usually receive cross subsidies. However, health care authorities usually lack the capacity to exert leverage against providers' dominance in negotiating service agreements (Zanetta and Casalegno 1999).
4. The NHS Community Care Act, 1990, established that the District Health Authorities (DHAs) became purchasers of the services provided by NHS Trusts and that their relationships are governed by 'contracts'. The contracts set out what services the Trusts would provide and how much the DHAs would pay.
5. Department of Health, *A Guide to NHS Foundations Trusts* (DOH, 2002).
6. The reserved places are as follows: one governor representing local NHS Primary Care Trusts; one governor representing local authorities in the area; three governors representing staff; a Chair; and one governor appointed from the local university, where applicable.
7. Thus, the regulator's power to make the Foundation Trusts accountable is significant, though this is different than traditional political accountability. Yet Foundation Trusts score lower to expected with respect to autonomy, when the contents of authorizations are considered. The more detailed and intrusive the standards contained in the licence, the less autonomy Foundation Trusts have in practice. The licence of Monitor identifies those services that

each Foundation Trust is obliged to provide and in what quantities (these are called regulated services). This provision is necessary to avoid distortive behaviours by which some trusts would stop providing non-profitable services. Emergency services are a clear instance of regulated services. The regulator, in deciding which services are 'regulated' and which are not, has the power to curtail the Foundation Trust's autonomy to change the services it was providing when it was granted Trust status. Thus, the degree of autonomy will depend on how authorizations are detailed and what is included and excluded from regulated services. What matters is that potentially Monitor has significant powers to curtail Trusts' autonomy, introducing another mechanism of accountability, noticeably of a non-political type.

8. Schedule 1, paragraph 15(2), 2003 *Health Care Act*, DOH, London.
9. Translation from French into English by the author.
10. Ordinance no. 406, 2 May 2005, *Dispositions relatives à la reforme des règles d'organisation et de fonctionnement des établissements publics de santé.*
11. *La situation des comptes sociaux en 2001*, Cour des Comptes, Paris.
12. Ordinance no. 406, 2 May 2005, Ministry of Health, Paris.
13. Circulaire no. 61, 13 February 2004, Ministry of Health, Paris.
14. Circulaire no. 61, 13 February 2004, Ministry of Health, Paris, regarding the implementation of the new hospital governance (*Modalités d'anticipation de la nouvelle gouvernance dans les établissements publics de santé autres que les hôpitaux locaux*).
15. *Code de la Santé Public*, Article L. 6143-6-1 CSP.
16. For the reforms of department into *poles d'activites*, see the dossier prepared by the DHOS entitled *De la reforme de la gouvernance hospitalierer*, January 2007.
17. The creation in 1996 of the regional hospital agencies (*Agences Régionales de l'Hospitalization–ARH*) was designed to allow for a decentralization of hospital services (Bouget, 1998). It has been argued that the setting up of these agencies was illustrative of NPM '*à la francaise*'. The regional agency has become the major actor for hospital planning, but is a local administrative extension of the central state. The process has been a classic case of administrative decentralization with little democratization, since ARHs are accountable upwards to the Minister. The ARH is responsible for the planning and financing of the whole hospital sector within its region. The 1996 decision to adopt administrative decentralization as part of the NPM has reduced the influence of regional elected officials, making the decision-making process less democratic (Minvielle, 1997: 761). It operates with hospitals on the basis of contracts on objectives and resources over the next five years.
18. Public hospitals in Germany account for approximately 38 per cent of the total number of hospitals and slightly over 50 per cent of the total number of beds (Statistisches Bundesamt, 2006). However, in 2006 the number of public hospitals having their legal form under private law was 51.2 per cent, in contrast with 28.3 per cent in 2002 (Statistisches Bundesamt, 2006).
19. At the time of writing, the German Ministry of Health is strengthening competition in Statutory Health Care.
20. The German model of health care organization is based on the Bismarckian social insurance scheme. There is a multi-payer system based on approximately 250 sickness funds remunerating care providers within a legal

framework, and primarily on a fee-for-service basis (Bode, 2006; Busse and Riesberg, 2004).

21. Sickness funds were governed by representatives of the insured, often trade unions, and of employers' associations.
22. *Zukunftsorientierte Verwaltung durch Innovationen*, Bundesministerium des Innern, 13 September 2006.
23. *Das Krankenhaus als Gesundheitszentrum: Leistungsangebot und Managementaufgaben*, in Das Krankenhaus Umschau, 10: 5, 1997, pp 2–8.
24. *Ergebnisse der Krankenhausplanung in der Zeit von 1990 bis 2004 in Berlin*, Senatsverwaltung für Gesundheit, Soziales und Verbraucherschutz, 2005. This document provides detailed information concerning the main achievements of hospital planning after the reunification, which includes 47 per cent reduction in hospital beds in ten years (from 43,000 to 23,000), and increasing costs since 1999.
25. The author interviewed him in Cologne on 18 December 2006.
26. LBK was handed over by the neoliberal government to the private group Asklepios in 2005.
27. LBK was a consortium of eight public hospitals. It had 7,000 beds. It employed 13,500 people and provided approximately 50 per cent of all hospital beds in Hamburg.
28. *Verordnung über die Satzung für den LBK Hamburg-Anstalt öffentlichen Rechts*, Hamburgisches Gesetz-und Verordungsblatt, 20 December 2004.
29. Interviews at Charité were conducted by the author during November and December 2006.
30. *Charité at a Glance*, Press Office, 2006.
31. Letter to Berlin's mayor concerning the restructuring of the Charité, unpublished document. The *Vorstand* calls for greater autonomy and entrepreneurial freedoms: 'nur in wirtschaftlicher Eigenverantwortung der universitärer Autonomie sowie unternehmerischer Freiheit kann die *Charité* die von ihr erwartete erfüllen'.
32. Interview, 12 December 2006.
33. *Berliner Universitatsmedizingesetz,* in Gesetz und Verordungsblatt für Berlin, no. 42, 15 December 2005. Article 12 establishes the responsibilities of the *Vorstand*, the management board and Article 10 of the *Aufsichtsrat*, the supervisory board.
34. In the supervisory board of the Charité a problem of dual leadership has been reported. The current situation has improved, but there has always been a latent competition between the Finance and Cultural Ministers. Surprisingly, the Minister for Health and Social Affairs is not a member. When the new law setting out the reorganization of the Charité was enacted in 2004, some concerns emerged about the dual leadership problem, but it remained unresolved.
35. *Berliner Universitaetsmedizingesetz*, December 2005.
36. Interview, 12 December 2006.
37. Interview with author, 13 December 2006.
38. *Berliner Markenzeichen*, Der Tagesspiegel, 19 November 2006.
39. Difficulties and poor administrative performance emerged immediately after the creation of the National Health Care Service in 1978. The 1978 reform was a response to the clientelistic system of health care of the 1960s and

1970s, based on 100 health care funds with huge indebtedness. See Mapelli (1999). Law no. 833 of 1978 offers universal access and democratic participation to all citizens. The reform is also the expression of the participatory culture supported by the unions and the Communist Party at the time. The law was passed by the National Solidarity Coalition which included Communists in the government for the first time. The creation of the national health care system was concurrent with regional reforms. Yet law no. 833 was not clear about the division of responsibilities between different levels of government, especially between municipal and regional ones.

40. F. De Lorenzo in *La Stampa*, 19 October 1992.
41. Executive board responsibilities include general policy guidelines, approval of the budget, oversight of administrative activities and division of local health care authorities in districts (law no. 111 and law no. 412 of 1991).
42. An executive board of five members appointed by the local councils was included in the delegating bill proposed by the government. The Senate maintained this provision. But in the final draft of Executive Decree no. 502/1992 presented to the parliamentary committees the executive board was abolished and the *direttore generale* remained the only decision-making authority of the local health care authorities.
43. The phrase 'privatisation of public-sector employment contracts' is used in the context of Italian administrative reforms to indicate the change of jurisdiction from public to civil law. This includes the possibility of having fixed-term contracts, or dismissing staff more easily or measuring results and performance.
44. Article 2 of the delegating law no. 421, 23 October 1992, is devoted entirely to the reform of public sector employment and civil service. It is stated that the purpose of the reform of public employment is to 'increase the efficiency of the administration to European standards, rationalise staff costs, and slowly integrate public and private law'. This reform is not as radical as the health care reform. There is no explicit reference to the possibility of using fixed-term contracts for other sectors, or flexibility in hiring, or performance-related pay. Access to all managerial positions remains firmly anchored in public competition. The health care reform seems to go further with regard to the highest level of medical managerial positions. Article 15 of the legislative decree regulates the functions and access to managerial positions for medical staff. Managerial levels are reduced from three to two, dropping the position of 'assistant doctors'. The highest-level doctors are appointed on the basis of a curriculum vitae and an interview by a committee chaired by the director general of the local health care authority. Unlike all the senior positions in other sectors, for this highest category of doctors the access is not through public competition.
45. Private sector contracts are regulated by the Civil Code, Volume V, Title II, Part 1, sections II and III.
46. The incompatibility is between the method of appointment, by an administrative act, and the employment contract regulated by private law. Since the appointment occurs through an administrative act, the content of the contract cannot be agreed between the two parties, as it would be in the private sector. The content of any contract for which an appointment is made is

decided by a ministerial administrative act, upon the proposal of the Minister of Health. See: Papadia (1993).
47. Interview with author, Rome.
48. Interview with author, Varese.
49. Interview with author, Rome.
50. Mr Bertoli, DC, Constitutional Affairs Committee Meeting, Lower Chamber, 25 September 1992.
51. Article 3 sections 6 and 9 and Article 4 section 1 of Executive Decree no. 502/1992.
52. Article 3 section 10 of Executive Decree no. 502/1992.
53. Antonio Tomassini, interview with author, Rome.
54. Article 3 section 1 of Executive Decree no. 502/1992. The Italian term is *azienda con personalità giuridica*, literally 'firm with juridical personality'. According to public law, a public body can only exist as an autonomous firm with respect to its economic and financial autonomy, not with respect to its juridical autonomy. Thus, a public firm is constrained by the principles of legality of acts, impartiality and good administration.
55. Article 6 of law no. 111/1991 anticipated the change established by Executive Decree no. 502/1992.
56. Article 32 of the Italian constitution: 'The Republic safeguards health as a basic right of the individual and as an interest of the community, and grants free medical assistance to the indigent'.

# 4 Patterns of Convergence in Educational Accountability in State Schools in Europe

1. The relatively ungenerous investment in public education in England has changed in recent years, due to an increase in public funding. According to OECD indicators, the UK has the highest percentage of GDP expenditure on educational institutions (excluding tertiary education), which amounts to 4.58 per cent of GDP (OECD Education at a Glance 2007, Indicator B6.1). The annual expenditure on educational institutions per student for all services in the UK is only second to France, respectively 7,290 US Dollar, and 8,653 (OECD, 2007).
2. In their classic work on European social policy and Europeanization, Leibfried and Pierson (1995) take a broad view of social policy, including education, focusing on policies which serve as mechanisms to modify market outcomes.
3. It is worth noting that the PISA survey and aggregated data include private schools.
4. By 'central' here I do not refer necessarily to the national level of government, but also to the state level of the Land in Germany.
5. From January to April 2007, a visiting fellowship at Somerville College, Oxford University, has offered to support the interview of head teachers and governors.
6. Interview with Cherwell head teacher, Oxford, April 2007.
7. Audit Commission, 1993, *Adding up the Sums: Schools' Management of their Finances*.

8.  In this chapter the main concern is not with the discussion of teaching and learning in secondary schools, but with the governance structures of autonomous schools and the changing balance between local schools' autonomy and local control by the LEAs. Consequently, issues of pedagogical autonomy will remain subordinate to the main focus on institutional autonomy and new governance structures established by the 2005 White Paper *Higher Standards, Better Schools for All*.
9.  'Blair Sweeps Aside Critics of School Reform', *Guardian*, 25 October 2005.
10. DfES, *Five-Year Strategy for Children and Learners*, Cm 6272, July 2004.
11. There were other important areas of policy developments, such as increasing diversity and choice in the provision of education, the greater participation of parents and pupils in improving standards of schools, the individualization of education tailored to individual needs, new measures to tackle failure and underperformance of schools and better discipline. In this section, I focus on the creation of Trust schools as new organizational arrangements emphasizing autonomy of schools and freedoms from the control of local educational authorities, rather than on what happens in schools and classrooms.
12. Ruth Kelly, Secretary of State for Education, House of Commons Debate, cols. 169 to 172, 25 October 2005.
13. DfES, *Five-Year Strategy for Children and Learners*, 2004.
14. 2005 *White Paper*, Chapter 2, Paragraph 2.16.
15. 2005 *White Paper*, Chapter 2, Paragraph 2.10 to 2.12.
16. Circulaire du 26 Juillet 1995.
17. Décret no. 85-924, 30 August 1985, created the EPLE. Law no. 2005-380, 23 April 2005, strengthened their autonomy and decentralization of secondary education.
18. *Bayerisches Gesetz über das Erziehungs- und Unterrichtswesen in der Fassung der Bekanntmachung*, Bayerisches Staatministerium für Unterricht und Kultus, 31 May 2000.
19. Ibid., Article 57, Schulleiterin oder Schulleiter.
20. *Modellprojekt Selbstverantwortung plus*, Teilprojekt 3: Organisationsstruktur, Hessisches Kultusministerium, 2005.
21. *Verordnung zur Durchführung des Modellvorhabens Selbständige Schule*, Ministerium für Schule, Jugend und Kinder des Landes Nordrhein-Westfalen, 12 April 2002; *Gesetz zur Weiterentwicklung von Schulen*, 27 November 2001.
22. For an overview of the main projects and activities of the Land Nordrhein Westfalen, see *'Projekt Selbständige Schule und andere Projekt-Aktivitäten'*, Ministerium für Schule, Jugend und Kinder des Landes Nordrhein-Westfalen, 23 October 2003.
23. *Schulgesetz für das Land Berlin*, 26 January 2004, GVBl. S. 26.
24. Secondary schools are of three types in Germany, as outlined in the 1959 *Rahmenplan* (Outline Plan): *Gymnasium* (grammar school), *Realschule* (intermediate school) and *Hauptschule* (main secondary school). This system is based on serving respectively three psychological and mental categories of pupils: the academic and theoretical, the technical and the practical. In comparison to other European systems, the German system is based on selection after two years of orientation and diagnosis of the students' ability

(*Orientierungstufe*). The Gymnasium is the most prestigious type and has a long and distinguished tradition dating from the days of Humboldt. Pupils of the *Realschule* would expect to become technicians, middle managers in industry, commerce and administration. This type has also its foundations in the nineteenth-century tradition and it was created to meet the needs of industry, commerce and the service sectors. The major aim of the *Hauptschule* is to prepare students for a period of qualified vocational education either in full-time education or in the 'Dual System' of education and training (Ertl and Phillips, 2000).

25. Luigi Berlinguer, 'Un'Anno di Svolta', in *Annali della Pubblica Istruzione*, 1 June 1997.
26. The Charter for the Service of Education was adopted by the Dini Government in 1995. It is one of the series of public service charters. The inspiration behind this initiative is the British model of the Citizens' Charter, 1991.
27. Decentralization of state administration is a broad phenomenon that involves most policy areas. Law no. 59, the Bassanini Law, named after the Minister of Public Service under the Prodi Government, gives authority to the government to decentralize powers to the regions and local administration. Education was also affected by these changes.
28. Bill No. 779, '*Riforma dell'amministrazione scolastica*', 17 November 1992.
29. Parlamento Italiano, VII Commissione Cultura, approved 15 December 2002.
30. Despite the characterization of the German system as a 'decentralised' one, in Archer's typology, the German Länder are extremely centralizing bureaucracies.
31. Corriere della Sera (2007), '*Italie: la gestion des établissement scolaires*', 27 November. See also: '*Ne foudrait-il pas éliminer les conseils des parents?*' (30 November 2007). The Corriere della Sera reported that parents' participation to governing bodies in secondary schools in Italy dropped dramatically from 60 per cent in 1975 to 15.9 per cent in 1985, and further to 10 per cent in 2006.

# 5   Towards the Managerial Welfare State: The Mechanism of a Silent Revolution

1. Sociological institutionalism in the late 1970s in the United States focused less on individual organizations and more on population of organizations. Institutional sociologists like DiMaggio studied what they defined as organizational 'fields' (DiMaggio and Powell, 1983). Such fields are formed by bodies ranging from public institutions (hospitals, schools, etc) to professional activities (doctors, teachers). The field in which a public system is embedded is studied as a whole, as an activity making rules, supervising and surveying. It defines an institutional context within which each single organization plots its courses of action. This book has adopted the same definition of field.

## 6   European Welfare States and Democracy: Marching to the Same Tune?

1. The definitive and constitutive element of political accountability in the book remained firmly anchored in the electoral process of accountability to democratic institutions, especially to elected representatives.
2. The different political use that politicians make of the organizational resources offered by schools and hospitals poses in turn different challenges to managers. On the one hand, in hospitals tensions and conflicts between the governance structures are frequent and the relationship between the supervisory boards and the management team may be conflictual. Managers of hospitals interviewed identified in political influence a major constraint to their operational autonomy. Interference takes the form of traditional means of political control, such as appointment of posts in the hospitals, including managers of medical divisions or the medical director of the management team. The direct interface between manager and politicians is much reduced and indirect in the case of schools' directors. Politicians do not represent a serious constraint to their decision-making process and internal running of schools.
3. This book has been mainly concerned with the effects of managerialism on politicians, but I have also touched upon the relationships between managerial and professional accountability. The findings presented in chapters 3 and 4 suggesting that it is not entirely accurate to identify professionals as the absolute losers of new managerialism (Clarke et al., 1994; 2000). A study of the internal governance of welfare institutions indicates how the relationship between managerial and professional accountability depends on the creation of new structural management arrangements for doctors and teachers. In France, Germany and Italy it was decided from the initial stage of reforms that professionals could not be isolated from the process of institutional change and it was not advisable to leave them outside the management frame of the new autonomous hospital enterprises. As analysed in Chapter 3, medical directors are part of the management team in German public hospitals and likewise all the heads of divisions of French hospitals are also members of the management team. Equally in Italy a new management structure was set up in hospitals in order to allow doctors to have an input in the decision-making process (Mattei, 2007b). Therefore, the widely claimed rivalry between managers and professionals should be also reappraised in comparative terms, contrasting Britain with the other continental European countries.

# Bibliography

Adams, J. and Kirst, M. (1999), 'New Demands and Concepts for Educational Accountability', in J. Murphy and K. Louis (eds), *Handbook of Research on Educational Administration* (San Francisco: Jossey-Bass), 463–89.

Allison, G. and Zelikon P. I. (1999), *Essence of Decision: Explaining the Cuban Missile Crisis*, 2nd ed. New York: Longman.

Allmendinger, J. and Leibfried, Stephan (2003), 'Education and Social Policy. The Four Worlds of Competence Production', *Journal of European Social Policy*, 13 (1), 63–81.

Altenstetter, C. and Busse, Reinhard (2005), 'Health Care Reform in Germany: Patchwork Change Within Established Governance Structures', *Journal of Health Politics, Policy and Law*, 30 (1–2), 121–42.

Ambler, J. (1985), 'Neo-Corporatism and the Politics of French Education', *West European Politics*, 8 (3), 23–42.

Anderson, Lesley (2001), 'A "Third Way" Towards Self-governing Schools?: New Labour and Opting Out', *British Journal of Educational Studies*, 49 (1), 56–70.

Archer, M. (1979), *Social Origins of Educational Systems* (London: SAGE).

Ashford, D. A. (1986), 'Structural Analysis and Institutional Change', *Polity*, 19 (1), 97–122.

——. (1986), *The Emergence of the Welfare States* (Oxford: Blackwell).

Assemblée Nationale (2003), *Les projets de loi de financement de la sécurité sociale*, Paris: Assemblée Nationale.

Aucoin, P. (1990), 'Administrative Reform in Public Management: Paradigms, Principles, Paradoxes and Pendulums', *Governance*, 3 (2), 115–37.

Audit Commission (1993), *Adding up the Sums: Schools' Management of Their Finances* (London: Audit Commission).

——. (2007), *Foundation Trust Accounts: A Guide for Non-Executives and Governors*, London: Audit Commission.

Bach, S. (1993), 'Health Care Reforms in the French Hospital System', *International Journal of Health Planning and Management*, 8, 189–200.

Backhaus-Maul, H. and Olk, T. (1994), 'Von Subsidiarität zum "outcontracting": Zum Wandel der Beziehungen von Staat und Wohlfahrtsverbänden in der Sozialpolitik', in Wolfgang Streeck (ed.), *Staat und Verbände* (Opladen).

Bacon, W. (1978), *Public Accountability and the Schooling System* (London: Harper & Row).

Balduzzi, R. and Di Gaspare, G. (2002), *Sanità e Assistenza dopo la Riforma del Titolo V* (Milano: Giuffrè Editore).

Baldwin, R. and Cave, M. (1999), *Understanding Regulation: Theory, State, and Practice* (Oxford: Oxford University Press).

Bandelow, N. and Hassenteufel, P. (2006), 'Mehrheitsdemokratische Politikblockaden und verhandlungsdemokratischer Reformeifer: Akteure und Interessen in der französischen und deutschen Gesundheitspolitik', *Koelner Zeitschrift für Soziologie*, 46, 320–42.

Banner, G. (2001), 'Kommunale Verwaltungsmodernisierung: Wie erfolgreich waren die letzten zehn Jahre?', in E Schröter (ed.), *Empirische Policy- und Ver-waltungsforschung: Lokale, nationale und internationale Perspektiven* (Opladen).
——. (2005), 'Aktivierend auch nach innen? Verwaltungsreformen zwischen Ländern und Kommunen', in F. Behrens, et al. (eds), *Modernisierung des Öffentlichen Sektors* (Berlin: Edition Sigma), 163–85.
Barzelay, M. (1992), *Breaking through Bureaucracy: A New Vision for Managing in Government*, Berkeley: University of California Press.
——. (2001), *The New Public Management* (Berkeley: University of California Press).
——. (eds) (2002), *Policy Dynamics* (Chicago: The University of Chicago Press).
Bayerisches Staatministerium für Unterricht und Kultus *(2000)*, *Bayerisches Gesetz über das Erziehungs- und Unterrichtswesen in der Fassung der Bekanntmachung* (Munchen: Bayerisches Staatministerium für Unterricht und Kultus).
Becher, T. Eraut, M. and Knight, J. (1981), *Policies for Educational Accountability* (London: Heinemann Educational).
Beck, U. (1992), *Risk Society: Towards a New Modernity* (London Sage).
Bennett, S. (1974), The School: An Organisational Analysis (Glasgow: Blackie).
Berger, S. (2006), 'Representation in Trouble', in P. Culpepper, Peter Hall, and B. Palier (eds), *Changing France. The Politics that Markets Make* (Basingstoke: Palgrave Macmillan), 276–92.
Bergman, T., Muller W., and K. Strom K. (2006), *Democratic Delegation and Accountability: Cross-National Patterns*, Oxford: Oxford University Press.
*Berliner Universitaetsmedizingesetz (2005)*, Gesetz und Verordungsblatt für Berlin, no. 42, 15 Dezember.
Besley, T. and Machin, S. (2006), 'Are Public Sector CEOs Different? Leadership Wages and Performance in School', (London: LSE), available at http://sticerd. lse.ac.uk/eopp/_new/research/public_sector_ceos.asp
Bevan, G. and Cornwell, J. (2006), 'Structure and Logic of Regulation and Governance of Quality of Health Care: Was OFSTED a Model for the Commission for Health Improvement?', *Health Economics, Policy and Law*, 1, 343–70.
Bevan, G. and Hood C. (2005), "Governance by Targets: Proportionality, Transparency, and Audit", In *Playing the Targets Game*, Oxford.
Blanchet, R. Wiener, C. and Isambert, J. (1999), *La revalorisation du role des chefs d'établissement de l'enseignement secondaire* (Paris: Ministère de l'Education Nationale).
Bode, Ingo (2006), 'Fair Funding and Competitive Governance. The German Model of Health Care Organisation Under Debate', *Revue francaise des affaires sociales*, 2 (3), 183–206.
Boedege, W. and Schellberg, K. (2005), *Organisationen der Sozialwirtschaft* (Baden-Baden: Nomos).
Boeri, T. Boersch-Supan A. and G. Tabellini (2001), 'Would You Like to Shrink the Welfare State? A Survey of European Citizens', *Economic Policy*, 32, 7–50.
Bogumil, J, Jann, W. and Nullmeier, F. (eds) (2006), *Politik und Verwaltung* (Wiesbaden: Vs Verlag für Sozialwissenschaften).
Bonoli, G., George, V., and Taylor-Gooby, P. (2000), *European Welfare States* (Cambridge: Polity Press).
Borgonovi, Elio (1988), *L'azienda sanità* (Milano: Franco Angeli).

Bottani, N. (2002), *Insegnanti Al Timone? Fatti E Parole Dell'autonomia Scolastica*, Bologna: Il Mulino.

Bouget, D. (1998), 'The Juppé Plan and the Future of the French Social Welfare System', *Journal of European Social Policy*, 8 (2), 155–72.

Bovens, M. (1998), *The Quest for Responsibility: Accountability and Citizenship in Complex Organisations* (Cambridge: Cambridge University Press).

——. (2006), 'Analysing and Assessing Public Accountability. A Conceptual Framework', *European Governance Papers (EUROGOV)*, No. C-06-01.

Brachetta, M. (2002), *Sulla riforma della scuola: per una scuola libera* (Roma: Armando).

Broadfoot, Patricia, et al. (1985), 'Changing Patterns of Education Accountability in England and France', *Comparative Education*, 21 (3), 273–86.

Brocca, B. (ed.) (1995), *Il futuro della scuola: idee e proposte per l'istruzione secondaria superiore* (Roma: Laterza).

Brocca, B. and Frabboni, F. (2004), *Dialogo sulla riforma della scuola* (Roma: Laterza).

Brodkin, Evelyn (1997), 'Inside the Welfare Contract: Discretion and Accountability in State Welfare Administration', *Social Service Review*, 1–33.

Buller, Jim and Flinders, Matthew (2005), 'The Domestic Origins of Depoliticisation in the Area of British Economic Policy', *British Journal of Political and International Relations*, 7 (4), 526–43.

Bundesministerium des Innern (2006) *Zukunftsorientierte Verwaltung durch Innovationen* (Berlin: Bundesministerium des Innern).

Bundesministerium für Gesundheit (1993), *Gesundheitsstrukturgesetz* (Bonn: Bundesministerium für Gesundheit).

——. (1998), *Act to Strengthen Solidarity in Statutory Health Insurance* (Bonn: Bundesministerium für Gesundheit).

——. (2007), *Gesetz zur Stärkung des Wettbewerbs in der Gesetzlichen Krankenversicherung* (GKV-Wettbewerbsstärkungsgesetz – GKV-WSG) (Berlin: Bundesministerium für Gesundheit).

Burnham, Peter (2001), 'New Labour and the Politics of Depoliticisation', *British Journal of Political and International Relations*, 3 (2), 127–49.

Busse, R. and Riesberg A. (2004), *Health Care Systems in Transition: Germany*, Copenhagen: European Observatory on Health Care Systems and Policies.

Caldwell, B. and Jim Spinks (1992), *Leading the Self-Managing School*, (London: The Falmer Press).

Callaghan, R. (1962), *Education and the Cult of Efficiency* (Chicago: University of Chicago Press).

Capano, G. (1992), *L'improbabile riforma. Le politiche di riforma amministrativa nell'Italia repubblicana* (Bologna: Il Mulino).

——. (2003), 'Higher Education Policy in Italy (1992–97): From Centralisation to Autonomy?', in R. Leonardi and M. Fedele (eds), *Italy: Politics and Policy* (Aldershot: Ashgate).

Carta dei Servizi della Scuola, Ministero della Funzione Pubblica, 1996.

Cassese, S. (2001), "La Storia e I Caratteri Dello Stato", In *Ritratto Dell'Italia* (ed.) by S. Cassese, Roma: Laterza.

Castles, F. Gerritsen, G., and Jack, R. (eds) (1996), *The Great Experiment: Labour Parties and Public Policy Transformation in Australia and New Zealand* (Sidney: Allen and Unwin).

Castles, F. (2005), 'Social Expenditure in the 1990s: Data and Determinants', *Policy and Politics*, 33 (3), 411–30.

——. (2004), *The Future of the Welfare State. Crisis, Myths and Crisis Realities* (Oxford: Oxford University Press).

Cavalli, A. and Ferratini P. (2003), "Scuola, Il Cambiamento da Condividere", *Il Mulino* 1, 108–18.

——. (2001a), 'New Public Management. The Effects of Contractualism and Devolution on Political Control', *Public Management Review*, 3 (1), 73–94.

——. (eds) (2001b), *New Public Management. The Transformation of Ideas and Practice* (London: Ashgate).

Christensen, Tom, Laegreid, Per, and Wise, Lois R. (2002), 'Transforming Administrative Policy', *Public Administration*, 80 (1), 153–78.

Chubb, J. E. and Moe, T. M. (1990), *Politics, Markets and America's Schools* (Washington, D.C.: The Brookings Institution).

Cipolla, C. and Giarelli, G. (eds) (2002), *Dopo l'aziendalizzazione. Nuove strategie di governance in sanità* (Milano: FrancoAngeli).

Clarke, John, Cochrane, Allan, and McLaughlin, Eugene (eds) (1994), *Managing Social Policy* (London: SAGE).

Clarke, John, Gewirtz, Sharon, and McLaughling, Eugene (eds) (2000), *New Managerialism. New Welfare?* (London: SAGE).

Clasen, J. (2005), *Reforming European Welfare States. Germany and the UK Compared* (Oxford: Oxford University Press).

Cole, Alistair (1997), 'Governing the Academies: Sub-Central Secondary Education Policy Making in France', *West European Politics*, 20 (2), 137–56.

——. (2001), 'The New Governance of French Education?', *Public Administration*, 79 (3), 707–24.

Cole, Alistair and Peter, John (2001), 'Governing Education in England and France', *Public Policy and Administration*, 16 (4), 106–25.

Cole, Alistair and Jones, G. (2005), 'Reshaping the State: Administrative Reform and New Public Management in France', *Governance*, 18 (4), 567–88.

*Corriere della Sera* (2007), 'Italie: la gestion des établissement scolaires', 27 November.

——. (2007) 'Ne foudrait-il pas éliminer les conseils des parents?', 30 November.

Cour des Comptes (2001), *La situation des comptes sociaux en 2001* (Paris: Cour des Comptes).

Cremadez, M. (1991), 'Gestion de l'hopital: le prix de la responsabilité', *Revue francaise de gestion*, September, 63–72.

Crozier, Michel (1964), *The Bureaucratic Phenomenon* (New York: Tavistock Publications).

——. (1970), *La Société Bloquée* (Paris: Editions du Seuil).

Dahl, David (1989), *Democracy and Its Critics* (New Heaven: Yale University Press).

Dale, R. (1980), *The State and Education* (Milton Keynes: Open University Press).

——. (1989), *The State and Education Policy* (London: Open University Press).

Das Krankenhaus (1997), 'Leistungsorientierte Fuehrungsstruckturen aus der Sicht des Krankenhausmanagements- Gib es "moderne" Fuehrungsstrukturen?' 12, 745–53.

Das Krankenhaus (1997), 'Das Krankenhaus als Gesundheitszentrum: Leistungsangebot und Managementaufgaben', 10 (5), 2–8.

Davies, Anne (2001), *Accountability: A Public Law Analysis of Government by Contract* (Oxford: Oxford University Press).

——. (2004), 'Foundation Hospitals: A New Approach to Accountability and Autonomy in the Delivery of Public Services', *Public Law*, Winter, 808–28.

Davies, L. (1990), *Equity and Efficiency? School Management in an International Context* (Lewes: Falmer Press).

Day, P. and Klein, Rudolph (1987), *Accountabilities* (London: Tavistock Publications).

Demailly, Lise (1993), 'L'evolution actuelle des methodes de mobilisation et d'encadrement des enseignants', *Savoir*, 5 (1), 24–46.

Demailly, Lise and Dembinski, O. (2002), 'La reorganisation manageriale à l'Ecole et à l'Hopital', *Education et Societes*, 6 (2), 43–64.

Dent, Mike, et al. (2004), 'Archetype Transition in the German Health Service? The Attempted Modernisation of Hospitals in a North German State', *Public Administration*, 82 (3), 727–42.

Dent, Mike (2005), 'Post-New Public Management in Public Sector Hospitals? The UK, Germany and Italy', *Policy & Politics*, 33 (4), 623–36.

Department of Education (1988), *Educational Reform Act* (London: Department for Education).

Department for Education and Skills (1998) *School Standards and Framework Act* (London: Department for Education).

——. *Higher Standards, Better Schools for All* (London: DfES).

——. (2004), *Five Year Strategy for Children and Learners* (London: DfES).

——. (2007), *A Guide to the Law for School Governors* (London: Department for Education and Skills).

Department for Health (DOH) (2000), *The NHS Plan: A Plan for Investment, a Plan for Reform* (London: Stationery Office).

——. (2001), *Shifting the Balance of Power Within the NHS: Securing Delivery* (London: Department of Health).

——. (2002), *A Guide to NHS Foundation Trusts* (London: Department of Health).

——. (2003), *Health and Social Care Act*, London: Department of Health.

——. (2006), *NHS Foundation Trusts: A Sourcebook for Developing Governance Arrangements* (London: DoH).

*Department of Health and Social Care (Community Health and Standards) Act* (2003), UK Parliament (London: HMSO).

Department of Health and Social Security (1983), *NHS Management Inquiry: Report to the Secretary of State for Social Services* (London: Department of Health and Social Security).

de Pouvourville, G. (1986), 'Hospital Reforms in France Under Socialist Government', *The Milibank Quarterly*, 64 (3), 392–413.

de Pouvourville, G. and Renaud, M. (1985), 'Hospital System Management in France and Canada: National Pluralism and Provincial Centralism', *Social Science and Medicine*, 20 (2), 153–67.

Desagnat, F. (2005), 'Les élus territoriaux au conseil d'administration', *Education and Management*, 28 (January), 38–9.

Deutsches Krankenhausinstitut (2007), *Krankenhaus Barometer. Umfrage* (Dusseldorf: Deutsches Krankenhausinstitut).

Diamond, J. (1993), 'The Experiences of Parent Governors', *Local Government Policy Making*, 19 (5), 21–4.

Diller, Matthew (2000), 'The Revolution in Welfare Administration: Rules, Discretion, and Entrepreneurial Government', *New York University Law Review*, 75 (5), 1121–220.

DiMaggio, Paul J. and Powell, Walter W. (1983), 'The Iron Cage Revisited: Institutional Isomorphism and Collective Rationality in Organisational Fields', *American Sociological Review*, 48 (2), 147–60.

Dixon, A. and Mossialos, E. (eds) (2002), *Health Care Systems in Eight Countries: Trends and Challenges* (London: European Observatory on Health Systems).

Döhler, M. (1995), 'The State as Architect of Political Order: Policy Dynamics in German Health Care', *Governance*, 8 (3), 380–404.

——. (1997), *Die Regulierung von Professionsgrenzen: Struktur und Entwicklungsdynamik von Gesundheitsberufen im internationalen Vergleich* (Frankfurt am Main: Campus Verlag).

Dorf, Michael and Sabel, Charles (1998), 'A Constitution of Democratic Experimentalism', *Columbia Law Review*, 98 (2), 267–473.

Dunleavy, P. (1991), *Democracy, Bureaucracy and Public Choice: Economic Explanations in Political Science* (New York: Wheatsheaf).

Dunsire, A., Hood, C., and Huby, M. (1989), *Cutback Management in Public Bureaucracies. Popular Theories and Observed Outcomes in Whitehall* (Cambridge: Cambridge University Press).

Dutercq, Y. (2007), 'Du management dans l'education', *Le management dans l'education* (18: Nouveaux regards).

Egeberg, M. (1999), "The Impact of Bureaucratic Structure on Policy Making", *Public Administration* 77, 155–70.

——. (2003), 'How Bureaucratic Structure Matters: An Organisational Perspective', in Guy Peters and J. Pierre (eds), *Handbook of Public Administration* (London: SAGE), 116–25.

Eisenstadt, S. N. and Roniger, L. (1984), *Patrons, Clients and Friends: Interpersonal Relations and the Structure of Trust in Society* (Cambridge: CUP).

Endrici, G. (2001), "Le Nomine Tra Giunta e Consiglio", *Rivista, Affari Istituzionali, Emilia Romagna* 1.

Ertl, Hubert and Phillips, David (2000), 'The Enduring Nature of the Tripartite System in Secondary Schooling in Germany: Some Explanations', *British Journal of Educational Studies*, 48 (4), 391–412.

Esping-Andersen, G. and Korpi, W. (1984). 'Social Policy as Class Politics in Postwar Capitalism' in J. Goldthorpe (ed.) *Order and Conflict in Contemporary Capitalism*. Oxford: Oxford University Press.

Esping-Andersen, Gosta (1990), *The Three Worlds of Welfare Capitalism* (Cambridge, UK: Polity Press).

——. (1999), *Social Foundations of Postindustrial Economies* (Oxford: Oxford University Press).

European Observatory on Health Care Systems (2000), '*Health Care Systems in Transition: Germany*' (Copenhagen: European Observatory on Health Care Systems).

——. (2001), *Health Care Systems in Transitions: Italy* (Copenhagen: European Observatory on Health Care Systems).

Eurydice (2005), 'Key Data on Education in Europe 2005' (Brussels: European Commission).

——. (2005), 'Key Data on Education in Europe 2005' (Brussels: Eurostat).

——. (2007), 'School Autonomy in Europe. Policies and Measures' (Brussels: Eurydice).

Fergusson, R. (1994), 'Managerialism in Education', in J. Clarke, A. Cochrane, and E. McLaughlin (eds), *Managing Social Policy* (London: Sage).

Ferlie, E. (1996) (ed.), *The New Public Management in Action*, Oxford: Oxford University Press.

Ferratini, P. (2002), "La Riforma Berlinguer-Moratti", *Il Mulino* 2, 259–69.

Ferrera, Maurizio (1989), "The Politics of Health Reformism: Origins and Performance of the Italian Health Service in Comparative Perspective", In *Controlling the Medical Professionals. The Comparative Politics of Health Governance* (ed.) by G. Freddi and James Warner Bjorkman, London: Sage.

——. (1995), 'The Rise and Fall of Democratic Universalism: Health Care Reform in Italy, 1978–94', *Journal of Health Politics, Policy and Law*, 20 (2), 275–302.

——. (1998), *Le Trappole del Welfare* (Bologna: Il Mulino).

Ferroni, G. (1997), *La scuola sospesa: istruzione, cultura e illusioni della riforma* (Torino: Einaudi).

Finer, H. (1941), 'Administrative Responsibility in Democratic Government', *Public Administration Review*, 1 (4), 335–50.

Fitz, John, Halpin, David, and Power, Sally (1997), "Between a Rock and a Hard Place': Diversity, Institutional Identity and Grant-Maintained Schools', *Oxford Review of Education*, 23 (1), 17–30.

Fixari, D. and Kletz, F. (1996), 'Pilotage d'etablissement scolaire: auto-évaluation et évaluation', *Politiques et Management Public*, 14 (2), 71–103.

Flora, P. and Heidenheimer, A. (1982), *The Development of Welfare States in Europe and America* (London: Transactions Books).

Flynn, N. and Strehl, F. (eds) (1996), *Public Sector Management in Europe* (London: Prentice Hall).

Foster, Christopher D. and Plowden, Francis J. (1996), *The State Under Stress* (Philadelphia: Open University Press).

Freddi, G. and Bjorkman J. W. (1989) (eds), *Controlling Medical Professionals: The Comparative Politics of Health Governance*, London: Sage.

Garrett, J. (1998), *Partisan Politics in the Global Economy* (Cambridge: Cambridge University Press).

Ginsborg, Paul (2001), *Italy and its Discontents 1980–2001: Civil Society, State* (London: Allen Lane).

Glennerster, Howard (1975), *Social Service Budgets and Social Policy: British and American Experiences* (London: Allen and Unwin).

Glennerster, Howard and Midgley, J. (eds) (1991), *The Radical Right and the Welfare State* (James Bennett Pty Ltd).

Glennerster, Howard (2000), *British Social Policy since 1945* (Oxford: Blackwell).

Goodin, R. and Dryzek J. (1986), "Risk-Sharing and Social Justice: The Motivational Foundations of the Post-War Welfare State", *British Journal of Political Science* 16, 1–34.

Goulder, A. W. (1954), *Patterns of Industrial Bureaucracy* (New York: Free Press).

Grace, Gerald (1993), 'On the Study of School Leadership: Beyond Education Management', *British Journal of Educational Studies*, 41 (4), 353–65.

Gray, Andrew and Jenkins, Bill (2003), 'Professions and Bureaucracy', in Baldock, Manning, and Vickerstoff (eds), *Social Policy* (Oxford: Oxford University Press).

Green, A. (1990), *Education and State Formation* (Basingstoke: Macmillan).

Green-Pedersen, C. (2002), 'New Public Management Reforms of the Danish and Swedish Welfare States: The Role of Different Social Democratic Responses', *Governance*, 15 (2), 271–94.

Grunow, D (1995), 'Zwischen Solidaritaet und Burokratie: Organisationsprobleme von Wohlfahrtsverbaenden', in T. Rauschenbach and T. Christoph (eds), *Von der Wertgemeinschaft zum Dienstleistungsunternehmen. Jugend und Wohlfahrtsverbaende im Umbruch* (Frankfurt: Suhrkamp), 253–79.

Hacker, J. (2002), *The Divided Welfare State: The Battle Over Public and Private Social Benefits in the United States* (Cambridge: Cambridge University Press).

——. (2004), *Privitizing Risk without Privitizing the Welfafre State: The Hidden Politics of Social Policy*, Cambridge: Cambridge University Press.

Hall, Peter (1993), 'Policy Paradigms, Social Learning, and the State: The Case of Economic Policymaking in Britain', *Comparative Politics*, 25, 275–96.

Halligan, J. (1997), 'New Public Sector Models: Reform in Australia and New Zealand', in J. E. Lane (ed.), *Public Sector Reform: Rationale, Trends, and Problems* (London: Sage), 17–46.

Halsey, J. (1993), 'The Impact of Local Management on School Management Style', *Local Government Policy Making*, 19 (5), 49–56.

Hammersley, M. (2000), 'The Relevance of Qualitative Research', *Oxford Review of Education*, 26, 393–405.

Handy, C. (1986), *Understanding Schools as Organisations* (London: Penguin Books).

Harding, A. and Preker, A. (1998), *Innovations in Health Care Delivery: Organisational Reforms Within the Public Sector* (Washington, D.C.: World Bank).

Harlow, Carol (2002), *Accountability in the European Union* (Oxford: Oxford University Press).

Harlow, Carol and Rawlings, Richard (2006), 'Promoting Accountability in Multi-Level Governance: A Network Approach', *European Governance Papers (EUROGOV)*, no. C-06-02.

Hasenfeld, Y. and English, R. (eds) (1974), *Human Service Organisations: A Book of Readings* (Ann Arbor: University of Michigan Press).

Hassenteufel, P. and Palier, B. (2005), 'Les trompe-l'oeil de la "gouvernance" de l'assurance malade', *Revue francaise d'administration publique*, 113, 13–28.

——. (2007), 'Towards Neo-Bismarkian Health Care States? Comparing Health Insurance Reforms in Bismarkian Welfare Systems', *Social Policy and Administration*, 41 (6), 574–96.

Hatzfeld, H. (1991), 'La Décentralisation du Système Educatif: les Régions à l'Epreuve', *Revue Politiques et Management Public*, 9 (4), 23–49.

Hayward, J. (1959), 'Solidarity: The Social History of an Idea in Nineteenth Century France', *International Review of Social History*, 4, 261–84.

——. (1975), *Political Inertia* (Hull: Lowgate Press).

——. (1976), "Institutional Inertia and Political Impetus in France and Britain", *European Journal of Political Research*, no. 4, 341–59.

——. (1998), 'The Normative, Political and Administrative Framework of Coordination', *Governing from the Centre* (Maison Francaise d'Oxford).

Healthcare Financial Management Association (2007), *Foundation Trust Accounts. A Guide for Non-Executives and Governors* (Bristol: Healthcare Financial Management Association).

Heclo, Hugh (1974), *Social Policy in Britain and Sweden* (New Haven: Yale University Press).

Heidenheimer, A. (1993), 'External and Domestic Determinants of Education Expansion: How Germany, Japan, and Switzerland Have Varied', *Governance*, 6 (2), 194–219.

Held, D. and McGrew, A. (2000), *The Global Transformations Reader: An Introduction to the Globalisation Debate* (Malden, MA: Polity Press).

Hennock, E. P. (2007), *The Origin of the Welfare State in England and Germany, 1850–1914*, Cambridge: Cambridge University Press.

Hessisches Kultusministerium (2005), *Modellprojekt Selbstverantwortung plus, Teilprojekt 3: Organisationsstruktur* (Hessen: Hessisches Kultusministerium).

Hine, D. (1993), *Governing Italy. The Politics of Bargained Pluralism*, Oxford: Oxford University Press.

Hirst, P. and Thompson, G. (1996), *Globalisation in Question* (Cambridge: Polity Press).

Holzinger, K. and Knill, C. (2005), 'Causes and Conditions of Cross-National Convergence', *Journal of European Public Policy*, 12 (5), 775–96.

Hood, Christopher (1991), 'A Public Management for All Seasons?', *Public Administration*, 69 (Spring), 3–19.

——. (1995), 'The New Public Management in the 1980s: Variations on a Theme', *Accounting, Organisations and Society*, 20, 93–109.

——. (1998), *The Art of the State. Culture, Rhetoric, and Public Management* (Oxford: Oxford University Press).

Hood, C., James, Oliver, and Scott, Colin (2000), 'Regulation of Government: Has it Increased, Is It Increasing, Should It Be Diminished?', *Public Administration*, 78 (2), 283–304.

Hood, C. (2007), 'What Happens When Transparency Meets Blame-Avoidance?', *Public Management Review*, 9 (2), 192–210.

Hopt, K. (2000), "Gemeinsame Grundsaetze Der Corporate Governance in Europa?" *Zeitschrift fuer Unternehmens-und Gesellschaftsrecht* 29, 779–84.

Huber, E. and Stephens, J. (2001), *Development and Crisis of the Welfare State* (Chicago: University of Chicago Press).

Hurrelmann, A., et al. (eds) (2007), *Transforming the Golden-Age Nation State* (Basingstoke: Palgrave Macmillan).

Immergut, E. M. (1992), *Health Politics, Interest, and Institutions in Western Europe* (Cambridge: Cambridge University Press).

Jann, Werner (2003), 'State, Administration and Governance in Germany: Competing Traditions and Dominant Narratives', *Public Administration*, 81 (1), 95–118.

Jann, Werner and Bogumil, J. (eds) (2004), *Status-Report Verwaltungsreform. Eine Zwischenbilanz nach zehn Jahren, Modernisierung des öffentlichen Sektors* (Berlin: Edition Sigma).

Jann, Werner (2005), 'Modern Governance: A European Perspective', in Geraldine Fraser-Moleketi (ed.), *The World We Could Win* (Amsterdam: IOS Press).

Jessop, B. (1990), *State Theory: Putting the Capitalist State in its Place* (Cambridge: Polity Press).

——. (1998), 'The Rise of Governance and the Risks of Failure: The Case of Economic Development', *International Social Science Journal*, 50 (155), 29–45.

Kaboolian, Linda (1998), 'The New Public Management: Challenging the Boundaries of the Management vs. Administration Debate', *Public Administration Review*, 58 (3), 189–93.

Kampe, D. M. and Kracht, P. J. (1989), *Management im Krankenhaus* (Berlin: De Gruyter Verlag).

Kauffman, F. (2002), *Sozialpolitik und Sozialstaat: Soziologische Analysen* (Opladen: Leske + Budrich).

Keohane, R. and Milner H. (1996) (eds), *Internazionalization and Domestic Politics*, Cambridge: Cambridge University Press.

Kettl, Donald (2000), *The Global Public Management Revolution* (Washington, D.C.: Brookings Institution Press).

KGSt (1993), *'Das Neue Steuerungsmodell. Begrundungen. Konturen. Umsetzungen'* (Cologne: KGSt).

——. (2003), *Selbstaendige Schule.nrw* (Cologne: KGSt).

Kickert, W. (ed.) (1997), *Public Management and Administrative Reform in Western Europe* (Cheltenham: Edward Elgar).

Kitschelt, Herbert (2001), 'Partisan Competition and Welfare State Retrenchment: When Do Politicians Choose Unpopular Policies?', in Paul Pierson (ed.), *The New Politics of the Welfare State* (Oxford: Oxford University Press).

Klein, R. (1982), "Performance, Evaluation and NHS: A Case-Study in Conceptual Perplexity and Organizational Complexity", *Public Administration* 60, no. 4, 385–407.

Klein, Rudolph (2001), *The New Politics of the NHS* (Essex: Prentice Hall).

Klein, Rudolf (2003), 'Mr Milburn's Flawed Model is a Cacophony of Accountabilities', *British Medical Journal*, 326 (25 January), 174–5.

Klein, Rudolph (2004), 'The First Wave of NHS Foundation Trusts', *British Medical Journal*, 328, 1332.

Kooiman, J. (2003), *Governing as Governance* (London: SAGE).

Koretz, D. (2008), *Measuring Up: What Educational Testing Really Tells Us* (Cambridge, MA: Harvard University Press).

Korpi, W. and Palme, J. (2003), 'New Politics and Class Politics in the Context of Austerity and Globalisation: Welfare State Regimes in 18 Countries, 1975–95', *American Political Science Review*, 97 (3), 425–46.

Kuhn, T. (1962), *The Structure of Scientific Revolutions* (Chicago: University of Chicago Press).

Laval, C. (2007), 'Contradictions et faux-semblants', *La management dans l'education* (8: Nouveaux regards).

Le Grand, J. and Bartlett, W. (eds) (1993), *Quasi-Markets and Social Policy* (Basingstoke: Macmillan).

Le Grand, J. Bartlett, W., and Roberts, J. A. (eds) (1998), *A Revolution in Social Policy: Quasi-Market Reforms* (Bristol: Policy Press).

Le Grand, Julian and Robinson, R. (eds) (1984), *Privatisation and the Welfare State* (London: Allen and Unwin).

Legrand, Andre (2005), 'Le rattachement des etablissements publics locaux d'enseignement à une collectivité territoriale et le controle de leurs actes', *Actualite Legislative*, 101 (January), 825–31.

Leibfried, S. (1994), *The Social Dimension of the European Union En Route to Positively Joint Sovereignty?* (ZeS-Arbeitspapier; Bremen).

Leibfried, S. and Pierson, Paul (eds) (1995), *European Social Policy. Between Fragmentation and Integration* (Washington, D.C.: The Brookings Institute).

Leibfried, S. and Zürn, M. (eds) (2005), *Transformations of the State?* (Cambridge: Cambridge University Press).

Leibfried, S. (2005), 'Social Policy', in H Wallace and W Wallace (eds), *Policy-Making in the European Union* (5th edn; Oxford: Oxford University Press).

Leisering, L. and Leibfried, S. (1999), *Time and Poverty in Western Welfare States. United Germany in Perspective* (Cambridge: Cambridge University Press).

Leisering (2007), *Die Kreativität des lokalen Sozialstaats. Die Modernisierung der kommunalen Sozialhilfeverwaltung in Deutschland (1990–2000) und internationale Reformerfahrungen* (Opladen: Leske und Budrich).

Le Point (2008), *Santé: enquete sur les scandales d'un système à about de souffle*, 10 April (Paris: Le Point), 76–86.

Lewis, J. and Glennerster, H. (1996), *Implementing the New Community Care* (Buckingham: Open University Press).

Lewis, J. (2001), *The Management of Non-Governmental Development Organisations* (London: Routledge).

Lewis, Jane, Evers, Adalbert, and Riedel, Birgit (2005), 'Developing Child-Care Provision in England and Germany: Problems of Governance', *Journal of European Social Policy*, 15 (3), 195–209.

Leys, Colin (2001), *Market-Driven Politics* (London: Verso).

Lijphart, Arend (1975), 'The Comparable Cases Strategy in Comparative Research', *Comparative Political Studies*, 8, 158–77.

Lingens, H. (2003) (ed.), *Uniting Europe: Initiatives in Education*, vol. 35, Issues and Studies in European Education.

Lipset, S. M. and Rokkan, S. (1967), *Party Systems and Voter Alignments* (New York: Doubleday).

Lowe, R. (1999), *The Welfare State in Britain since 1945* (2nd edn.; Basingstoke: Macmillan).

Lukes, Stephen (2004), 'Invasions of the Market', in M. R. Dworkin (ed.), *From Liberal Values to Democratic Transition. Essays in Honor of Janos Kis* (Budapest: Central University Press).

Mair, P. (2005), "Democracy Beyond Parties", In *Center for the Study of Democracy*, University of California, Irvine.

Majone, Giandomenico (1996), *Regulating Europe* (London: Routledge).

——. (1998), 'Europe's 'Democratic Deficit': The Question of Standards', *European Law Journal*, 4 (1), 5–28.

Manning, N. and Shaw, I. (eds) (2000), *New Risks, New Welfare* (Oxford: Blackwell).

Manow, Philip (2004), *Federalism and the Welfare State: The German Case* (ZeS-Arbeitspapier; Bremen).

Mapelli, Vittorio (1999), *Il sistema sanitario italiano* (Bologna: Il Mulino).

March, James G. and Simon, Herbert (1958), *Organisations* (New York: Wiley).

March, James G. and Olsen, Johan P. (1984), 'The New Institutionalism: Organisational Factors in Political Life', *The American Political Science Review*, 78 (3), 734–49.

March, James G. (1988), *Decisions and Organisations* (London: Blackwell).

March, James G. and Olsen, Johan P. (1989), *Rediscovering Institutions. The Organisational Basis of Politics* (New York: The Free Press).

Marmor, Theodore (2004), *Fads in Medical Care Management and Policy* (London: The Nuffield Trust).

Marshall, T. H. (1950), *Class, Citizenship and Social Development* (Cambridge: Cambridge University Press).

Martini, A. (2002), "La Scuola Italiana Nei Confronti Internazionali", *Il Mulino* 6, 1133–42.

Mattei, Paola (1999), 'The Impact of New Public Management Ideas on Italian Administrative Reforms in the 1990s', M.Phil. Thesis.

——. (2004), 'The Administrative Framework of Intergovernmental Relations: Italian Regions and Communes after the Health Care Reforms of the 1990s', *Regional and Federal Studies*, 14 (4), 538–53.

——. (2005a), 'Party System Change and Parliamentary Scrutiny of the Executive in Italy', *The Journal of Legislative Studies*, 11 (1), 1–22.

——. (2005b), 'The Modernisation of the Welfare State in Italy: Dynamic Conservatism and Health Care Reforms, 1992 to 2003 ', PhD Thesis. Department of Government, London School of Economics and Political Science.

——. (2006), 'New Public Management and Health Care Reforms', *Public Administration*, 84 (4), 1007–27.

——. (2007a), 'Managerial and Political Accountability: An Anglo-German Comparison of the Transformations of Social Services', *IRAS*, 73 (3).

——. (2007b), 'From Politics to Management? The Transformation of Local Welfare in Italy', *West European Politics*, 30 (3), 595–620.

——. (2007c), *The Welfare State and a New Challenge From the Back Door* (TranState Working Paper; Bremen).

Mayntz, Renate and Streeck, Wolfgang (eds) (2003), *Die Reformierbarkeit der Demokratie. Innovationen und Blockaden* (Frankfurt: Campus).

McCubbins, M., Noll, R., and Weingast, B. (1987), 'Administrative Procedures as Instrument of Political Control', *Journal of Law, Economics and Organisation*, 3 (2), 243–77.

McKee, Martin and Healy, Judith (eds) (2002), *Hospitals in a Changing Europe* (Buckingham: Open University Press).

Melis (1996), *Storia dell'amministrazione italiana, 1861–1993* (Bologna: Il Mulino).

Meny, Y. and Wright, Vincent (eds) (1994), *La riforma amministrativa in Europa* (Bologna: Il Mulino).

Merchel, J. (2003), *Traegerstrukturen in der sozialen Arbeit. Eine Einfuhrung.* (Weinheim: Juventa Verlag).

Metcalfe, L. and Richards, S. (1987), 'Evolving Public Management Cultures', in J. Kooiman and K. Eliassen (eds), *Managing Public Organisations* (London: Sage).

Meyer, John W. and Rowan, Bryan (1977), 'Institutionalized Organizations: Formal Structure as Myth and Ceremony', *The American Journal of Sociology*, 83 (2), 340–63.

Milewa, T., Valentine, J., and Calnan, M. (1998), 'Managerialism and Active Citizenship in Britain's Reformed Health Service: Power and Community in an Era of Decentralisation', *Social Science and Medicine*, 47 (4), 507–17.

Mill, John Stuart (1962), *Representative Government* (London: Everyman's Library).

Ministère de la Santé (2007), *Plan Hospital*, (Paris: Ministère de la Santé).

———. *Projet HOPITAL 2007. Mission sur 'La modernisation des statuts de l'hopital public et de sa gestion sociale'* (Paris: Ministère de la Santé).

———. (2004), *Circulaire* no.61, *Modalités d'anticipation de la nouvelle gouvernance dans les établissements publics de santé autres que les hopitaux locaux* (Paris: Ministère de la Santé).

———. (2005), *Ordinance* no. 406, *Dispositions relatives à la reforme des régles d'organisation et de fonctionnement des établissements publics de santé* (Paris: Ministère de la Santé).

———. (2007), *De la reforme de la gouvernance hospitaliere* (Paris: Ministère de la Santé).

Ministère de l'Education Nationale (2000), *Décentrralisation et projet d'établissement* (Paris: MEN).

———. (2002), *Au niveau de l'établissement scolaire* (Paris: MEN).

———. (2006), *Guide juridique du chef d'établissement* (Paris: MEN).

Ministero della Funzione Pubblica (1996), *Carta dei Servizi della Scuola* (Roma: Ministero della Funzione Pubblica).

Ministerium für Schule, Jugend und Kinder des Landes Nordrhein-Westfalen (2002),*Verordnung zur Durchführung des Modellvorhabens Selbständige Schule* (Cologne: Ministerium für Schule, Jugend und Kinder des Landes Nordrhein-Westfalen).

———. (2001) *Gesetz zur Weiterentwicklung von Schulen.*

———. (2003) *Projekt Selbständige Schule und andere Projekt-Aktivitäten.*

Ministero dell'Istruzione, Università e della Ricerca (2002), *Norme concernenti il governo delle istituzioni scolastiche* (Roma: Ministero dell'Istruzione).

———. (2003), *'Le parole di una scuola che cresce: piccolo dizionario delle riforme'* (Roma: Ministero dell'Istruzione).

Ministero per la Funzione Pubblica (1982), *Rapporto sui principali problemi dell'amministrazione dello Stato* (Roma: Funzione Pubblica).

Mintzberg, H. (1979), *The Structuring of Organisations* (Hemel Hempstead: Prentice Hall).

———. (1990), "The Manager's Job: Folklore and Fact", *Harvard Business Review* 90, no. 2, 163–76.

Minvielle, E. (1997), 'Beyond Quality Management Methods: Meeting the Challenges of Health Care Reform', *International Journal for Quality in Health Care*, 9 (3), 189–92.

Moe, T. (1984), 'The New Economics of Organisation', *American Journal of Political Science*, 28 (4), 739–77.

Monitor (2006), *The NHS Foundation Trust Code of Governance* (London: Monitor).

Moran, M. (1998), 'Explaining the Rise of the Market in Health Care', in Wendy Ranade (ed.), *Markets and Health Care: A Comparative Analysis* (London: Longman).

Mossialos, E. and Julian Le Grand (1999) (eds), *Health Care and Cost Containment in the European Union*, London: Ashgate.

Mossialos, Elias, Saltman, Richard, and Busse, Reinhard (eds) (2002), *Regulating Entrepreneurial Behaviour in European Health Care Systems* (Buckingham: Open University Press).

Mossialos, Elias and Thompson, Sarah (2004), 'Health Care Systems in Transition: France' (European Observatory on Health Systems and Policies).

Mulgan, Richard (2000), '"Accountability": An Ever-Expanding Concept?', *Public Administration*, 78 (3), 555–73.

Murphy, J. and Seashore, K. (eds) (1999), *Handbook of Research on Educational Administration* (San Francisco: Jossey-Bass Publishers).

National Commission on Excellence in Education (1983), '*A Nation at Risk: The Imperative for Educational Reform*' (Washington, D.C.: National Commission on Excellence in Education).

Newman, J. and Kuhlmann, E. (2007), 'Consumers Enter the Political Stage? The Modernisation of Health Care in Britain and Germany', *Journal of European Public Policy*, 17 (2), 99–111.

NHS Community Care Act *(*1990), UK Parliament (London: HMSO).

Obinger, Herbert, Leibfried, Stephan, and Castles, Francis (eds) (2005), *Federalism and the Welfare State. New World and European Experiences* (Cambridge: Cambridge University Press).

OECD (1981), *The Welfare State in Crisis*, Paris: OECD

——. 'Governance in Transition' (Paris: OECD).

——. (1996), 'Globalisation: What Challenges and Opportunities for Governments?' (Paris: OECD).

——. (2001), 'Knowledge and Skills for Life' (Paris: OECD).

——. (2003), 'PISA' (Paris: OECD).

——. (2005), ' Modernising Government and the Way Forward' (Paris: OECD).

——. (2007a), 'PISA 2006: Science Competencies for Tomorrow's World' (Paris: OECD).

——. (2007b), 'Education at a Glance: Indicators' (Paris: OECD).

Olla, Giovanni and Pavan, Aldo (eds) (2000), *Il management nell'azienda sanitaria* (Milano: Giuffré).

Osborne, David E. and Gaebler, Ted (1992), *Reinventing Government: How the Entrepreneurial Spirit is Transforming the Public Sector* (New York: Plume).

Ouchi, William G. (1979), 'A Conceptual Framework for the Design of Organisational Control Mechanisms', *Management Science*, 25 (9), 833–48.

Page, Edward C. (1992), *Political Authority and Bureaucratic Power. A Comparative Analysis* (2nd edn.; Hemel Hempstead: Harvester Wheatsheaf).

Page, Stephen (2006), 'The Web of Managerial Accountability. The Impact of Reinventing Government', *Administration and Society*, 38 (2), 166–97.

Papadia, V. (1993), "Il Nuovo Ordinamento Del Servizio Sanitario Nazionale", *Sanità Pubblica* 6.

Parsons, T. and Smelser N. (1956), *Economy and Society*, New York: Free Press.

Peters, Guy (1992), 'Government Reorganisation: A Theoretical Analysis', *International Political Science Review*, 13 (2), 199–217.

——. (1996), *The Future of Governing: Four Emerging Models* (Kansas: University Press of Kansas).

Peters, T. and Watermann, R. (1982), *In Search of Excellence* (New York: Harper and Row).

Phillips, David (1987), 'Lessons from Germany? The Case of German Secondary Schools', *British Journal of Educational Studies*, 35 (3), 211–32.

Pierre, J. (ed.) (1995), *Bureaucracy in the Modern State: An Introduction to Comparative Public Administration* (Aldershot: Edward Elgar).

Pierre, J. and Peters, Guy (eds) (2001), *Politicians, Bureaucrats and Administrative Reform* (London: Routledge).

Pierru, F. (1999), 'L'hopital-enterprise. Une *self-fulfilling prophecy* avortée', *Politix*, 46, 7–47.

Pierson, Paul (1994), *Dismantling the Welfare State? Reagan, Thatcher, and the Politics of Retrenchment* (Cambridge: Cambridge University Press).

——. (1996), 'The New Politics of the Welfare State', *World Politics*, 48 (2), 143–79.

——. (ed.) (2001), *The New Politics of the Welfare State* (Oxford: Oxford University Press).

Pipan, T. (1995), "Culture Del Servizio Pubblico e Identità", *Rivista di Scienza dell'Amministrazione* 1.

Pollitt, C. et al. (1991), 'General Management in the NHS: The Initial Impact 1983–8', *Public Administration*, 69 (Spring), 61–83.

Pollitt, C., Birchall, J., and Putnam, K. (eds) (1998), *Decentralising Public Service Management* (Basingstoke: Palgrave Macmillan).

Pollitt, C., and Bouckaert, Geert (2000), *Public Management Reform. A Comparative Analysis* (Oxford: Oxford University Press), 314.

Pollitt, C. (2001), 'Convergence: The Useful Myth?', *Public Administration*, 79 (4), 933–47.

——. (2003), *The Essential Public Manager* (Oxford: Oxford University Press).

Pollock, A. (2004), *NHS PLC: The Privatisation of Our Health Care* (London Verso).

Powell, Walter W. and DiMaggio, Paul J. (eds) (1991), *The New Institutionalism in Organisational Analysis* (Chicago: University of Chicago Press).

Power, M. (1997), *The Audit Society: Rituals of Verification*, Oxford: Oxford University Press.

Pugner, K. (2000), 'Hospital Governance in England and Germany in the 1990s',(London: London School of Economics).

Ragin, C. (1987), *The Comparative Method: Moving Beyond Qualitative and Quantitative Strategies* (Berkeley: University of California Press).

Ranade, Wendy (ed.) (1997), *A Future for the NHS? Health Care for the Millennium* (New York: Longman).

——. (ed.) (1998), *Markets and Health Care: A Comparative Analysis* (London: Longman).

Rebora, Gianfranco (1995), *Organizzazione e politica del personale nelle amministrazioni pubbliche* (Milano: Guerini Scientifica).

——. (1999), *Un decennio di riforme: nuovi modelli organizzativi e processi di cambiamento delle amministrazioni pubbliche: (1990–9)* (Milano: Guerini e Associati).

Reichard, C. (1994), *Umdenken im Rathaus. Neue Steuerungsmodelle in der deutschen Kommunalverwaltung. Modernisierung des öffentlichen Sektors* (3; Berlin: Sigma).

——. (1998), 'Der Produktansatz im Neuen Steuerungsmodell – von der Euphorie zur Ernüchterung', in D Grunow and Hellmut Wöllmann (eds), *Lokale Verwaltungsreform in Aktion. Fortschritte und Fallstricke* (Basel).

Rhodes, R. A. W. (1994), 'The Hollowing Out of the State', *Political Quarterly*, 65, 138–51.

——. (1997), *Understanding Governance: Policy Networks, Governance, Reflexivity, and Accountability* (Buckingham: Open University Press).

Rhodes, Martin (1997), 'The Welfare State: Internal Challenges, Institutional Constraints', in Martin Rhodes, Paul Heywood, and Vincent Wright (eds), *Developments in West European Politics* (Basingstoke: Palgrave Macmillan).

Richardson, Jeremy (ed.) (1993), *Pressure Groups* (Oxford: Oxford University Press).

Rieger, E. and Leibfried, Stephan (2003), *Limits to Globalization: Welfare States and the World Economy* (Cambridge: Polity Press).

Robinson, R. (2002), 'NHS Foundation Trusts: Greater Autonomy May Prove illusory', *British Medical Journal*, 325, 506–7.

Robinson, R. (1989), 'Self Governing Hospitals', *British Medical Journal*, 25 March.

Robinson, S. B. and Kuhlman, J. C. (1967), 'Two Decades of Non-Reform in West German Education', *Comparative Education Review*, 11 (3), 311–30.

Robson, Colin (2002), *Real World Research. A Resource for Social Scientists and Practitioner-Researchers* (Oxford: Blackwell).

Romzek, Barbara and Dubnick, M. J. (1987), 'Accountability in the Public Sector: Lessons from the *Challenge* Tragedy', *Public Administration Review*, 47, 227–38.

Romzek, Barbara (1996), 'Enhancing Accountability', in James Perry (ed.), *Handbook of Public Administration* (San Francisco: Jossey-Bass Publishers), 97–114.

Rose, R. and Terence K. (1984), *Inertia or Incrementalism? A Long-Term View of the Growth of Government*, Glasgow: Centre for the Study of Public Policy.

Rubin, Herbert J. and Rubin, Irene S. (1995), *Qualitative Interviewing. The Art of Hearing Data* (London: SAGE Publications).

Ruef, Martin and Scott, Richard (1998), 'A Multidimensional Model of Organisational Legitimacy: Hospital Survival in Changing Institutional Environments', *Administrative Science Quarterly*, 43 (4), 877–904.

Saltman, R., and Figueras, J. (eds) (1997), *European Health Care Reform: Analysis of Current Strategies* (Copenhagen: World Health Organisation).

Saltman, R., Figueras, J., and Sakallarides, C. (eds) (1998), *Critical Challenges for Health Care Reform in Europe* (Philadelphia: Open University Press).

Saltman, R., Busse, Reihnard, and Mossialos, Elias (eds) (2002), *Regulating Entrepreneurial Behaviour in European Health Care Systems* (Buckingham: Open University Press).

Sartori, Giovanni (1970), 'Concept Misformation in Comparative Politics', *American Political Science Review* (64), 1033–53.

Scharpf, F. (1999), *Governing in Europe: Effective and Democratic?* (Oxford: Oxford University Press).

Schattschneider, Elmer Eric (1975), *The Semisovereign People: A Realist's View of Democracy in America* (Hinsdale: Dryden Press).

Schnapp, F. (1998), 'Soziale Selbstverwaltung vor der Agonie?', *Staatswissenschaften und Staatspraxis*, 9 (2), 149–62.

*Schulgesetz für das Land Berlin* (2004), Berlin: Senatsverwaltung für Bildung, Wissenschaft und Forschung.

Schwartz, F. W., and Busse R. (1997), "Germany", In *Health Care Reform: Learning from International Experience* (ed.) by C. Ham, Buckingham: Open University Press.

Secretaries of State for Health, Wales, Northern Ireland and Scotland (1989), *Working for Patients*, (London: HMSO, CM 55).

Seeleib-Kaiser, Martin and Bleses, P. (2004), *The Dual Transformations of the German Welfare State* (New York: Palgrave Macmillan).

Self, Peter (1993), *Government by the Market? The Politics of Public Choice* (Basingstoke: Macmillan).

Selznick, P. (1948), 'Foundations of the Theory of Organization', *American Sociological Review*, 13 (1), 25–35.

Senatsverwaltung für Gesundheit, Soziales und Verbraucherschutz (2005), *Ergebnisse der Krankenhausplanung in der Zeit von 1990 bis 2004* (Berlin: Senatsverwaltung für Gesundheit, Soziales und Verbraucherschutz).

Sepe, V. (1995), *Amministrazione e storia* (Rimini: Maggioli).

Sharpe, L. J. (1970), 'Theories and Values of Local Government', *Political studies*, 18, 153–74.

——. (ed.) (1993), *The Rise of Meso Government in Europe* (London: SAGE).

Shapiro, I. (1999) (ed.), *Democracy's Value*, Cambridge: Cambridge University Press.

Simon, Herbert (1945), *Administrative Behaviour* (New York: Free Press).

Sinclair, Amanda (1995), 'The Chameleon of Accountability: Forms and Discourses', *Accounting, Organisation, and Society*, 20 (2/3), 219–37.

Soubie, R. (1993), 'Santé 2010' (Paris: Commissariat Général du Plan).

Starke, P. (2007), *Radical Welfare State Retrenchment. A Comparative Analysis* (Basingstoke: Palgrave Macmillan).

Stewart, John and Walsh, Kieron (1992), 'Change in the Management of Public Services', *Public Administration*, 70.

Stoker, G. (2006), *Why Politics Matters. Making Democracy Work* (Basingstoke: Palgrave Macmillan).

Strange, S. (1996), *The Retreat of the State: The Diffusion of Power in the World Economy*. Cambridge: Cambridge University Press.

Suleiman, Ezra (2003), *Dismantling Democratic States* (Princeton: Princeton University Press).

Swank, D. (2002), *Global Capital, Political Institutions, and Policy Change in Developed Welfare States* (Cambridge: Cambridge University Press).

Tarrow, Sidney, Graziano, L., and Katzenstein, P. (eds) (1979), *Territorial Politics in Industrial Nations* (New York: Prager).

Taylor-Gooby, P. (ed.) (2004), *Making a European Welfare State? Convergences and Conflicts Over European Social Policy* (Oxford: Blackwell Publishing).

Taylor-Gooby, P. and Lawson, R. (eds) (1993), *Markets and Managers: New Issues in the Delivery of Welfare* (Buckingham: Open University Press).

Thatcher, Mark and Stone Sweet, A. (eds) (2002), *The Politics of Delegation* (London: Frank Cass).

Thatcher, Mark (2005), 'The Third Force? Independent Regulatory Agencies and Elected Politicians in Europe', *Governance*, 18 (3), 347–73.

*The Guardian* (2005), 'Blair Sweeps Aside Critics of School Reform', 25 October.

Thoenig, Jean-Claude (2003), 'Institutional Theories and Public Institutions: Traditions and Appropriateness', in Guy Peters and Jon Pierre (eds), *Handbook of Public Administration* (London: SAGE), 127–37.

Thomas, H. and Bullock, A. (1994), 'The Political Economy of Local Management of Schools', in S. Tomlinson (ed.), *Educational Reforms and its Consequences* (London: IPPR/Rivers Oram Press), 41–52.

Titmuss, Richard (1958), *Essays on 'the Welfare State'* (London: Allen & Unwin).

——. (1968), *Commitment to Welfare* (London: Allen &Unwin).

——. (1970), *The Gift Relationship: From Human Blood to Social Policy* (London: Allen and Unwin).

Tomlinson, S. (2001), *Education in a Post-Welfare Society* (Buckingham: Open University Press).

Tsebelis, George (2000), *Veto Players: How Political Institutions Work* (Princeton: Princeton University Press).

Tuohy, Carolyn (1999), *Accidental Logics, the Dynamics of Change in the Health Care Arena in the U.S., Britain and Canada* (Oxford: Oxford University Press).

Tyler, W. (1988), *School Organisation: A Sociological Perspective* (Oxford: Routledge).

van Zanten, A. (2000), *L'école, l'état des savoirs* (Paris: La Découverte).

Ventura, Sofia (1998), *La politica scolatisca* (Bologna: Il Mulino).

Verhoest, Koen, et al. (2004), 'The Study of Organisational Autonomy: A Conceptual Review', *Public Administration and Development*, 24 (2), 101–18.

*Verordnung über die Satzung für den LBK Hamburg-Anstalt öffentlichen Rechts* (2004), Hamburgisches Gesetz-und Verordungsblatt, 20 December.

Vickerstaff, Sarah (2003), 'Education and Training', in J. Baldock, N. Manning, and S. Vickerstaff (eds), *Social Policy* (Oxford: Oxford University Press), 362–86.

Weaver, R. K. (1986), 'The Politics of Blame Avoidance', *Journal of Public Policy*, 6 (4), 371–98.

Weber, Max (1991), *From Max Weber: Essays in Sociology*, eds H., Gerth and C., Wright Mills (London: Routledge).

West, A. and Pennell, H. (2005), 'Market-oriented Reforms and "High Stakes" Testing: Incentives and Consequences', *Cahiers de la recherche sure l'éducation et les savoirs* (1), 181–99.

West, A. and Currie, P. (2008), 'The Role of the Private Sector in Publicly Funded Schooling in England: Finance, Delivery and Decision Making', *Policy and Politics*, 36 (2), 191–207.

Westoby, A. (ed.) (1988), *Culture and Power in Educational Organisations: A Reader*.

Whitty, G., Power S., and Halpin D. (1998), *Devolution and Choice in Education: The School, the State, and the Market*, Bristol: Open University Press.

Wilde, Stephanie (2002), 'Secondary Education in Germany 1990–2000: "One Decade on Non-Reform in Unified German Education?"', *Oxford Review of Education*, 28 (1), 39–51 (Milton Keynes: Open University Press).

Wolf, F. (2007), 'Die Bildungsausgaben der Bundeslaender: Bestimmungsfaktoren und sozialpolitische Relevanz', *Zeitschrift für Sozialreform*, 53 (1), 31–56.

Wöllmann, Hellmut (2001), 'Germany's Trajectory of Public Sector Modernisation: Continuities and Discontinuities', *Policy & Politics*, 29 (2), 151–70.

Wössmann, L. (2007), 'International Evidence on School Competition, Autonomy, and Accountability: A Review', *Journal of Education*, 82 (2–3), 473–97.

Wright, Vincent and Meny, Y. (eds) (1985), *Centre-Periphery Relations in Western Europe* (London: Allen and Unwin).

Wright, Vincent and Muller, W. (eds) (1994), *The State in Western Europe: Retreat or Redefinition?* (London: Cass).

Wright, Vincent (1994), 'Reshaping the State: The Implications for Public Administration', *West European Politics*, 102–37.

——. (ed.) (1994), *Privatisation in Western Europe: Pressures, Problems and Paradoxes* (London Pinter).

Wright, Vincent and Cassese, Sabino (eds) (1996), *La recomposition de l'Etat en Europe* (Paris: La Découverte).

Wright, Vincent and Page, Edward C. (eds) (1999), *Bureaucratic Elites in Western European States* (Oxford: Oxford University Press).

Yin, Robert (1994), *Case Study Research. Design and Methods* (2nd edn., Applied Social Research Methods Series, 5; London: SAGE).

Zanetta, Gianpaolo and Casalegno, Cristiana (1999), *Le leggi della nuova sanità* (Milano: Il Sole 24 Ore).

Zay, D. (1994), 'Etablissements et partenariats', *Savoir*, 6 (1), 33–44.

Zürn, M. and Leibfried, Stephan (2005), 'A New Perspective on the State. Reconfiguring the National Constellation', *European Review*, 13 (1), 1–36.

# Index

Page numbers followed by t refer to tables. Endnotes are indicated by n between the page and note numbers.